D1765624

understanding **naturalism**

OXFORD BROOKES
UNIVERSITY
LIBRARY

00 860814 02

Understanding Movements in Modern Thought
Series Editor: Jack Reynolds

This series provides short, accessible and lively introductions to the major schools, movements and traditions in philosophy and the history of ideas since the beginning of the Enlightenment. All books in the series are written for undergraduates meeting the subject for the first time.

Published

Forthcoming titles include

understanding **naturalism**

Jack Ritchie

ACUMEN

ACC. NO. 86081402   FUND THEOP
LOC. ET   CATEGORY STkw   PRICE 14.94

12 FEB 2009

CLASS No. 146   RIT

OXFORD BROOKES
UNIVERSITY LIBRARY

© Jack Ritchie, 2008

This book is copyright under the Berne Convention.
No reproduction without permission.
All rights reserved.

First published in 2008 by Acumen

Acumen Publishing Limited
Stocksfield Hall
Stocksfield
NE43 7TN
www.acumenpublishing.co.uk

ISBN: 978-1-84465-078-1 (hardcover)
ISBN: 978-1-84465-079-8 (paperback)

British Library Cataloguing-in-Publication Data
A catalogue record for this book is available from the British Library.

Typeset by Type Study, Scarborough.
Printed and bound by Biddles Limited, King's Lynn.

To my parents, Anne and John Ritchie

Contents

Acknowledgements

I am greatly indebted to all my philosophy teachers, especially John Worrall, Craig Callender and Luciano Floridi. Most of this book was written while I was an Irish Research Council for the Humanities and Social Sciences post-doctoral fellow at University College Dublin. I thank the IRCHSS for their support and for allowing me to pursue a project outwith my original research proposal. While a post-doctoral fellow I benefited enormously from the support and interest of all my colleagues in University College Dublin and later at Trinity College Dublin. I would especially like to thank John Callanan for keeping me straight on Kant. I had the opportunity to try out the basic ideas presented in the first half of the book on a MA class at University College Dublin and a fourth-year class at Trinity. The enthusiasm of the students was a great encouragement to me. They helped me simplify and clarify a lot of the material. The influence of many non-philosopher friends (they know who they are) is evident throughout the book. I thank them for the support they gave me during this project; support that endured even when they discovered that the book, despite its potentially misleading title, contained no photographs and no chapter on volleyball.

Special thanks must go to John Ritchie who read an almost complete early draft, and to an anonymous referee. Both suggested many improvements in both form and content. Elizabeth Teague and Sue Hadden did excellent work on the final manuscript and were extremely patient with an inveterate fiddler. I must also thank my editors at Acumen, Tristan Palmer and Steven Gerrard, first for suggesting the project to me and then for their incredible patience when the book was much delayed by new jobs, a wedding and a move to the other side of the world. But most of all, I'd like to thank Aoife Lennon-Ritchie, who had to endure first a boyfriend, then a fiancé and finally a husband seemingly continually distracted by the need to finish off the last few chapters of the book. Without her support those last few chapters would never have been completed.

Introduction

Rationalism, empiricism, structuralism, scepticism, existentialism, pragmatism . . . Philosophers like to talk of their great and dead predecessors in terms of –isms. Lecture courses, seminar series and conferences are organized under the heading of one –ism or another. But if you were to ask a contemporary philosopher in the English-speaking world – one of the living and thus not so great – to classify her philosophical position, I would wager that the most common answer would be: "I'm a naturalist". It is certainly the answer I would give. Naturalism is the current philosophical fashion, at least in this part of the world.

What, then, is this fashionable naturalism? It is certainly true that all naturalists share an admiring attitude towards science; and like all philosophical positions naturalism has its slogans: "There is no first philosophy"; "Philosophy is continuous with the natural sciences". But like most slogans, they tell us little. Philosophers are inclined to think that when a term is in common usage, without a clear definition, that is when they are most needed. They roll up their sleeves and set to work to find necessary and sufficient conditions for something to be X. That is not what I intend to do in this book. I doubt if there is any such definition for naturalism. Like most of the other –isms in philosophy, naturalism embraces many differing views.

To understand adequately the various things that naturalism can and might mean we shall need to look in detail at the many different naturalist philosophers and examine their points of agreement and difference. Part of the aim of this book is to map out the most prominent variations in naturalist thinking over the last fifty or so years. In subsequent chapters we shall look at naturalist ideas in epistemology, the philosophy of science, metaphysics and the philosophy of language. But before attending to the detail of various naturalist positions, I want to think a little about the word "natural". Even if we cannot offer necessary and sufficient conditions for what constitutes naturalism, we can throw some light on the various things different philosophers might mean by natural, and thus naturalism, by contrasting it with three other terms: the supernatural, the artificial and the normative.

Natural versus supernatural

Naturalists oppose the supernatural. They deny the existence of ghosts, goblins, gods and other spooky entities.

This seems like a statement about what there is, a piece of metaphysics, but it may also be taken in a methodological way. Naturalists oppose tarot-card readings and séances, and other strange ways of finding out about the world.

This is far from a trivial doctrine. Many people believe in ghosts and astrology. Many more believe in some religion. Declarations of atheism are not just controversial in some parts of the world, but positively dangerous. These claims by themselves are, however, unlikely to cause much excitement among philosophers. One would have to look long and hard to find a philosopher who defends the existence of goblins or the use of tarot cards to predict the future. God might seem to be a different matter. It is likely that the population of philosophers (both past and present) is as theistic as the population at large, but mere atheism is not enough to characterize an interesting philosophical position. Many philosophers who call themselves existentialists, such as Sartre, or positivists, such as Carnap, or critical theorists or postmodernists are atheists but not happily classified as naturalists.

We might label the kind of naturalism represented by these general statements – a rejection of astrology, God and goblins – as popular naturalism. It is an important view. It stands opposed to many current views in our culture, some or all of which one might argue have dangerous consequences. But popular naturalism is not the subject of this book. Philosophical naturalism has other targets.

Those targets are of course the views of other philosophers. Have philosophers postulated the existence of entities or methods that are spooky? Certainly we can find philosophers talking about abstract entities such as universals, Fregean senses, numbers and the like, which do not seem to be found in any science, as well as methods such as phenomenological reduction, transcendental philosophy and intro-spection, which seem to differ from scientific methods. Are these supernatural or spooky? We would like to do more than rest on our intuition here.

One possible way of being more precise about what things are super-natural is offered by naturalists who call themselves physicalists. According to these philosophers everything in the universe is physical. Anything postulated to exist that is not physical is therefore spooky. This provides a clear programme for the naturalist. Many things like minds and numbers don't seem to be physical, so the naturalist has to show that these apparently non-physical things really are physical or, if they are not, that we can do without them. We look at this programme in Chapter 5.

Physicalism provides some guidance for the metaphysical part of naturalism, but how can we be more precise about the methodologi-cal strand, which is opposed to supernatural methods? In Chapter 1 and throughout the first half of the book we shall discuss some of those special methods adopted by philosophers – why they felt the need to adopt them and why some who call themselves naturalists reject them. In Chapter 4 we shall try to see if we can be more precise about what the methods of science are. If we can be clear about what is wrong with those philosophical methods and what the scientific methods are that the naturalist thinks should replace them, then again we should have a clear outline for what a naturalist philosophy might be.

Natural versus artificial

One use of the word "natural" confronts me every morning at break-fast. My orange juice announces that it is 100 per cent natural. Natural means here not mucked about with; nothing is added. Some philoso-phers have a similar sense of natural in mind when they call their position naturalist.

The philosopher of science Arthur Fine expresses what he calls NOA (the natural ontological attitude) this way: "The attitude that marks [my naturalism] is just this: try to take science on its own terms, and try not to read things into science" (Fine 1996: 149). Penelope Maddy, a philosopher of mathematics, has a very similar conception of her own naturalism: "Philosophy is not in the business of criticizing and recommending reforms of mathematics on extra-mathematical grounds" (Maddy 1997: 171).

> To judge mathematical methods from any vantage point outside mathematics ... seems to me to run counter to the spirit that underlies all naturalism: the conviction that a successful enterprise ... should be understood and evaluated on its own terms. (*Ibid.*: 184)

This suggests a kind of deflationary philosophical position. Philosophers should not try to interfere with successful practices like science but simply accept that science (or mathematics) is successful and strive to understand its success.

The two senses of natural that I have highlighted are obviously compatible but might, when used as the basis for a philosophical naturalism, come into conflict. Imagine physicists, working away in their laboratory, decide that in order to explain a particularly strange particle interaction a new mechanism needs to be postulated – ghosts are intervening in the normal working apparatus and swallowing particles that the theory predicts should otherwise be observable. Obviously there is a lot of fuss in the physics community when this mechanism is first postulated, but when no one succeeds in thinking up a ghost-free rival theory that explains these funny results, physicists begin over time to talk quite happily about ghost-induced anomalies in experiments.

What should a naturalist make of these scientific developments? The naturalist who opposes the supernatural should be appalled. Science is invoking entities that he believes do not exist. The naturalist who opposes placing artificial constraints on science should, on the other hand, be relaxed. After all, it is not for philosophers to dictate to scientists which entities exist and which do not.

My story is pretty silly. Physicists are not going to postulate the existence of ghosts. There is, though, a real historical case that highlights the same tension between these two naturalist inclinations.

When Isaac Newton first presented his universal theory of gravitation, there was an outcry among his fellow scientists and philosophers. Gravity was to them a mysterious force. Some contemporaries of Newton called it "occult", which is just another name for supernatural. Gravity gave them no explanation of the motion of planets, or terrestrial bodies. Good science explained motion in terms of pushes and pulls through direct contact. Newton's gravitational force acts instantaneously through empty space. To many this was just weird. How could something have an effect without that being mediated by some contact between the bodies?

The spectacular success of Newton's theory eventually swung the argument in his favour. Gravity and the idea of force came to be accepted by practising scientists and the worries of Newton's critics were judged to be misplaced. Newtonian science has taught us that there are causal interactions other than pushes and pulls. There is an obvious lesson here for someone who thinks of naturalism as a metaphysical doctrine. What scientists decide is an acceptable kind of entity or process to postulate changes as science develops. Gravity was once supernatural and now is not. Physical entities once had to have a definite position in space and time but now quantum theory suggests to us that this is misguided. Given that we expect science to tell us more and more about the world in the future and force us to change further our views about the sorts of things that exist, it is going to be hard for a philosopher to provide a definite and precise list of what is natural (or physical) and what is not. We shall worry about this further throughout Chapter 6 when we look at naturalist philosophers who challenge physicalism.

There is an equally serious worry that arises for philosophers such as Maddy and Fine. If philosophers have to take science on its own terms, what work is there for philosophers to do? Should good naturalists just give up and retrain as scientists? What about if scientists start making claims that we might think to be socially dangerous – say that women are less intelligent than men? Should naturalists of Maddy and Fine's stripe just shrug their shoulders and say that if that is what good scientists recommend, then that is what we should believe?

My own form of naturalism is, I think, fairly close to Fine and Maddy's views; and as I do not want to be unemployed or find myself supporting ethically dubious claims, this question matters to me. I hope to show in Chapter 4 and in the conclusion that there is plenty of room for both something called philosophy and for criticism of particular scientific claims if we accept a deflationary naturalism. To give a hint of the answers to come, taking science on its own terms is not something philosophers have had much practice at, so there is a great deal of work to be done in trying to articulate exactly what the different sciences and their methods are. Moreover, scientists criticize each others' theories all the time. There seems no need to worry about whether we can be critical of scientific theories if we adopt a deflationary naturalism; the hard work will be in deciding what counts as good scientific criticism.

Natural versus normative

Scientific theories tell us how things are: that electrons are negatively charged; that male seahorses give birth to their young; that the gene for sickle-cell anaemia is recessive. But we are not merely interested in how things are; we are also interested in how things should be. We want to know the *right* way to infer a conclusion from premises, the *right* way to lead our lives. We have a vocabulary full of evaluative terms – good, bad, ugly, silly, valid, breathtaking – with which to express our values. If science only describes the world, what are naturalists to make of normative or evaluative claims?

One might think that the contrast between the natural and the normative is just a special case of the contrast between the natural and the supernatural. Naturalists' attitude to it should be the same as it is towards other problematic items like numbers and minds. They need to demonstrate that although norms do not seem to be natural or physical things, they can with sufficient hard work be shown to be so, or perhaps that we can do without them. Many philosophers, though, would claim that norms are a special case. Any attempt to draw evaluative or prescriptive conclusions from descriptive premises is a fallacy, the naturalistic fallacy. No matter how much we know about how things in fact are, that tells us nothing about whether they are good, right or beautiful. The point is well summed up in a famous passage from David Hume:

> In every system of morality which I have hitherto met with I have always remarked that the author proceeds for some time in the ordinary way of reasoning, and establishes the being of God, or makes observations concerning human affairs; when of a sudden I am surprised to find, that instead of the usual copulations of propositions, *is* and *is not*, I meet with no proposition that is not connected with an *ought* or *ought not* ... [A]s this *ought* or *ought not* expresses some new relation or affirmation, it is necessary that it should be observed and explained; and at the same time that a reason should be given for what seems altogether inconceivable, how this relation can be a deduction from others that are entirely different.
>
> (Hume 1739: III.I.i)

If Hume is right and prescriptions about what one ought to do are just different from descriptions, then it will be impossible to capture normative notions in natural or physical terms. If science just describes, it can tell us nothing about what is right and wrong. This is worrying for anyone trying to defend naturalism because it is not as though we can do without norms either. Science, the thing most admired by naturalists, is full of norms. Scientists need to know the *right* way to set up an experiment, the *right* way to draw conclusions from the evidence they have collected. For example, it seems *right* to infer on the basis of the fossil record, geology and our understanding of genetics that we have evolved from apes, and *wrong* to infer that human beings and everything else on the earth were created 4,000 or so years ago. Scientific research can be done well or badly, so the naturalist needs some account of norms to make sense of his favourite disciplines.

I think that making sense of the normative is the hardest task for naturalists. It is a worry that will emerge and re-emerge throughout this text. In our discussion of Quine's work in Chapter 2 and naturalized philosophy of science in Chapter 4 we shall look at the various ways naturalists have tried to accommodate norms in science. In Chapter 7 we shall turn to the equally hard question of what sense the naturalist can make of other normative notions such as truth and meaning.

However, before we begin to entertain the problems of naturalism, we must try to understand the motivations and arguments in favour of naturalist philosophies. The best way to begin is to look at some of the traditional philosophical problems and projects that naturalists react against.

one

First philosophy

One of the slogans of naturalism mentioned in the introduction is that "there is no first philosophy". In this chapter we shall try to make sense of the idea of first philosophy – what it is and why many philosophers have thought we needed such a thing. What follows is a potted history of first philosophies – enough for us to understand both the motivations for first philosophy and to highlight some of the problems that cause naturalists to reject the very idea.

A first philosophical problem: scepticism

One philosopher proclaiming precisely that he is undertaking first philosophy is René Descartes. The full title of Descartes's most celebrated work is *Meditations on First Philosophy*. Descartes's aim is to rebuild our knowledge on solid foundations. He begins in a negative mode; and it is the negative aspect of Descartes's philosophy that will concern us here. He starts by questioning on what basis we can claim to know anything.

For certain cases answers readily present themselves. For example, I know that I am sitting at my desk right now with my laptop in front of me because I can see my desk, my laptop and my hands moving over the keyboard. That seems like a very good answer to the question: how do you know that you are now sitting at your desk typing on your laptop?

Descartes proceeds in the First Meditation to offer us reasons to doubt the adequacy of the simple idea that we know things about the world by looking, touching and using our other senses. First Descartes points out that the senses often deceive us. Sticks that we know are straight look bent when half-submerged in water. So we cannot always trust what we see. Most of us are not likely to be impressed by this argument for doubting what we sense since we know that the stick is really straight only because we can feel it. We need to use information from our other senses, in this case the sense of touch, to see that we have made a mistake. Descartes agrees and quickly moves on to provide other more substantial reasons for doubting what we see. Could it not be the case that, even though I think I am sitting here writing, I might really be dreaming? After all, I would have exactly the same sensations I have now but I would not in fact be sitting at my desk writing this book.

In the final few paragraphs of the First Meditation Descartes provides another, very striking tale which casts doubt on everything we think we know:

> I will suppose . . . some malicious demon of the utmost power and cunning has employed all his energies in order to deceive me. I shall think that the sky, the air, the earth, colours, shapes, sounds and all external things are merely the delusions of dreams which he has devised to ensnare my judgement.
>
> (Descartes 1641: 22–3)

Many contemporary philosophers, less enamoured of talk of demons, offer alternative tales. How do we know that we are not just a brain-in-a-vat with a mad scientist manipulating everything we think we see and feel? How do we know that we are not like the many human beings in the film *The Matrix*, human batteries, which are fed images of the world that are nothing like the dark and terrible reality?

The upshot of all these stories is the same. We do not really know for certain anything about the world around us. All we actually know are our own thoughts. I do not doubt, I cannot doubt, that I think I am writing. But I do not know for certain that is how things really are.

Descartes's understanding of the relation of our ideas to the world beyond us can be pictured as in Figure 1.1. On one side we have the contents of our minds, our ideas. On the other side we have the world beyond us. We think that the cause of many of our ideas is something external to us – like laptops and desks. But when we reflect, we realize

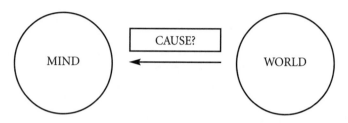

Figure 1.1 Descartes's view of the relation of ideas to the world

that things other than those objects might cause the same ideas. Maybe I am dreaming so I am the cause of those ideas, or maybe I am being deceived by some external agent so she is the cause of those ideas. Knowledge of the external world, in Descartes's picture, is mediated by ideas. Once we admit this, we have a worry about whether the cause of those ideas is really what we ordinarily take it to be. We have to worry about whether my representation of reality is anything like the way the world really is. This is what philosophers refer to as the problem of scepticism.

Descartes's own solution is famously unsatisfactory. He "proves" the existence of a God by starting from his idea of God. Since God is a non-deceiver, we are guaranteed not to be systematically mistaken about the world. We do not need to go into the details of Descartes's proof and its problems. (See Cottingham 1986 and Williams 1978 for a detailed and clear discussion.) Suffice to say that, had Descartes really been able to prove the existence of God he would be a far more famous philosopher than he already is.

Despite the failure of his solution to the problem of scepticism, Descartes presents in a vivid way a very general problem about our knowledge: how can we be sure that we know anything at all? Importantly, the way that he has done this makes it clear that it is the sort of question only a philosopher could answer. If a scientist tried to explain how I know about the objects in front of me and began talking about light reflecting off the surface of the laptop, which is then focused onto my retina by the lens of my eye (among other things), where it is converted into an electric signal and sent via the optic nerve to my brain, and so on – however full and complete that answer seemed, it would not answer Descartes's worry. If we take Descartes seriously, we cannot be certain that any of those objects referred to in the scientist's explanation exist. So we cannot use them to answer Descartes's question.

Here, then, is a problem that sets philosophy radically apart from science. It is also a problem that we must answer before we can place full trust in the results of any science. If we are worried about our knowledge of anything and everything, then all our scientific knowledge must be in question too. We can see the sense in calling this *first* philosophy. Until this philosophical question is answered we cannot claim knowledge of anything.

Another first philosophical problem: induction

The problem of scepticism calls all our beliefs into doubt. Another more modest form of scepticism, most vividly presented by the great Scottish philosopher, David Hume, raises doubts about the legitimacy of our scientific knowledge.

Scientific theories make predictions about how things will turn out in the future. Astronomers, for example, predict that there will be a total solar eclipse visible over the UK and Ireland on 23 September 2090. Less exactly, but perhaps more importantly, doctors predict that smokers are likely to die younger than non-smokers.

Simplifying somewhat, science can do this because scientists discover laws or regularities in nature that are the basis of this prediction. Here is a very crude version of the sort of inference a scientist makes: every morning I get up and I see the sun rise, so I conclude that the sun will rise every morning. My inference starts with some claims about how things have been in the past and then makes a prediction about how things will turn out in the future. Similarly, when a drug goes through clinical trials and is declared safe for human consumption, the same sort of inference has taken place. Because the drug was shown not to cause harmful side-effects on our trial patients, we can conclude that future patients who use this drug will not suffer any adverse side-effects either. We call such inferences, which go from how things have been in the past to how things will turn out in the future, inductions; and in all such arguments we must assume that how things have gone in the past is an indication of how things will turn out in the future.

The first problem with an inductive argument is, as Hume points out, that its conclusion is not guaranteed to be true. "That there is no demonstrative argument in this case seems evident; since it implies no contradiction that the course of nature may change" (Hume 1748: 35). In other words, everything we know about the past may be true and yet it would be quite consistent for the world to behave differently tomorrow; for the sun not to rise or new patients who took the drug in question to start having severe allergic reactions. The idea that the future will resemble the past is not a logical truth.

This seems undeniable but perhaps not very worrying. Even if what we learn from the past does not *guarantee* that the future will turn out as we predict, it at least, we might think, makes it probable. Hume rejects this too. He wrote that we cannot "so much as prove by any *probable* arguments that the future must be conformable to the past" (Hume 1740).

Consider a simple case of something we know to be probable. When we roll a fair die we believe that there is an equal chance that it will land on any side. So it is very probable that we will not roll a 6. But how do we know that in the future rolls of the die will conform to the pattern described here, so that throws of 6's are relatively improbable. Well, we might appeal to our knowledge of the mathematics of probability. Given that we assume an equal probability that any side might turn up, it is far more probable that we shall roll a number between 1 and 5 than a 6. This is, as it stands, a truism. It follows simply from the way we have fixed the probabilities in this case. The real question is why we should believe that the probability of any side landing face up is the same for each side. No formal mathematical theory can tell us why because formal theories do not, by themselves, say anything about real objects. One obvious response is that our knowledge that the die is fair is based on experience. We might have rolled the die thousands of times and found that, roughly speaking, each side came up equally frequently. But to use this evidence for future rolls of the die we would have to assume that the future resembles the past – which is precisely the claim that we are looking to justify.

To make sense of the claim that something is probable you need to assume that the event in question conforms to some pattern, a pattern in which events of that type occur more often than not. But even if events in the past have conformed to that pattern, that gives no reason to assume that events in the future will continue to do so. Just as it is logically possible that the sun will not rise, it is also possible that a die that used to be fair will suddenly start to become biased so that every time we throw it in the future it turns up a 6.

Inductions, whether we use probabilities or not, require us to assume that the future is in some way like the past. Hume has shown us that we have no way of demonstrating that this is the case. Nevertheless, we might think that even if we cannot demonstrate that the future will be like the past, we have very good reasons for believing it. My experience teaches me that the future resembles the past. For example, last week I made the prediction that the sun would indeed rise in the east and today, lo and behold, it did. So it turned out that I was right to think the future would resemble the past; and this is not of course just a one-off. Throughout our lives, we and scientists make predictions about how the future will turn out based on what we know about the past: that there will be a solar eclipse at such and such a time; that a certain drug is safe; that (as my experience quickly taught me) a 7 kg turkey needs to be cooked for more than two hours. So we might claim that we know as well as we know anything from experience that the future resembles the past.

Hume has an answer here too. "Our experience in the past can be a proof of nothing for the future but upon the supposition that there is a resemblance between them. This, therefore, can admit of no proof at all" (Hume 1740).

Our argument says that because, as it were, past futures have resembled past pasts, we have good reason to assume that future futures will also resemble the past. To make that a good inference we have to assume that the past (in which past futures have resembled past pasts) will resemble the future. But that is the very thing we wanted to prove. Trying to justify the claim that the past resembles the future by appealing to our experience is to argue in a circle.

This is very worrying. It suggests that all of our science rests on an unjustified assumption. Again we can see why a problem like this might be called first philosophy. The problem of induction calls into question all scientific results. No science can provide an answer to the problem because all sciences rely on induction and any such answer would be circular. Only philosophy could provide an answer, if an answer can be given at all.

Hume's solution

Hume claims that it is impossible to justify our belief that the future will resemble the past, but we can explain where we get the belief from.

> The experimental reasoning itself [what we are calling induction], which we possess in common with the beasts, and on which the whole conduct of life depends, is nothing but a

species of instinct or mechanical power, that acts in us unknown to ourselves . . . [I]t is an instinct which teaches man to avoid the fire; as much as that, which teaches the bird, with such exactness, the art of incubation, and the whole economy and order of its nursery.   (Hume 1748: 108)

So we have an inborn instinct to reason inductively, according to Hume. It is just what we do and as a matter of fact it seems to work pretty well for us – but we have no justification for it. As we shall see, Hume's answer to the problem of induction has much in common with later naturalists' attitudes towards sceptical problems.

Kant and transcendental philosophy

So far we have looked just at first philosophical problems. Now, I want to look at what a first philosophical solution to these problems might be. By far the most important, influential, interesting and, unfortunately, complicated approach is Immanuel Kant's transcendental idealism. I shall not try here to give anything like a full account of Kant's philosophy. I shall sketch the general position quickly first and point out a couple of obvious problems, problems that are of particular interest to naturalists suspicious of first philosophy.

To begin our discussion of Kant we start with two other big figures from modern philosophy, Locke and Berkeley. Locke is, according to Kant, a transcendental realist. Like Descartes, Locke thinks that we know our own ideas directly. Some aspects of our ideas, such as shape and texture, match up to how things really are in the external world. These Locke calls primary qualities. Some aspects, such as colour and smell, do not. They are just caused in us by the powers of objects. These Locke calls secondary qualities. The problem for Locke is identical to the one Descartes encountered: how, given that we only know our ideas directly, can we be sure that they really match up with the world outside in the way Locke claims?

Berkeley has a very simple and utterly weird-sounding solution to Descartes's and Locke's problem. Deny the existence of the external world completely. When we talk about objects that we normally take to exist in the external world, for example apples, what we are really referring to is a certain cluster of ideas that go together. In the case of apples, a certain sort of round shape, green colour, and appley taste and smell. There can be no sceptical worries about how we know about apples since all there is to apple is this cluster of ideas that we know directly. Kant calls Berkeley's view empirical idealism.

Kant's own view rearranges the labels he uses to describe Berkeley and Locke. Kant claims to be both a transcendental idealist and an empirical realist.

It is easiest to explain Kant's transcendental idealism and empirical realism by thinking about a particular dispute in metaphysics, the nature of space. We need again to introduce the ideas of two great thinkers that preceded Kant – Isaac Newton and Gottfried von Leibniz. Newton thought that space was a real thing, something like a giant box. All objects have a definite position in this real space; and even if there were no objects, space would still exist. Leibniz thought otherwise. Space is, he claimed, ideal. It is something we construct out of the relations between objects. So if there were no objects and no us to do the constructing, then there would be no space.

Kant's own view is a synthesis of these two seemingly contradictory ideas. The idea of space is a precondition for the possibility of the perception of any object. When we think of objects at all, we must think of them as in some space (and time). But we do not get the idea of space from experience. We supply the idea of space without which experience would be impossible. How is this a synthesis of Newton's and Leibniz's views? Looked at one way, Newton is right to say that space is perfectly real and objective. Given the framework of spatial and temporal representations that we must bring to any perception, there are perfectly objective facts about when and where objects are located. This is the standpoint Kant calls empirical realism. Crudely, from the empirical realist standpoint the world is largely as we find it to be. This is the perspective of common sense and science. Looked at another way, though, Kant's views are much closer to those of Leibniz. Space abstracted from our perception of things is nothing at all. It is a precondition of any experience. "Space and . . . time and with them all appearances are nothing but representations and cannot exist outside our mind" (Kant A490–1/B518–8). This is the perspective that Kant calls transcendental idealism. It is the special perspective of the philosopher; and the special task of the philosopher is to work out what the "conditions of possible experience" are – in other words, to work out what must be the case in order for us to have any perceptions at all.

Kant's account of space illustrates what he called his "Copernican revolution" in philosophy. "Hitherto it has been assumed that all our knowledge must conform to objects" but Kant thinks that we must "make trial whether we may not have more success in the tasks of metaphysics, if we suppose that objects must conform to our knowledge" (Bxvi). It is a way of understanding how we represent the world (and ourselves) that rejects the Cartesian picture illustrated above. Descartes assumes that having perceptions and ideas is basic and unproblematic. The problem is to reassure ourselves that the ideas that we have match up with how things really are. Kant thinks that Descartes (as well as Locke and Berkeley) have failed to ask a more important question: what must be the case to have any perceptions or representations at all?

What Kant claims about space, he also claims about a great many other things. The ideas of time, causality and substance are all preconditions for the possibility of experience. Space and time are what Kant calls the pure forms of our intuitions. Substance and causality are pure concepts of the understanding. An intuition is a representation of a particular thing. The content or matter of an intuition I get through experience, from something outside me, but the form of that experience, that it occurs at a particular place or time, comes from me. A concept is a representation of an object "by means of a feature which several things may have in common" (A220/B377) – in other words as a certain kind of thing. Knowledge requires both. "Thoughts without contents are empty, intuitions without concepts are blind" (A51/B75). The scheme of pure forms of intuition and pure concepts of the understanding is a framework to which all experience and knowledge must conform. Our knowledge of objects considered within this framework is knowledge of what Kant calls phenomena or appearances. Kant also talks of noumena or things-in-themselves. These are the objects considered independently of the framework of concepts and intuitions that constitute the phenomenal object. Noumena are in some sense the source of our representations. They supply the matter or content of our intuitions. We supply the form. However, since our intuitions and concepts do not, in fact cannot, apply to these things, we can have no knowledge of noumenal objects.

The fact that in order to have any experience we must first have pure intuitions and concepts is used by Kant to explain how we can know certain things independently of experience. Our pure intuition of space explains how we can come to know geometrical truths. Geometry is in effect the consideration of our pure intuition of space through the mental construction of lines and shapes. That space is Euclidean space. It follows that all objects of which we have experience must conform to the principles of Euclidean geometry. Kant offers analogous considerations to explain the *a priori* nature of arithmetic and the fundamental principles of Newtonian physics. Again this has the very strong consequence that all our experience of the external world must fit with the principles of Newtonian mechanics.

I have just presented the results of Kant's transcendental philosophy. Kant has a great many subtle arguments to justify his picture of representation. But we have enough here to give us an idea of how Kant's system helps us answer the first philosophical problems of Descartes and Hume, and to highlight some problems.

As we noted above, Kant rejects Descartes's picture of representation. What we call external objects, things such as the laptop here in front of me, are in fact representations conforming to the framework of pure concepts and intuitions which come from me. So I have no need to infer the existence of the external world from my ideas. Objects of the external world are not inferred from my ideas, they are known directly and as certainly as representations of my inner self.

Some readers of Kant find this unsatisfactory. We may know about the phenomenal world, but what about the noumenal reality or the things-in-themselves? Isn't that what we really want to know about? From Kant's perspective this kind of question represents a confusion. Knowledge is necessarily limited to objects that fit the framework of our representations. To ask to know what the world is like independently of this framework is to ask to know what the world is like when it is not known. It is an incoherent request.

Kant can also answer Hume's scepticism about induction. For experience to be possible, it must conform to our pure concepts of understanding, in particular to our concept of causation. Experience is only possible if we can relate representations in time as cause and effect. So I know independently of any actual experience of the world that my representation of objects must conform to the principle of universal causation; every event has a cause and like causes must produce like effects. Actually, we know more than just this. As we remarked earlier, the principles of Newtonian mechanics are also preconditions for the possibility of experience. Hence we know that Newton's laws will be true of all the events in the world in both the past and in the future.

Some problems with Kant's transcendental philosophy

Let's look at some of the difficulties with Kant's philosophy which might be relevant to someone suspicious of first philosophy.

The first problem concerns whether we can really make sense of Kant's system within Kant's system. Knowledge, recall, is necessarily limited to the phenomenal realm. We can have no knowledge of noumena. But it looks as if Kant's system involves many knowledge claims that make direct reference to noumena. Noumena are supposed to be the source of our intuitions. Moreover, we need to have some idea of noumena in order to make sense of the distinction between the empirical and transcendental levels. Phenomenal objects are objects considered at the empirical realist level. Noumena are objects considered at the transcendentally ideal level. But how can we even make sense of that if noumena are not things that fit our framework of understanding and so cannot be objects of knowledge? We need the idea of noumenal objects to make sense of the project of transcendental philosophy, but it looks as if within transcendental philosophy we cannot make sense of the idea of noumenal objects. So it looks as if we cannot make sense of the possibility of transcendental philosophy within transcendental philosophy.

More worrying than any of this, and of particular interest to naturalists, is the problem that Kant's system encounters when it comes up against developments in later mathematics and physics. Let us look at space again. Kant claims that the form of our intuition of space is Euclidean geometry and so all objects, whether imagined or experienced, must conform to the principles of that geometry. In the nineteenth century non-Euclidean geometries were developed by Reimann and Lebochowski. It became clear then that it was possible to think of space differently from the way Kant claimed was necessary. Worse yet, with Einstein's theory of relativity came a conception of the world that rejected Kant's pure forms of space and time in favour of a new conception of four-dimensional space-time. What Kant claimed we know independently of experience as a necessary truth was shown to be false by developments in science and mathematics. Other Kantian claims are also undermined by twentieth-century physics. The law of universal causation, that every event has a cause, one of the pure concepts of the understanding, is undermined by empirical discoveries and quantum physics. When radioactive atoms decay, this is a random, apparently uncaused, process.

The internal difficulties of Kant's system and the fact that claims touted as necessary truths turn out to be revisable in the light of our experience can only lead us to the conclusion that Kant's attempt at first philosophy is a failure. Mathematical and scientific findings undermine the pretensions of his first philosophy.

Kant's project is an outstandingly ambitious one. He not only tries to explain how knowledge of the external world is possible, but also provides explanations for our understanding of geometry, arithmetic and the principles of Newtonian mechanics. Perhaps it is no surprise that his project is not a success. Maybe we should not give up on first philosophy yet. After all, we still have the twin problems of scepticism and induction to deal with. A more modest form of first philosophy could succeed where Kant fails.

Frege: logic is special

A first step in constructing a more modest first philosophy is to think about logic. A hasty response to the problems with Kant's system would be that all our knowledge is empirical knowledge. Developing this thought with regard to logic, we might be tempted to say that logic describes the way we reason; and if people reasoned differently from us, then a different logic would be appropriate to describe their thinking. Take a logical form of argument such as *modus ponens*: if *p*, then *q*; *p*; therefore *q*. For example:

If Inverness Caledonian Thistle beat Celtic, then Jack is very happy.
Inverness Caledonian Thistle beat Celtic.
Therefore Jack is very happy.

Modus ponens on this view then is just a law that describes how we move from thoughts that make up the premises to the thought that makes up the conclusion, just as Galileo's law of free-fall motion describes how objects fall close to the earth's surface. This kind of view of logic and thought is called psychologism.

Some nineteenth-century thinkers (whom we might identify as early naturalists) held this view of logic. Gottlob Frege argued that their views rested on a profound misunderstanding of logic and truth. "Just as 'beautiful' points the way for aesthetics and 'good' for ethics, so do words like 'true' for logic . . . From the laws of truth [logic] there follow prescriptions about asserting, thinking, judging, inferring" (Frege 1918–19: 58). Logic, Frege argued, is not concerned with the way people actually reason. A deduction is not valid because it correctly describes how human beings move from one thought to the next. It is valid because it preserves truth in our judgements. Deductive logic ensures that we move from true premises to true conclusions. Equally, just because people are disposed to make certain kinds of inferences, this does not mean that those inferences should be endorsed by logic. Many people are prone to infer from: if p, then q; q; therefore p. For example: if I have measles, then I will have spots. I have spots. Therefore I have measles. This is just a (deductive) mistake. The two premises can be true but the conclusion false. I might have spots for other reasons; maybe I have chickenpox, for example.

According to Frege, logic is concerned not with how we *do* reason but how we *should* reason to ensure that we proceed from truth to truth. It is not a descriptive science of thought but a prescriptive or normative one. If Frege is right, then we have grounds for thinking that logical truths are quite different from scientific claims. Science describes how the world is; logic tells us how we *must* think if we wish to preserve truth in our inferences.

Frege is most famous for doing two things. First, he articulated a formal system that expressed what he believed were the fundamental and eternal truths of logic – what we now call classical logic. Secondly, along with Bertrand Russell, he instituted the logicist programme in the philosophy of mathematics. Frege's goal was to provide a definition of number using only the resources of naive set theory and logic, and then show that the basic axioms of arithmetic can be proved from the fundamental logical laws. It is not necessary here to offer any details of this intriguing and difficult project. Suffice to say that Frege's view that logic has a special status and that mathematics could be grounded in logic offered certain early twentieth-century philosophers, the logical positivists, a framework in which to develop a sophisticated empiricist first philosophy.

Logic and empiricism

The most interesting and detailed account of this early positivist programme can be found in Rudolf Carnap's *The Logical Structure of the World*. The basic elements are as follows. The logical system bequeathed to the positivists by Frege provided a universal framework for all logical thought. To this is added the empiricist idea that knowledge of the world about us comes from experience – but with a linguistic twist. All languages have a primitive kind of vocabulary that picks out our basic experiences. It is difficult to provide concrete examples of sentences in this "primitive" vocabulary, but they would have been sentences such as "I see red now". The universal logic and the universal language for describing primitive experiences can then be combined to formulate sentences that it can be decided are true or false in the light of some experience. Positivists, like Carnap, believed that all meaningful sentences in any language must be in principle translatable into a very complicated sentence making use only of the basic vocabulary that refers to primitive experience plus classical logic. If a sentence could not be so translated and was not a logical truth, it was meaningless.

The job for philosophy was to effect these translations. A correct translation would yield one of two results. If the claim being put forward were a mathematical or an *a priori* truth, such as "all bachelors are unmarried men", then analysis should turn that statement into a logical truth or tautology. If the claim being put forward were an empirical or scientific claim such as "light bends round heavy objects", then analysis would reveal the long and complicated sentence that employed only the primitive vocabulary equivalent to the ordinary scientific sentence. It would thereby make explicit the range of experiences that confirm the sentence and the range of experiences that would disconfirm it. Carnap thought that this would help to explain why scientists were all able to agree so much. The translations of scientific discourse into primitive vocabulary make explicit what counted as empirical evidence in favour of a theory and what counted against the theory.

This approach to language can also provide an answer to the problem of scepticism. The sceptic says that we can imagine two scenarios: one in which our experiences are caused by the external world, and one in which they are caused by something else – a malicious demon or a mad scientist. By hypothesis there is no experience that can distinguish these different scenarios. Given the positivists' criterion for meaningfulness of sentences, then these two apparent alternative hypotheses must actually be identical. Whatever additional, non-empirical assertions we think distinguish the brain-in-the-vat hypothesis from the hypothesis that the world exists must, since they make no difference to experience, be meaningless.

The later Carnap

Carnap's early project turned out to be a heroic failure. Despite a great deal of ingenuity on his part, he was never able to offer the reductions of theoretical sentences into sentences making use of a vocabulary referring only to primitive experiences. Moreover, the idea that classical logic represented the one true set of rules for all correct thinking was challenged by the development of other, non-classical logics, such as the intuitionist logic of Brouwer. (Certain claims that are logical truths in classical logic are not in intuitionist logics, e.g., that either p or not-p.) These problems led Carnap to develop a more liberal form of logical empiricism.

The key notion in Carnap's later work is that of a linguistic framework. It is helpful to think of what Carnap means by this idea by imagining what someone must do if they are constructing a language or part of a language from scratch. Say, for example, we wish to introduce the concept of number into a language where this concept does not already exist. How do we do that? "If someone wishes to speak in his language about a new kind of entities, he has to introduce a system of new ways of speaking, subject to new rules" (Carnap 1950a: 73). The relevant rules for number terms would involve introducing names for individual numbers, such as "three"; a general name for all numbers, such as "numbers"; some names for properties of numbers, such as "odd" and "even"; and rules describing the relations and functions in which numbers appear, e.g. "plus", "multiplication" and so on. These rules would define how to use the new number terms, what could be truly said about numbers and what could not. We could introduce similar definitions for all other terms in a language. For example, we would define the rules for (and thus the meaning of) a theoretical term such as "electron" by outlining rules relating it to other terms, say "charge", "mass" and "electromagnetic field". Since the term "electron" also features as part of a scientific theory, the rules of the framework specify relations to what Carnap called protocol sentences – sentences expressing possible observations that may confirm or disconfirm the theory in which electrons feature. Our framework rules will also tell us to what degree these observations confirm or disconfirm the theory.

The idea of a linguistic framework is more liberal than the earlier Carnap's account for two reasons. First, the idea of translating sentences involving non-empirical terms into sentences making use solely of the primitive empirical vocabulary has been replaced with the less demanding idea of specifying the rules that link theoretical terms to one another and ultimately to the set of protocol sentences that would confirm or disconfirm them. Secondly, Carnap allows that there can be many different mutually incompatible linguistic frameworks: frameworks employing classical logic and others employing intuitionistic logic; frameworks in which there are numbers and others where there are no numbers; frameworks in which there are electrons and others where there aren't.

Carnap advocated what he called the Principle of Tolerance towards different frameworks: "*In logic there are no morals.* Everyone is at liberty to build up his own logic, i.e. his own form of language, as he wishes" (Carnap 1934: 52). Our decision to use one framework rather than another is precisely that: a decision. There is nothing in reality or the structure of language that forces one choice on us as the correct one. There is no such thing as the correct framework.

Once we have decided to make use of one of these frameworks, we can ask perfectly intelligible questions about how things are in the world. For example, once we have fixed on the rules for the use of terms such as "horse" and "white", we can ask the question: are there white horses? And our linguistic framework tells us which protocol sentences would make this sentence true and which would make it false. Once our framework is in place, the claim that there are white horses is either true or false, depending on how we find things in the world.

Carnap's liberalism towards different frameworks gives traditional questions about the existence of problematic entities a new form. Consider, for example, a question that concerns many philosophers of mathematics: do numbers exist? Within Carnap's system, this question can be understood in two ways – as what Carnap calls either an internal or an external question. Understood as an internal question, it is about whether, given some linguistic framework, numbers exist; and the answer will always be a trivial one. If we are working with a linguistic framework in which we have introduced the rules for defining numbers and the related arithmetical relations, then it follows just from the rules of the framework that numbers exist. If we are working in a linguistic framework without such rules, then we shall get the opposite answer.

Anyone who pursues such a question in the philosophy of mathematics is likely to find this kind of answer unsatisfactory. They want to know whether numbers *really* exist; not just if we talk one way, then we shall say they do, and if we talk another way, then that they do not. One way such a philosopher might put this question to someone like Carnap is to ask which linguistic framework is the right one. Which framework reflects the correct ontology – the one with numbers or the one without? Now we are asking a question not within a framework but one about which commitments involved in adopting a framework are the right ones to make. This is an external question.

We state such questions as though they concern factual matters, questions about what really exists. Carnap insists that this is to misunderstand them. Once we have the idea of a linguistic framework in place, we can see that they are better understood as questions of the following form: should we adopt a linguistic framework that contains number terms? A question about which framework to adopt, what language in which to express your science, is no more a factual question than whether it is better to express one's science in English or in French. It is a purely pragmatic matter. What we need to decide is whether things would be easier for us in our science if we adopted number talk.

Similarly with physical objects. There is no objective, self-standing truth about whether there are physical objects. There is just a practical decision we need to make about whether to adopt object talk (what Carnap calls the thing-language) or not. Sceptical problems dissolve. Talk of evil demons is just a florid, metaphorical way of introducing a linguistic framework without physical objects. All we have to decide is which is more convenient. Clearly, for most of us most of the time, talking of objects is a simpler, more fruitful way to go. The fact that we all "choose" to talk that way outside the philosophy classroom (and normally inside too) shows this to be the case. But the decision is not forced on us. There may be circumstances in which it is more convenient to adopt a language without commitment to physical objects.

Carnap's linguistic frameworks also offer some sort of solution to the problem of induction. Within our linguistic framework we can say precisely to what degree some hypothesis is confirmed by the evidence. The framework provides us with rules about how to assess and adapt our empirical beliefs in light of new evidence.

We can summarize the later Carnap's views as follows. Assertions about how the world is can be analysed in two parts. First, the meaning of the terms used in the sentences is provided by a framework of rules that defines their use. A framework is adopted for conventional or pragmatic reasons – because we find it useful. The rules adopted in the framework explain the *a priori* truths of mathematics and logic. *A priori* truths are just those that follow from the conventionally adopted rules of the framework. Secondly, in the case of genuinely factual claims, whether a statement is true or false is then decided by experience. In the case of theoretical science the framework articulates which observations are important for confirming the theory and to what extent the theory is so confirmed. Correspondingly there are two sorts of changes to our assertions that we might make as we undertake some investigation – what we might call internal and external revisions. If I am working in a framework and my theory makes an incorrect prediction, then I should revise one of my beliefs according to the rules of the framework. For example, if I am working in a framework that includes the term "swans" and the colour terms, then I might assert: "All swans are white". If, during the course of experience, I discover a black swan, then I should give up this belief and instead say: "Not all swans are white". Internal changes like this are prompted by experience and justified by the rules of the framework. An external change involves changing the linguistic framework. It is prompted by pragmatic considerations of simplicity and fruitfulness.

There is clearly a close parallel between Carnap and Kant. Carnap has transformed Kant's framework of pure intuitions and categories that marks the limits of possible experience and thought into a linguistic framework that marks the limits of meaningful assertion. Kant's ideal framework is a set of necessary *a priori* truths; Carnap's is a conventionally adopted system. But both serve the same purpose: to show that certain philosophical questions such as the problem of scepticism or the existence of numbers rest on a misunderstanding of the essential preconditions of thought or language. And both do so by invoking two levels of enquiry: the transcendental and the empirical in Kant, and the external and the internal in Carnap.

Carnap's account has certain clear advantages over Kant's too. Kant's system cannot account for the changes in twentieth-century physics that massively altered our views of space, time and causality. Carnap's can. The change from Newtonian physics to relativity can be thought of as a change of linguistic framework. We get rid of a framework involving terms such as "space", "time" and "straight line" and replace it with a framework including terms such as "space-time", "geodesic" and so on.

First philosophy then becomes the task of making explicit the many different linguistic frameworks, so that mathematicians, scientists and others can choose the most useful one for their purposes. Philosophers provide a clear articulation of the possible linguistic forms that any enquiry might utilize.

Problems with Carnap's view

The similarities with Kant stretch further than those we have already sketched. The problems we encountered with Kant's system resurface in Carnap.

A problem for Kant that we touched on above is how to make sense of the distinction between the transcendental and empirical levels given the strictures he placed on knowledge. If the noumenon or thing-in-itself does not conform to the categories of understanding, how can we even conceive of it? Similarly there are problems in making sense of Carnap's two levels and his distinction between internal and external questions. Consider our "decision" to adopt the number language or not. We are supposed to make an assessment of the fruitfulness and simplicity of this scheme relative to others. But when we are entertaining thoughts about the relative fruitfulness of two frameworks, what language are we doing that in? If I say, for example, "the number language is more fruitful than the nominalist language", then what linguistic framework am I making use of? The worry here is serious. After all, I cannot say anything at all without making use of some language, and so presumably some linguistic framework. Is the framework I am using to make this decision just one among many meta-frameworks or is it special in some way? If it is just one among many that I might adopt, then surely it is possible that within other frameworks I might reach different decisions about which is, pragmatically speaking, the best framework to apply. Could there be a meta-framework, for example, in which the Principle of Tolerance is rejected? Should we be tolerant of such meta-frameworks? Or is there a way to decide between these competing meta-linguistic frameworks? What framework would we do that in? What would its status be? The same questions would presumably arise at this higher level.

Once we begin to think along these lines, we quickly lose the sense of what we are talking about. It is unclear how tolerant judgements about competing frameworks could genuinely be applied to these meta-frameworks. That might suggest to us that Carnap should be committed to a special meta-language in which objective verdicts about the fruitfulness of competing frameworks can be made. But such a framework must have a logic. So we should, surely, contrary to Carnap's aims, be committed to that being ultimately the right logic. Presumably it must involve further ontological commitments. Surely, then, these would come out as just plain facts, not dependent on a framework in any way. If matters concerning frameworks can be decided objectively here, then why do we not adopt this master framework for all our deliberations? In either case the distinction between internal and external questions on which Carnap's position rests looks threatened. In the first case, external questions turn out to be internal questions in competing meta-frameworks, ones that perhaps offer different standards for deciding between frameworks, so there is no way to judge objectively the relative merits of competing frameworks. In the second case, the existence of an objective meta-framework makes it mysterious why we ever needed to introduce different linguistic frameworks in the first place. Surely the master framework is the right place to decide all questions objectively.

These issues threaten the coherence of Carnap's philosophy, and there seem to be no clear answers to the questions we have raised in his writings. But, as in the case of Kant, that is not the end of his problems. Even if Carnap could address the worries we have just identified, there are other reasons to be sceptical of his position. In Chapter 2 we shall look at some criticisms of Carnap's first philosophical project that motivate the rejection of first philosophy outright.

two

Quine and naturalized epistemology

Carnap's theory of linguistic frameworks (and the distinction between internal and external questions which comes with it) is in many ways an appealing approach to philosophy. It offers us a way of explaining the special *a priori* status of mathematics and logic; it allows us to dismiss a great many metaphysical questions as pseudo-questions; and, unlike the Kantian picture, it can accommodate the radical changes in our ideas of space, time and causation that took place in the twentieth century.

We need to grasp this Carnapian picture if we are to understand the most prominent naturalist philosopher of the twentieth century: Willard van Orman Quine. Quine's naturalism emerges from his criticism of Carnap's philosophy. In particular, as we shall see, Quine raises serious questions about the different ways internal and external questions are supposedly settled according to Carnap.

Recall that, according to Carnap, within a framework an internal question (if it is empirical) is settled by appeal to empirical evidence; external questions, such as whether to adopt the thing-language, are settled by pragmatic considerations of simplicity, fruitfulness of the framework, etc.

Let us think about a piece of science conducted within the thing-language. Suppose I have some astronomical theory that predicts the motions of the planets. Let us say I am a nineteenth-century astronomer testing Newton's theory of gravitation. Newton's theory all by itself does not predict anything. I need to combine it with other claims. I need to assume the rest of Newton's theoretical framework, including the laws of motion. I need to make assumptions about how my measuring instruments work, and about the position, size and mass of the planets that I am observing. I need to assume certain claims of mathematics to make a quantitative prediction; and in making my deductions from the theory I need to assume the truth of deductive logic. So to deduce a prediction I shall need to assume a great deal in addition to my theory of gravitation. My prediction, written out explicitly, will look roughly as follows:

1. Newton's law of gravitation and
2. Newton's laws of motion and
3. Assumptions about planetary position and
4. Theory of how my telescope works and
5. Mathematics and
6. Logic

Entails prediction P: Planet X will be in position d at time t.

This is an illustration of what Quine calls "holism". No scientific statement can be tested all by itself. It also highlights one serious problem for the early Carnap's project. We cannot reduce a sentence of a scientific theory to one that makes use of logic alone and refers to basic experiences because there is no set of experiences that will confirm or falsify the sentence all by itself. Only when this sentence is combined with many others can we generate a prediction. This point is accommodated in the later Carnap's account. Scientific sentences only entail protocol sentences when combined with the rules in the linguistic framework and other scientific claims. But the later Carnap has other problems, as we shall see.

Let us imagine that I observe the motion of some distant planet and find that it does not fit with my theory's prediction. What should I do? Perhaps Newton's theory is wrong. Perhaps there is something wrong with the telescope I am using. Perhaps the earth's atmosphere is affecting the light travelling from the star and distorting its apparent position. Perhaps there is another planet close by, one that I cannot see, which is affecting the orbit of the planet. Any of these explanations is possible. In fact it follows logically that since all the assumptions listed above are necessary to generate my prediction, we could revise any one of them in order to avoid the conflict between my prediction and my observation. How do we decide which revisions we should make? A sensible answer seems to be that we look for a revision of our knowledge that makes our overall theory as simple as possible, or revisions that suggest new interesting phenomena to investigate. For example, our nineteenth-century astronomer would not reject Newton's theory of gravity because he has no theory with which to replace it. That would not be very fruitful. Similarly, just saying his telescope is not working does not sound like a very interesting or productive hypothesis, particularly if it has seemed to work perfectly well up until now. So he might judge that the simplest and most fruitful explanation for the discrepancy between his prediction and his observation is that some unseen planet is affecting the orbit of the planet he has been viewing through the telescope. This decision is not forced on him. Perhaps other astronomers will come to different conclusions. But they too will have to make a judgement about which sort of adjustment is most likely to bring theory and observation into agreement. Decisions about which revision is simplest or most fruitful are, obviously, pragmatic decisions. So pragmatic considerations do not just bear on what Carnap calls external questions, an element of pragmatism is present at the empirical or internal level too.

Analogously, what initially prompts us to search for what Carnap might describe as a different framework are often empirical considerations. We drop Euclidean geometry and adopt a non-Euclidean geometry in part because of experiments and observations that suggest something is wrong with the Newtonian framework.

Once we admit this, we might wonder what is the point of drawing a distinction between the internal and the external perspective. This is precisely how Quine sees the matter:

> Carnap ... take[s] a pragmatic stand on the question of choosing between language forms, scientific frameworks ... I espouse a more thorough pragmatism. Each man is given a scientific heritage plus a continuing barrage of sensory stimulations; and the considerations which guide him in warping his scientific heritage to fit his continuing sensory promptings are, where rational, pragmatic. (Quine 1980: 46)

By making this suggestion, Quine embraces what he calls "methodological monism". Carnap is, Quine claims, wrong to believe that there are two ways in which beliefs are revised: one corresponding to adjustments demanded by the rules of the framework, and one corresponding to changes in the framework motivated by pragmatic considerations. Rather, in all cases experience prompts us to revise our beliefs, and pragmatic considerations guide those revisions. For Quine those pragmatic considerations include, as well as simplicity and fruitfulness, conservativeness (try to change as few of your beliefs as possible), modesty and refutability (make sure your revisions give rise to further testable consequences).

Quine has other more sophisticated arguments against Carnap's philosophy. In particular, he has detailed criticisms of Carnap's use of concepts such as convention and analyticity. But I think his overriding motivation for rejecting Carnap's account is just the simple one that I have explained above. Carnap's distinction between internal and external questions is a distinction without a difference. The methods we adopt to evaluate and revise all our beliefs are the same: a mixture of the pragmatic and the empirical.

If there is no special separate philosophical task of clarifying and explicating linguistic frameworks, then what is left for philosophy? It, like everything else, must find a home within the methods and theories of science. One of Quine's favourite metaphors nicely sums up the position: "Neurath has likened science to a boat which, if we are to rebuild it, we must rebuild plank by plank while staying afloat in it" (Quine 1960: 3). "The naturalistic philosopher begins his reasoning within the inherited world theory as a going concern. He tentatively believes all of it, but believes also that some unidentified portions are wrong. He tries to improve, clarify and understand the system from within. He is the busy sailor adrift on Neurath's boat" (Quine 1975: 72).

Here, then, we have the rejection of first philosophy. We have not arrived here by showing that first philosophy is impossible. Rather, we have found that the attempts to carve out a first philosophy due to Kant and Carnap have failed in revealing ways. The best reasons for rejecting pure forms of intuition and understanding as necessary truths are empirical. The methods Carnap claims we use to choose between competing linguistic frameworks are the same methods we use to choose between competing scientific beliefs. Claims that are held up to be special, distinct or required as a foundation for science turn out to be provisional and open to empirical refutation in the same way that ordinary scientific theories are. Methods held up to be distinctly philosophical turn out to be part of the methods employed by scientists.

Some qualifications to Quine's holism

Before beginning to think about how philosophy looks from this naturalist standpoint, more needs to be said about Quine's holism.

Quine states his holism using a variety of metaphors that require some explanation. In one of Quine's most famous papers, "Two Dogmas of Empiricism", he explains the idea as follows:

> The totality of our so-called knowledge or beliefs, from the most casual matters of geography and history to the profoundest laws of atomic physics or even pure mathematics and logic, is a man-made fabric which impinges on experience along the edges. Or, to change the figure, total science is like a field of force whose boundary conditions are experience. A conflict with experience occasions readjustments in the interior field . . . If this view is right, it is misleading to speak of the empirical content of an individual statement – especially if it is a statement at all remote from the experiential periphery of the field. (Quine 1980: 42–3)

In other writings Quine talks of our science as a "web of belief". Webs too have peripheries and interiors. This invites us to think that our beliefs are ordered in a certain way. Some claims, such as the fundamental laws of physics, are highly general; some, like my report of a planet's position, are highly specific. The most abstract beliefs are near the centre; the more concrete and specific beliefs towards the edge. Thus logic and the fundamental laws of physics are near the centre of our web of beliefs, claims about the workings of telescopes, or the positions of various planets, are further out still, and the reports of our observations are right at the edge.

Another way to think of Quine's image of a belief's distance from a sensory periphery is to think of how much work we need to do to make our beliefs consistent if we find ourselves confronted with an observation that is inconsistent with our predictions. Let us go back to our astronomer. Let us suppose he decides that the reason for his false prediction is that another unseen planet's gravitational attraction is affecting the orbit of the planet we are interested in. To make this change, very few other beliefs need to be revised. However, if he thought that the best way to deal with the problem was to revise the fundamental laws of physics, then he would need to make many other adjustments too. Fundamental theories have many more connections with our other beliefs than less abstract claims. The closer towards the centre of the web you go, the more connections those beliefs will have to others, and so the greater the effect on the rest of your beliefs a revision will have.

The metaphor of centrality, then, can be made sense of in two ways. Beliefs nearer the centre are more abstract, more distant from actual observations, and changes in these beliefs require more radical changes in the rest of our science. There is therefore a difference of degree between our beliefs – some are less abstract than others; some can be revised more easily than others – but there is no difference in principle as Carnap's account requires.

In "Two Dogmas of Empiricism" Quine draws a very radical conclusion from his holism:

> The unit of empirical significance is the whole of science.
> (Quine 1980: 42)

> Any statement can be held true come what may, if we make drastic enough adjustments elsewhere in the system. Even a statement very close to the periphery can be held true in face of recalcitrant experience by pleading hallucination or by amending certain laws of the kind called logical laws. Conversely, by the same token, no statement is immune to revision. Revision of the logical law of excluded middle has been proposed as a mean of simplifying quantum mechanics; and what difference is there in principle between such a shift and the shift whereby Kepler superseded Ptolemy, Einstein Newton or Darwin Aristotle? (*Ibid.*: 43)

> A recalcitrant experience [one that does not match our science's predictions] can ... be accommodated by any of various alternative reevaluations in various alternative quarters of our conceptual scheme. (*Ibid.*: 44)

Statements such as this can make Quine's holism seem extreme and implausible in two related ways. First, Quine seems to be suggesting that all our beliefs, what he calls our total science, are involved in generating a prediction. Secondly, when prediction and observation fail to match up, we are free to change any part of our total science in order to make our beliefs consistent.

We can make these worries more vivid by considering an imagined case. I predict that I will meet a friend of mine, Dan, in the pub in 45 minutes. We spoke on the phone and we both agreed we would be there by then. But 45 minutes later I am there but he is not. How can I explain this? Quite easily, most probably. He has been delayed and so is late.

Now on the extreme reading of Quine, there seem to be many other things I could say. All of my science is involved in generating that prediction, so I could in theory revise any one of my beliefs. I could for example deny:

1. What I obviously seem to see, which is that my friend is not now here; or
2. That the laws of quantum theory hold; or
3. Some fundamental law of logic or mathematics.

All three of these denials seem on the face of it absurd. Quine, I think, would agree. We might think he would have a simple justification for the absurdity of these revisions: the pragmatic considerations that guide the revision of our beliefs should rule out any of these revisions. Quine does say this, but there are additional reasons within Quine's system for thinking that such changes are unwarranted. By thinking about each in turn, we shall learn a little more about Quine's holism.

Let us start with denial of belief 2. The idea that we might revise quantum theory to explain my friend's failure to turn up seems absurd because, on the face of it, quantum theory has nothing to do with why I predicted that my friend would turn up at the pub in 45 minutes. Quine agrees: "It is an uninteresting legalism . . . to think of our scientific system of the world as involved *en bloc* in every prediction. More modest chunks suffice, and so may be ascribed their independent empirical meaning" (Quine 1981: 71). So in practice I need only consider revising parts of the more modest chunk that are necessary to generate my prediction.

This is sensible but it does not help us see why we are reluctant to claim that we could revise either belief 1 or 3. Both are necessary in generating the conflict between our prediction and our observation. Without the observation that my friend is not actually there, there would be no conflict at all. Without the rules of logic and simple arithmetic, I could not generate my predication. If I phoned my friend at 7.05, I would expect him to be there at 7.50. Part of that prediction depends on the simple arithmetic claim that $5 + 45 = 50$. So we need to say something else about these cases.

Let us take observations first. We all agree that in certain circumstances it can be right to deny what you think you see. Quine provides us with one example: hallucination. Perhaps if I am waiting in the pub and I am very drunk, that might give me another reason to doubt what I think I see. I also know that I am less reliable as an observer when I do not wear my spectacles. But in general just denying what I observe does not seem a reasonable strategy to adopt. One Quinean reason for this could, as we noted earlier, appeal to our pragmatic standards. To deny what we see introduces unwanted complexity into our system. It is usually simpler to deny one of my other beliefs. There is, though, a more important reason for giving additional credence to our observations. The whole point of our beliefs, from common sense to science, according to Quine, is to predict the future course of experience: "[W]hen I cite predictions as the checkpoint of science . . . I see it as defining a particular language game . . . the game of science. A sentence's claim to be scientific rests on what it contributes to a theory whose checkpoints are in prediction" (Quine 1990: 20). If we systematically reject any data that come into conflict with our predictions, then we have given up on the game of science. We have a responsibility to take our observations seriously if we are to do science at all. Quine is not a simple-minded coherentist. The aim of science is not simply to arrive at a set of beliefs that are consistent with each other. Our system of beliefs must make correct predictions. We should deny our observations only if we have good reason to think they might be error.

What then of the third category? This is the most interesting case because it seems doubtful that we can even make sense of the possibility of revising statements such as $2 + 5 = 7$ or some of the laws of logic. Part of the attraction of the Kantian and Carnapian systems, whatever their faults, is that they recognize a difference between the claims of mathematics and logic, and those of science; and both Carnap and Kant try to offer some explanation of the apparently special status of these disciplines. Is there anything Quine can say to explain or explain away why we think that logic and mathematics are special in this way?

A first effort to explain what Quine might mean here is to note that revision of a claim such as $2 + 5 = 7$ is of course possible in one sense. We could change what we meant by the symbols. If we decided to represent what we now call "2" by the symbol "3" and what we now call "3" by the symbol "2", then in our new language we would have to say $2 + 5 = 7$ is false and in fact $3 + 5 = 7$. But this wouldn't be a very interesting change. It is nothing more than a change of symbolism: $2 + 5$ still equals 7, but we've just chosen to represent 2 in a different way. It is impossible to see how any change like this could help us when confronted with a mismatch between predictions and observations.

Even if we grant that we cannot see how to revise mathematical statements in ways that are not trivial, Quine is not forced to grant a special status to logic or mathematics. He can claim that the fact that we cannot imagine changes in simple arithmetic is a psychological fact about us. It does not mean that they are unrevisable in principle. To make this plausible, we need only consider the case of Euclidean geometry. For an eighteenth-century thinker, someone like Kant, it would have been impossible to imagine revising statements such as "the internal angles of a triangle add up to 180 degrees". With the development of non-Euclidean geometry, it became possible to think that this statement might be false; and with the development of Einstein's theory of general relativity, we began to think that in fact it was false (as a claim about physical space at least). We may be in the same situation with regard to our basic logic and arithmetic as the eighteenth-century thinker was with regard to geometry.

The claim that we might revise *any* of our beliefs is motivated by both logic and the history of science. Logic tells us that, given that any prediction involves the conjunction of a large set of beliefs, any one of those could be revised to remove the contradiction between our prediction and the evidence. The history of science shows us that many claims that philosophers have thought to be special, distinct and unrevisable have turned out to be false – and so revised.

We can summarize the more nuanced claims of Quine's holism by picturing his field of belief as divided into three layers (see Figure 2.1). In the first layer we have observation statements. All our predictions have ultimately to be tested against these. In the second layer we have what we shall broadly call science. It includes highly abstract beliefs such as the claims of quantum theory as well as highly specific but non-observable claims, such as where I thought I left my stapler. In the third and central layer we have our logic and mathematics. Logic plays a role in the deduction of any prediction; mathematics plays a role in most serious science. These claims are at this time psychologically imposs-ible for us to question, but we must remain open to at least the possi-bility that in the future things may be different.

The business of science is largely concerned with making revisions within limited bundles of beliefs in the middle layer so that they come into agreement (or at least no longer conflict) with beliefs in the outside layer. The divisions between these layers are porous. We can deny observations in special circumstances. Maybe I am hallucinating. Beliefs that we might not think are relevant to our prediction may through further work come to be seen as relevant. Perhaps my friend Dan has disappeared down a spontaneously generated black hole. Then maybe I shall need to reconsider my beliefs about fundamental physics.

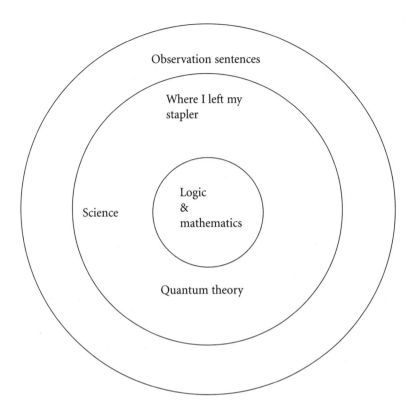

Figure 2.1   Quine's field of beliefs

And beliefs that now seem impossible to revise may in time become revisable. Such might be the fate of logic and mathematics.

Naturalized philosophy

With this more carefully articulated account of Quine's holism in place, let us return to naturalism. Carnap's view allowed him to dismiss certain metaphysical questions as pseudo-questions. If we ask whether there are really physical objects or numbers, we are not really asking a question about how the world is; we are just wondering what might be the most fruitful linguistic framework in which to couch our science. Quine rejects this separate philosophical perspective and so for him questions about what exists are to be decided in the same way as any ordinary scientific question: "Our acceptance of an ontology is, I think, similar in principle to our acceptance of a scientific theory . . . Our ontology is determined once we have fixed upon the overall conceptual scheme which is to accommodate science in the broadest sense" (Quine 1980: 16–17). Quine's view of ontology has some surprising consequences. Mathematics is an indispensable part of our science. It makes assertions about abstract objects such as numbers and sets, so we as good naturalists should accept mathematical objects into our ontology.

In Chapter 4 we shall look in more detail at Quine's ideas about ontological questions and the surprising consequences he draws. In the rest of this chapter, I want to concentrate on what epistemology looks like from Quine's naturalist perspective. According to Quine:

> Naturalism does not repudiate epistemology, but assimilates it to empirical psychology. Science itself tells us that our information about the world is limited to irritations of our sensory surfaces, and then the epistemological question is in turn a question within science: the question how we human animals can have managed to arrive at science from such limited information. (Quine 1981: 72)

This, in a nutshell, is Quine's naturalized epistemology. Part of what we need to do is to see how, if at all, Quine's empirical epistemology has connections with the more traditional philosophical enterprise of epistemology as providing a ground or foundation for our knowledge. In particular, will the naturalist be able to provide a theory of our knowledge that will help solve the twin problems of scepticism and induction?

I shall tackle Quine's naturalized epistemology in two parts. First, I shall abstract away from Quine's particular account of naturalized epistemology. We shall investigate to what extent an empirical theory that explains how we "arrive at science from such limited information" can help us with the traditional preoccupations of epistemology. In the second part, we shall look at Quine's positive proposals for explaining how we go from what he calls the meagre input of sensory stimulations to the torrential output of our science.

Naturalized epistemology and traditional epistemology

Let us imagine then we have a very complicated theory, let's call it theory X, which explains how it is that any individual forms the beliefs that he does on the basis of certain experiences. Theory X will have to use the resources of many different sciences. We shall need a story about how our senses work, how we learn a language, possibly also a story about how our beliefs are shaped by those around us. Let us just assume that all of this is in place. In what sense would we want to say that theory X is epistemology?

The kind of explanations theory X would provide have strong similarities with the work of certain classical epistemologists. The British empiricists, Locke, Berkeley and Hume, were all interested in questions about the origins of our ideas. Take Hume's story about causation. When we see one billiard ball hit another ball and the second ball move off, we think that the impact of the first ball caused the movement of the second ball. Where do we get such an idea? According to Hume there are only three possible sources for ideas: reason, experience or the imagination. Our idea of causation cannot come from reason because there is no contradiction in imagining that when ball 1 strikes ball 2, ball 2 does not move off. We cannot get the idea from experience since all we actually see is one ball moving up to the other ball and the second rolling off. We do not see the cause. So the idea must come from our imagination. We project the idea of cause and effect on to what we see because we have seen many billiard-ball collisions and that has led us to believe that whenever we see a moving billiard ball collide with a stationary one, the stationary one will in turn move. Theory X would in a similar but scientifically more sophisticated way provide an explanation for the origin of our beliefs.

In other ways, though, theory X seems irrelevant to epistemology. We expect an epistemology to answer the problems of scepticism and induction that we introduced in Chapter 1. Any empirical theory just takes it for granted that we have knowledge of the external world or that we can reason from the past experience to the future. Naturalized epistemology in this respect can seem inferior to the first philosophies of Kant and Carnap. Whatever their faults, both philosophers have a way of solving or dissolving the problems of scepticism and induction.

This may make us wonder whether naturalized epistemology is really epistemology at all. In many of his writings, Quine has attempted to respond to this worry. He has tried to show that there are important connections between his conception of naturalized epistemology and the traditional problem of scepticism. The key to understanding these further connections between Quine and earlier epistemology is his claim that properly understood sceptical worries arise within science.

The challenge runs as follows. Science itself teaches that there is no clairvoyance; that the only information that can reach our sensory surfaces from external objects must be limited to two-dimensional optical projections and various impacts of airwaves on the eardrums and some gaseous reactions in the nasal passages and a few kindred odds and ends. How, the challenge proceeds, could one hope to find out about the external world from such meager traces? In short, if our science were true, how could we know it?   (Quine 1981: 2)

This does indeed sound like an important challenge, but it does not on the face of it sound like the traditional problem of scepticism. The challenge of traditional scepticism is more radical: how can we know anything at all?

Again, Quine justifies this picture of the epistemologist's task by invoking the work of previous philosophers. "Berkeley was bent on deriving depth from two-dimensional data for no other reason than the physical fact that the surface of the eye is two-dimensional" (*ibid.*). Berkeley's worry arises from his scientific understanding of vision. Similarly, modern epistemologists do not in general motivate scepticism by appealing, like Descartes, to malicious demons. They prefer to ask: how do we know that we are not brains-in-a-vat being manipulated by a mad scientist? The appeal of this picture, one could argue, is again based on our scientific understanding. Science teaches us that our knowledge of the external world is mediated through stimulations of our brains in various ways. The naturalized epistemologist differs from his more traditional colleagues in recognizing the proper source of these doubts. Once we recognize that it is within science that sceptical doubts arise, then we are quite at liberty to use our scientific theories to answer these questions. We might for example be able to use our imagined theory X to show that the brain-in-a-vat hypothesis is impossible. Maybe the only way your brain can in fact be stimulated to produce the rich representation of the world you currently enjoy is if you are, in fact, a brain-in-a-body interacting with the world about you.

For a traditional epistemologist that would miss the point. Sceptical worries are worries about our knowledge *en bloc*. No science can help us answer them. Using science to justify science is, from this perspective, as we saw Chapter 1, just circular reasoning. One way to highlight this difference is again to contrast our theory X with more traditional philosophical accounts of how knowledge is possible. Let us take

Descartes's theory as our contrast. Descartes's ultimate justification for the reliability of our knowledge of the external world is that God exists and he is no deceiver. However, Descartes's arguments for the existence of God are, frankly, hopeless. This is devastating for his epistemological project. Without the guarantee that God exists and is no deceiver Descartes cannot claim to know anything at all. Naturalized epistemology is not like this. Suppose we discover that theory X is not as perfect as I have described. Perhaps theory X works for most human beings but, for some reason, when tested on Christian fundamentalists, things go wrong. The theory predicts that, given their experience and background, they should say and believe things such as, "The earth is millions of years old" and "The Bible is not to be taken literally", but for some reason they do not. This discovery would not undermine the rest of our knowledge. It would just show that we needed to refine theory X in some way. Our scientific theory of how we form beliefs is just one of the planks that make up Neurath's boat. It too can be revised if our predictions fail to match up with experience.

The traditional epistemologists and the Quinean naturalist have two different perspectives on the question of knowledge. The traditional epistemologist starts with sceptical doubts, uncertain of anything, and wonders how he can ever recover his knowledge. The naturalized epistemologist starts afloat Neurath's ship, standing on the planks of scientific and common-sense knowledge. Doubts about any one of our beliefs might arise but the only possible source of this doubt is the rest of our science and experience.

Changing the subject?

Quine admits that his attitude to the epistemological project is "no minor deviation from the Cartesian paradigm". If the question of Cartesian scepticism is definitive of epistemology, then naturalists such as Quine are indeed advocating a change of subject. The question of interest for us is to consider whether or not Quine has good reasons for motivating this change of subject.

One obvious reason to give up on the project of finding an answer to the sceptical problem is because it seems hopeless. All the answers given in the history of philosophy, through Descartes to Kant to Carnap to the present day have (most people would agree) failed. So part of the naturalist's attitude might be: why bother with a question that we cannot answer? Let us try something fruitful.

Quine adds to this pessimistic survey of past philosophical attempts to answer the sceptic a logical point. If we are, broadly speaking, empiricists and think that our knowledge of the world comes to us ultimately through our senses and that an answer to the sceptic's worries requires that we have certainty about our beliefs, then our task is impossible. Part of the lesson of failures of early empiricist attempts to reduce talk of objects to talk of sense-data is that what is implied by a scientific theory always outstrips any actual evidence we have for that theory. In the jargon used by contemporary philosophers, scientific theories are underdetermined by our evidence. This is one way to think of what Quine calls the gap between meagre input and torrential output. It is also a way to think about the problem of induction. The evidence we have from the past now does not determine how things will go in the future. Quine does not in fact think there is an answer to Hume's problem: "the Humean predicament is the human predicament" (Quine 1969: 72), as he pithily puts it. From the Quinean perspective, what this shows us is that we cannot have absolute certainty that our (scientific) beliefs are true. This fact in itself, though, should not undermine our confidence in our science. The mere fact that we might be wrong should not by itself shake our belief in any part of our science. Rather it should cultivate in us an attitude of modesty towards it. We should always remain open to the possibility that future knowledge or experience could force us to revise any of our beliefs.

Another reason for rejecting the Cartesian project is suggested by Christopher Hookway (1988: 197–8). Descartes's worry is that our beliefs may not match up with how things are in reality. To make sense of this picture we need to have some idea of what we mean by "reality" that is theoretically quite independent from how things are in our heads. For Descartes the answer to this is intimately bound up with his theology. The way the world really is for Descartes is the way that God knows it to be. The aim of his epistemology, if you like, is to know the world as God does. Modern, secular epistemologists cannot share this conception of either reality or what epistemology is ultimately striving to discover. Naturalists, like Quine, will claim that *our* conception of reality is just the one we get from our science; and *our* conception of the epistemological task is simply: how do we know about those things like wombats, DNA and electrons that our science talks about?

This response may seem unsatisfactory given that almost all of us, when we first read Descartes, find ourselves persuaded that there is a real problem here. But as Hookway suggests, there are two things the naturalist might say in response. First, he might claim that the doubts we feel on reading the First Meditation are not real. No one really believes that they are being deceived by a malicious demon. These doubts are merely a kind of game of make-believe that we indulge in while in the philosophy classroom but have no bearing on what we think of as knowledge or knowledge claims in our actual lives. Secondly, he might claim that the real force of the sceptical argument is found precisely in the kind of scepticism that Quine allows. What we are responding to is not the imaginary cases Descartes presents. Rather, what Descartes's stories help us recognize is the big gap between the causal interactions with the world that are the source of our knowledge and the elaborate and complex beliefs we have about the world. This is of course precisely the relationship that Quine's naturalized epistemology is supposed to address.

I leave it to the reader to decide whether these considerations do enough to motivate the subtle change of subject that Quine recommends.

Worries about justification

We have traced some connections between Quine's programme and traditional problems of scepticism, and have been forced to admit that in certain ways Quine is suggesting a change of subject. I have tried to suggest that change of subject is well motivated from the naturalist standpoint. Even if you are persuaded that such a change is indeed motivated, there are other reasons for thinking that Quine's project does not engage with the real concerns of epistemology.

Consider again our theory X. Imagine now two individuals Peter and Simone who have very different beliefs. Peter believes that the earth is flat, that God created the earth and mankind 4,000 years ago, and that the world will end within the year. He knows all this, he claims, because God communicates with him every night and tells him such things. Simone is a scientist. She believes that the world is roughly round but flat at the poles, that all life on our planet, including ourselves, slowly evolved over millions of years and that the world will probably end in about 5 billion years when the sun becomes a red giant star. She knows this because she has been to school and learnt such things; and she knows many more specific facts about the world directly related to her research. If theory X is as I described it, then it should be able to account for the beliefs of both these individuals. We should be able to tell a scientific story that explains Peter's peculiar beliefs and Simone's sensible ones. But of course this just shows that our scientific theory X omits something important. Simone's beliefs are, we are inclined to think, *justified*. Peter's beliefs are not. A scientific story that merely explains how any individual as a matter of fact came to have the beliefs he does cannot distinguish between beliefs that are justified and those that are not.

Here, then, is a second important reason for thinking that what Quine is suggesting is not epistemology. Even if we are not worried about sceptical problems, an epistemology should tell us something about when beliefs are justified and when they are not. Epistemology is in part a normative discipline, telling us when it is right to believe something and when not. A merely descriptive psychology or science cannot fill this role.

What we need to add to our theory X and Quine's naturalized epistemology is a naturalized account of epistemic norms. Two sorts of response suggest themselves. One strategy would be to try to provide a naturalistic account of justification. If we can do that, then we can explain in a naturalistically respectable way why Simone's views are justified and Peter's are not. The subject of Chapter 3, reliabilism, suggests one way that this might be done. The second response, more in line with the elements of Quine's philosophy that we have laid out above, would be to reject a general characterization of justification and instead try to give an account of the norms involved in science. The naturalist would hope that these norms could be described and defended without having to appeal to anything that look liked first philosophy. Quine gives some indication of what he thinks those norms would be. Theory revision is governed by the pragmatic standards of simplicity, conservativeness and fruitfulness, among others. In later writings he has suggested further ways in which naturalized epistemology can suggest norms to the scientist: "Insofar as theoretical epistemology gets naturalized into a chapter of theoretical science, so normative epistemology gets naturalized into a chapter of engineering: the technology of anticipating sensory stimulation" (Quine 1990: 19). Just as physics tells the engineer how he should build the bridge if he wants it to support the weight of traffic, descriptive epistemology can tell us how we should pursue science if we want our theories to stand up to empirical test. Furthermore, one very fundamental norm emerges for naturalized epistemology. "The most notable norm of naturalized epistemology actually coincides with that of traditional epistemology. It is simply the watchword of empiricism: *nihil in mente quod non prius sens* [Nothing in the mind, without first being in the senses]" (*ibid.*). Science itself teaches us that we learn about the world through our senses. So naturalized epistemology counsels us only to take seriously those theories and ideas that come from empirical research. These very general remarks are by themselves enough to begin to form a case against Peter and in favour of Simone. Simone's views stand up to observational evidence, Peter's, for the most part, do not. Unfortunately Quine's remarks here are at best indicative of a general approach we might take. In Chapter 4, when we turn to philosophy of science, we shall see if some of Quine's ideas can be developed into a defence of naturalized philosophy of science.

Let us review our general assessment of naturalized epistemology before looking in detail at what Quine actually thinks a theory that explains how we go from sensory stimulations to science will look like. Quine's project has similarities with past epistemologies. Like the British empiricists, Quine is interested in how we come to have the beliefs we do. However, naturalized epistemology does not seek an ultimate justification of science from outside science. That would be to attempt to do first philosophy. We need then to understand traditional epistemological questions differently. The sceptical challenge is not a demand for an ultimate grounding for science but a picturesque way of formulating problems that arise within it, specifically the problem of how we are able to form such elaborate theories about the world on the basis of the small amount of information we obtain through our senses. The role of our naturalized theory of knowledge is not to provide a foundation on which the remainder of our science is supposed to rest. It is just another part of our scientific picture. It can be revised while holding on to (most of) the rest of our scientific beliefs. Thinking of our epistemology as merely like any scientific theory leads us to the problem we noted above. Epistemology involves normative or evaluative notions such as justification. Science just describes. So an epistemology that is identified with a certain kind of scientific theory cannot perform the role of a normative epistemology. Something else needs to be added.

Quine's account of naturalized epistemology

Let us turn now to the details of Quine's own vision of naturalized epistemology. Given that Quine claims that epistemology is "assimilated to empirical psychology", we might expect his account of naturalized epistemology to be filled with references to contemporary work in psychology and cognitive science on such subjects as perception and language acquisition. Surprisingly, it is not. What we get is a story from the armchair about how it is that we human individuals go from initial stimulation of our senses to the production of sentences making reference to objects far removed from any direct sensory access.

One way to think of what Quine is doing is that he is providing a naturalistically respectable reinterpretation of Carnap's early project. The Carnap of the *Logical Structure of the World* wanted to tell a story about how to reconstruct our knowledge from elementary experiences plus logic and mathematics. Quine replaces elementary experiences with the scientifically more respectable triggering of sensory receptors but asks essentially the same question: how can we construct our knowledge of the world from such triggering?

Quine's story can be broken down into a series of stages. We start with an experience that triggers a class of sensory receptors. Quine calls this the global stimulus. The same sort of global stimulus will produce the same sorts of triggering. Quine calls this receptual similarity. Different experiences are classed together as what Quine calls perceptually similar when they produce the same or similar reactions in us (or indeed any animal). When we see a rabbit, we may not always see it from the same place or angle. We might on occasion be able to see only its ears, on others its tail. However, all these experiences cause us to react in similar ways; we react to the salient, rabbity features of these different experiences. "Perceptual similarity is the basis of all expectation, all learning, all habit formation. It operates through our propensity to expect perceptually similar situations to have sequels perceptually similar to each other. This is primitive induction" (Quine 1990: 20). Without these primitive inductive abilities no creature would be able to recognize food or a dangerous predator. These primitive inductive habits are a gift, Quine speculates, from evolution. For some creatures, "birds, apes and humans", natural selection has been even more generous. We are able to share information. Human beings can speak. We learn to do so by associating the sounds of a language with perceptually similar stimuli.

The most primitive form of speech, what Quine calls our entering wedge into the language, are *observation sentences*. An observation sentence is understood initially, as Quine puts it, holophrastically. It has no internal structure. A sound, say "Mama", is linked to some global stimulus some part of which is made salient by the language teacher by pointing or perhaps shaking the object in front of the child. ("Mama" from the point of view of a mature language user is an elliptical way of asserting "that's Mama" and is in Quine's view a one-word sentence.) The child quickly learns many observation sentences and soon in turn picks up the use of various logical connectives, such as "not" and "and". We might learn "not", for example, when corrected by the language teacher. The most significant novel form of compound observation sentences the child learns, though, is predication. When the child learns the sentences, "swan" and "white", he can join these to make the new sentence "white swan"; and he learns in the process that the connection between these two sentences is tighter than merely conjoining them with "and". It is only correct to utter "white swan" if the white part of the observed scene overlaps entirely the swan part. This is the first hint of the introduction of entities into our world-view since predication suggests a spatial clustering of features; and objects, says Quine, are in the first instance recognized as such spatial clusterings.

Observation sentences may be conjoined in other useful ways. They may be used to form what Quine calls observation categoricals. Here we use language not just to report what we sense but to formulate a primitive law about the future course of experience. They are sentences such as: "When it snows, it's cold" and "When there's lightning, there's thunder".

Full-blown science requires laws, universal generalizations such as "All swans are white". This is the final stage in Quine's story and requires what he calls reification. We cannot get such universal generalizations from observational categoricals alone. The sentence "When there are swans, there is white" does not quite do it. That sentence could be true if there were black swans that happened, say, to be always accompanied by white doves. We need to introduce what Quine calls the essential indexical. Our sentence should become "When there is a swan, *it* is white":

> The pronoun "it" is a vital new link between the component observation sentences . . . It posits common carriers of the two traits. The carriers are [swans], bodies. I see this pronominal structure achieving objective reference. An observational categorical of this strengthened sort, "Whenever . . ., it . . ." I call a *focal* observational categorical. The earlier ones [such as "when there's thunder, there's lightning"] are *free* observational categoricals. (Quine 1990: 27)

Here, then, objects enter Quine's story. They are posited to provide these stronger forms of observational categoricals. The rest of what we call common sense or science is just more of the same. Further entities are posited – electrons, genes and superegos – in the hope of producing categorical sentences that can be combined with other sentences to predict the future course of sense experience. Once we have introduced objects, they feed back into the holophrastically learned observation sentences and provide them with some structure. The sentence "swan" can now be understood to be making a commitment to the existence of the object swan. When, given our more sophisticated theory, we understand our observation sentences as referring to objects, we understand them as Quine puts it "analytically"; that is, as now having some structure.

We can schematize the progress from stimulation to science as follows:

> Triggering → observation sentences → combinations of observation sentences (conjunction, predication, etc.) → free observational categoricals → focal observation categorical (and reference and bodies) → science

What we have is a story that tells us how we are able to produce the complex web of beliefs which constitutes our science from basic sensory stimulation. This is just what Quine promised us: a story that takes us from stimulus to science.

The return of scepticism

Many commentators have noted a similarity between Quine's naturalized epistemology and Descartes's supernatural epistemology. Descartes's system introduces a fundamental distinction between our ideas about the world and the way the world is. Sceptical worries arise because we cannot see how to bridge the gap or how to rule out deviant causes of our ideas, such as evil demons. Quine's system seems to embody a similar distinction. Between our beliefs about the world and the objects those beliefs are about are the triggerings of our nerve endings and holophrastically understood observation sentences. As with Descartes, it seems possible to imagine that the causes of those triggerings might be quite different from what we ordinarily take them to be.

For example, it seems possible that what causes the sensory triggerings that prompt assent to the sentence "swan" are swans for me but ducks for you. Worse yet, it could be the case that what causes those sensory triggerings for me is not anything in the physical world at all but could instead be our fabled mad scientists manipulating my brain-in-a-vat. If our knowledge of the world is ultimately based on such triggering, and all the objects and things we take to exist are just theoretical postulates employed to aid our prediction of the future course of experience, it seems that we have no guarantee that the way our science describes the world matches up with how things are. Naturalized epistemology seems to lead to scepticism.

In fact, Quine seems in an even worse position than Descartes. At least Descartes can be certain of the contents of his own mind. Quine's starting point in epistemology is not something we are directly aware of; the naturalized epistemologist begins with causal input into our sensory system. But that input is itself something postulated by our science. If the science we construct can be as massively wrong as the brain-in-a-vat hypothesis suggests, then we cannot even be certain that there are inputs of the kind Quine describes.

There is a real problem here, or more accurately a set of problems. There are, I think, at least three things people are alluding to when they claim that Quine's naturalized epistemology leads to scepticism, and I shall try to tease these out below. The first can be answered quite easily. The other two suggest that there is perhaps something wrong with Quine's account of language.

The first and least troubling problem is that we might be looking for some kind of guarantee that similar sensory triggerings have similar causes. We want some way to rule out my suggestion that what causes me to assent to the sentence "swan" are swans but, for you, ducks. Quine has a good naturalistic answer to this. Evolution has made us in the same way, so we respond in the same fashion to the same stimulus: "So we see a preestablished harmony of perceptual similarity standards ... This public harmony of private standards of perceptual similarity is accounted for by natural selection" (Quine 1990: 21).

A second way of understanding the objection is more subtle and, for Quine, more difficult to address. The problem does not concern epistemology so much as semantics, and has been most forcefully put by Quine's one-time student Donald Davidson (2001). That semantic issues are raised by Quine's account is no surprise. The naturalized epistemology of Quine that I have just sketched is an account of how we first acquire a language, and a story about how words first come to mean anything at all for us. So worries about meaning seem appropriate when thinking about Quine's epistemology.

Davidson's point is that in order to communicate successfully, we must share meanings. If I say "there's a rabbit", then unless you understand by the term "rabbit" the same thing that I do, we have failed to communicate. The worry then becomes something like this. The meaning of theoretical sentences is linked to the world via observation sentences. Our observation sentences mean what they do in virtue of the sensory stimulations that prompt them. But sensory stimulations are, as philosophers would say, private. I cannot share my sensory stimulations with you, any more than I can share my headache with you. So there is nothing in Quine's story to explain how it is that we can ever come to share meanings. This issue is difficult and complex. To address it properly we would have to consider in detail Quine's theory of meaning and concepts such as radical translation, which we have not touched on here. I leave this worry about language and meaning to one side for now, but we shall return to these issues in Chapter 7.

The core of the third and perhaps most pressing problem is that Quine's naturalized epistemology seems to employ a distinction between data on the one hand (sensory triggerings) and projected theory on the other. And the way that connection is described is, as it were, loose enough to admit sceptical possibilities. Barry Stroud makes the point well:

> [A] completely general distinction between everything we get through the senses, on the one hand, and what is or is not true of the external world, on the other, would cut us off forever from knowledge of the world about us. That general epistemic distinction is fatal to the naturalizing project. It has the effect of casting us out of our knowledge of the world, as it were, and leaving us with no independent reason to suppose that any of our projections are true. (Stroud 1984: 248)

Given my earlier general remarks about naturalized epistemology, this seems an unlikely conclusion. Epistemology was supposed to be just one part of our total science. Worries about our epistemology should not threaten the rest of our science. How has Neurath's ship been sunk by sceptical worries? In part, the problem arises for us because we are tempted to understand Quine's story in the Cartesian spirit. Reading it in that Cartesian way can make scepticism seem unavoidable. We begin with nothing and ask how it is that we get knowledge. But from the naturalist perspective that is the wrong way to think of the problem.

The naturalist does not start with a general doubt about how the world is. He starts within science. He believes in objects and events in a world that exists beyond his skin. We appeal to those objects and events in order to make sense of how it is that we come to have beliefs at all. Given that we have such beliefs about the world, if we come up with an epistemological story that makes it seem impossible that we ever arrived at such beliefs or even why we should have these beliefs rather than others, then something is wrong with that story. We need to revise our epistemology, not abandon our science. If we are to be fair to Quine, objections to his naturalized epistemology must be seen in that spirit. So is it the case that Quine's epistemology is just a bad theory?

One reason to think it is bad is Davidson's. It cannot be an adequate account of language because it fails to explain how communication is possible. It fails to explain how we can relate to others when we talk since all communication depends upon something private. Stroud is making a related point. Quine's account of language fails to explain how we can relate to objects in the outside world, again because all our talk seems to depend on something private, our sensory stimulations. What is the relation between our sentences and the world that allows us to say that any of our scientific claims are true? Quine often talks of language as an instrument. Language is "a conceptual apparatus that helps us to forsee and control the triggerings of sensory receptors" (1980: 1). Objects are referred to as "posits". If language is just an instrument, if the things that we take to exist are "posits" or "projections", then why should we think of any of the claims we make as true, rather than just useful for getting by? Here then we have another problem for Quine's account of language. It is difficult to see how our words hook up with objects in the world. It is difficult to see how things in the world can or could make certain sentences true. I think Stroud is right that it is this aspect of Quine's naturalized epistemology that produces sceptical worries. The naturalist wants to stand firm on the planks of his best science when investigating the world and people's knowledge of it. Quine's story undermines the naturalist's confidence that those planks are as sturdy as he thinks. For it turns out that, if Quine is right, all those entities – chairs, electrons, people – that he believes in are just projections from his sensory stimulations. Why, having learnt this, should he continue to take these projections seriously?

Another reason, not related to the sceptical problem, to be dissatisfied with Quine's account is that it fails to explain why we are justified in believing the claims of our science. The problem with Quine's talk of sensory triggerings and the positing of objects is that it does not seem relevant to our understanding of the success of our science. When we think of evidence for or against some theory, we tend as scientists not to ask the question: how have I, as an individual, come to know that such and such is the case? Rather, we ask what facts about the world supports our scientific conclusions. If I am asked what evidence there is in favour of the constancy of the speed of light, then, if I know my stuff, I shall say that this is a theoretical consequence of Maxwell's equations. I shall also point to the evidence of the famous Michelson and Morley experiments, which show that the speed of light is constant and independent of the direction in which light travels near the earth's surface. An additional story about how as a matter of fact various causal processes in my sensory system caused me to have this belief is irrelevant. This is again a point that we have already made. Quine's story is descriptive. We need to understand what justifies my beliefs, not simply what caused them.

If a naturalist is going to provide an adequate account of our knowledge of the world, he has to be able to explain certain facts about language that seem mysterious on Quine's account. How is it that sentences come to have meaning so that we may communicate? In virtue of what is it that certain sentences are true? What is the relation between words and the world that explains truth and falsity? And there remain unanswered worries about the normative aspect of epistemology. How are we to find a place for the norms of justification and scientific method within a naturalistic world-view? These are the topics of Chapters 3, 4 and 7. Without answers to these questions, traditional epistemologists are entitled to think that Quine's story fails to provide an account of what knowledge is and how it is possible.

Quine the unscientific naturalist

One obvious further reason to be dissatisfied with Quine's naturalized epistemology should be underlined. Quine's account of language acquisition is an entirely *a priori*, armchair piece of theorizing. It pays no heed to and shows no interest in anything that modern psychology or linguistics has to say about perception or language learning. I find Quine's attack on first philosophy with which we began this chapter compelling, but his attempts at naturalized philosophy disappointing. As we try to articulate a more convincing form of naturalism throughout the remaining chapters, we shall have to leave behind the comfy armchair speculation of Quine's philosophy and begin to think in detail about the content of real science and its methods of justification.

three

Reliabilism

Sceptical worries have been at the centre of most of our discussions about knowledge so far. A different but perhaps more common approach to epistemology is to seek out an analysis of what knowledge is. If we can say what knowledge is, then we should be able to identify in particular cases if we know or not. The subject of this chapter, reliabilism, grew out of this tradition of philosophy.

Justified true belief

Our story begins this time with Plato rather than Descartes. Knowledge, Plato tell us in the *Theaetetus*, is justified true belief. That knowledge requires truth seems straightforward enough. If my belief is not true, it is mistaken and mistakes cannot possibly be knowledge. It also seems very reasonable that knowledge requires justification. For example, I might be asked to guess how many grains of sand there are in a bucket. Let us say I guess there are 3,127 and I form a belief that there are 3,127 grains of sand in the bucket. It just so happens to turn out that my belief is correct, so I have a true belief. Nobody would describe this as knowledge. I am just lucky that my belief corresponds to how things are. The difference between mere true belief and genuine knowledge appears intuitively to be that in cases of genuine knowledge I am justified in asserting my belief. I can offer some reason in virtue of which I am entitled to say what I believe. For example, I might believe truly that there are 27 students in my philosophy class. The reason I believe this is that I have counted them. This provides a proper justification for my belief and so I would be entitled to say that I know that there are 27 students in the class.

This simple, intuitive definition of knowledge was challenged in a famous paper by Edmund Gettier (1963). Gettier pointed out that there were conditions under which somebody might have a true justified belief but we would not describe them as knowing. For example, suppose I believe that Inverness Caledonian Thistle won their last match. The reason I believe this is because I read in the paper that Inverness won their last match. I know that newspapers generally report these things accurately so I have a justification for my belief. It just so happens, though, that the paper I read was a week old and referred not to the last match played but to the one before last. Nevertheless it turns out that Inverness did win their last match. So I have a true justified belief that Inverness won their last match. But because of the way this has been justified, by referring to a paper that is a week out of date, it does not really seem to be a case of knowledge. It just seems to be a lucky coincidence that Inverness won last week and the week before. My justification does not seem to link up in the right way with my belief.

The idea that true justified belief is an adequate analysis of knowledge can be challenged in another way. Gettier-style examples challenge the sufficiency of the definition. They suggest that there could be cases where there is true justified belief but that does not amount to knowledge. There are other cases in which having a true justified belief is not a necessary condition for knowledge; that is, somebody can have knowledge despite the fact that they do not have a true justified belief. This idea is suggested by reliabilists.

Reliabilists claim that I can know something even though I can offer no justification for my belief. What is important about knowing, according to reliabilists, is not in fact that I can offer an explicit justification for my beliefs but rather that the process by which I acquired my belief is a reliable one, where by reliable we just mean that it is more likely to produce true beliefs than false beliefs. The idea was first presented by Alvin Goldman (1979) and has been refined and developed in a variety of ways by a number of different philosophers, prominent among them Fred Dretske (1981). The basic idea is easy to motivate.

An example can illustrate the appeal of reliabilism. Apparently the sex of chickens is something that is very difficult to determine just by looking. You can, though, train individuals to identify the sex of chickens very successfully. Somehow in the process of training, of looking at the appropriate chicken bits and being told by an expert which sex the bird is, individuals simply catch on to something that helps them to identify the chicken's sex. If you ask them why they believe that the particular chicken that they have identified is female, say, they cannot give an answer. Nevertheless appropriate tests show that these individuals are very reliable discriminators between the sexes of chickens. So, the thought would go, it seems reasonable to say that these chicken sexers *know* whether a chicken is male or female, and we can say that they know not because they can offer a reason or a justification for their belief. They can't. But because the mechanism, unknown to them, by which they identify the sex of chickens reliably generates true beliefs.

If the traditional account of knowledge is correct, and knowledge requires us to be able to offer explicit justifications for our beliefs, then very few creatures can be classed as knowers. Animals and pre-linguistic children, since they cannot ever offer reasons, cannot be knowers. This to me at least seems counterintuitive. If a dog buries his bones in my neighbour's back garden and can reliably dig them up when he fancies a gnaw, I am inclined to say that the dog has some knowledge – knowledge that his bones are buried in a certain part of my neighbour's garden. I say this, reasonably, I think, because he is a reliable bone locator. Whatever state in his brain encodes the location of the bones can be described as a state of knowing. If you agree with me, then you should reject the standard requirement that knowledge requires justification, if by justification we mean explicitly offering a reason.

Here then we have the basic idea and motivation for reliabilism. What distinguishes knowledge from mere true belief is not that we can offer justifications for our beliefs, but that the mechanism by which we have acquired those beliefs reliably generates truth. As an account of knowledge this has clear appeal to a naturalist. We noted in Chapter 2 that justification, being a normative notion, creates difficulties for a naturalized epistemology; however, the idea of reliability, which has replaced justification, is straightforward. (I say "replaced", but some reliabilists think that what they have actually done is to explain what a good justification is. A belief is justified if it is generated by a reliable mechanism. Nothing much hangs on whether you prefer to say replaced or explained.) Obviously, whether or not a process is reliable, whether or not it generates more true beliefs than false beliefs, is a fact plain and simple. If reliabilists are right that knowledge consists in true belief generated by a reliable mechanism, then this holds out the hope that we can give a fully naturalistic account of what knowledge is. If we can give a naturalized account of what belief and truth are, then we will have a fully naturalized account of knowledge.

Reliabilism and scepticism

Before assessing the adequacy of the reliabilist's definition of knowledge, I want to think about how reliablilism can, if at all, address some of the problems we raised in Chapter 1. What will reliabilists say about the problems of scepticism and induction?

The problem of scepticism as normally understood takes for granted that we have knowledge of our ideas or our sense impressions, or what we think we know and see. We then wonder how, if at all, those ideas match up with things in the outside world. It seems as if a straight answer to the sceptical problem requires us to offer some justification that our ideas about the outside world really are, in the main at least, true. Descartes offers us one possible answer. We are justified in thinking that our beliefs about the outside world are true because God exists and is no deceiver, and moreover Descartes takes himself to have proved explicitly these "facts" starting only with those ideas of which we are certain. Reliablism does not offer us anything like Descartes's solution. What distinguishes knowledge from mere true belief is something the subjects themselves may know nothing about. The chicken sexers are an example of such subjects. They know but they do not know that they know.

Reliabilism is for this reason classed as a version of epistemological externalism. What makes the difference between mere true belief and knowledge is not something that the subjects themselves are aware of. It is a fact outwith their conscious grasp. An answer to the traditional problem of scepticism seems to insist on the opposite: internalism. An adequate answer to sceptical worries requires that we demonstrate that we know that we know; or at least that we know that we are not systematically deceived. So whatever its other virtues or vices, reliabilism cannot be thought of as an answer to the sceptic; in this way, at least, it is similar to Quine's naturalized epistemology.

A great deal of the controversy over reliabilism concerns the plausibility or otherwise of externalism, and not just from philosophers fascinated by the sceptical problem. Robert Brandom (2000), for one, has argued that phenomena reliabilists appeal to, in order to motivate the importance of reliable belief-forming processes over justifications, are marginal at best. Generally if someone is unable to provide any reason for their belief, we shall be reluctant to credit them with knowledge. If, for example, our chicken sexers do not know that they are reliable discriminators of a chicken's sex, then we shall question their right to even *believe* that the sex of a chicken is one sex or the other. Without knowledge of their own reliability it seems no more than an opinion, and a responsible careful enquirer should acknowledge this.

Brandom asks us to consider a community of believers who all have reliably formed beliefs but never offer reasons for them.

> Its members can serve as measuring instruments – that is as reliable indicators – both of perceptible environing states and of one another's responses. But they cannot treat themselves or one another as doing that. For they do not discriminate between reliable indication and unreliable indication. Absent such discrimination, they cannot be taken to understand themselves as *indicators* at all.   (Brandom 2000: 107)

Even though the community members satisfy the reliabilist's requirements for knowledge, they would themselves have no concept of knowledge. Since they are *never* able to provide reasons for their beliefs, they will never be able to form a belief about the reliability or otherwise of themselves or some other individual. If they cannot recognize these facts about each other and how they connect to the *justification* of their belief, they will not have any concept of belief either, claims Brandom. He goes further and questions whether any such community can be described as a community of *believers* at all. "[S]tates that do not stand in inferential relations to one another, that do not serve as reasons one for another, are not recognizable as beliefs at all" (*ibid.*: 108).

One reason to insist upon this is that otherwise too many things will count as knowers. Anything that reliably indicates some state of the world could be said to have knowledge. For example, a parrot trained to utter "red" in the presence of red things is a reliable indicator of red. But, claims Brandom, no one would credit the parrot with the *belief* that there is something red in front of it. Worse yet, rusting iron is a reliable indicator of moisture in the air. But we definitely do not want to say that the iron *knows* that there is moisture in the air.

The issue here concerns under what conditions it is appropriate to say that something *believes*. Clearly being a kind of thing that merely correctly registers certain changes in the environment is not enough, otherwise rusting iron can come out as a believer or knower. Brandom thinks that beliefs "are essentially things that can serve as premises and conclusions of inferences" (*ibid.*). If we believe that something is red, we are

> adopting a stance that involves further consequential commitments (for instance, to the object perceived as being coloured), that is incompatible with other commitments (for instance, to the object perceived being green) . . . no response that is not a node in a network of such broadly inferential involvements is recognizable as the application of *concepts*. And if not, it is not recognizable as a belief, or the expression of a belief, either.
>
> (*Ibid.*: 108–9)

Brandom's point, as I understand it, then is that internalists are right to insist on the importance of giving explicit reasons as part of our account of knowledge since only an animal that is in a position to give such reasons can count as a believer in the first place. Much here hangs on one's intuition about whether animals and other non-linguistic creatures can be said to know anything at all. Brandom's view clearly rules out the possibility of the dog mentioned above having knowledge that bones are buried in a certain place. If reliabilists are right that knowledge does not require us to be able to offer justifications, then they require an account of belief that is different from Brandom's. It must be possible to form beliefs without undertaking "such broadly inferential commitments". So reliabilism involves non-trivial semantic commitments. As we shall see in Chapter 7, one way of developing a naturalistic theory of meaning, and so belief content, is precisely to appeal to reliable indication. The problem Brandom raises for any such position is that reliabilists must have a principled way of distinguishing things that are clearly not believers and knowers – rusting iron, for example – from creatures that are, the likes of you and me. I leave discussion of this issue until Chapter 7.

However, Brandom's imagined community of reliable belief formers who never offer justifications provides us with an insight into the interest and importance of reliabilism. Clearly we are not such a community. We do have beliefs about other people's beliefs. We do offer explicit justifications for our beliefs. If the reliabilist account of knowledge is correct, then it provides us with a way of understanding what we are trying to do as responsible enquirers seeking knowledge. What we are looking for are reliable ways to form our beliefs. What distinguishes sophisticated human enquirers from other animals is that we set out (or should set out) explicitly to control how we come to form beliefs so that they are produced by reliable mechanisms. Perhaps this is the right way to think about what scientists are doing. The carefully controlled experiments, mathematical techniques and methods of peer review used in the sciences are to be held in high regard precisely because they are reliable mechanisms for producing true beliefs. So, even if reliabilism does not answer sceptical worries, it arguably does something more important. It tells us what self-conscious subjects who pursue knowledge should be looking for – reliable belief-forming mechanisms. Where the reliabilist differs from someone like Brandom is just that they do not make being a self-conscious subject a precondition of being a knower. Animals or children with reliable belief-fixing mechanisms can be knowers too. Being a self-conscious enquirer allows you to refine your methods of forming beliefs to become a better knower, and reliabilism tells you what sort of refinement you are looking for.

If this is right, the issue of externalism is of importance only in terms of the pressure it puts on naturalists to provide a certain kind of theory of meaning. What is really important, epistemologically, is that reliabilism provides a naturalistic account of knowledge that tells us what we should be trying to do if we wish to increase our knowledge.

Reliabilism and the problem of induction

With this in mind, we might think that reliabilism can throw some light on the inductive methods in the sciences and why they should be pursued. The reliabilist answer to the problem of induction looks, on the face of it, straightforward: if inductive methods generate true beliefs more often than false beliefs, then those methods are reliable and so any true belief formed using the inductive methods should count as knowledge. That seems all right as far as it goes, but what we as self-conscious enquirers might want to know is why we should believe that inductive methods are reliable. The reliabilist, externalist that he is, could of course refuse to answer that question. No one need know that inductive methods are reliable for beliefs arrived at via these methods to constitute knowledge. But then reliabilism would not be doing what I suggested it should be doing: offering us an insight into the methods adopted by science. At best it would involve the mere and apparently unwarranted assertion that induction is reliable. Some reliabilists, at least, think that is not good enough. For example David Papineau has said:

[The] demand for a defence of the claim that induction yields knowledge is not being made of ordinary knowers who are using inductions, but rather of us philosophers who are talking about inductions, and in particular about the question of whether inductions yield knowledge. We reliabilist friends of induction are explicitly claiming that inductive inferences yield knowledge because they reliably yield truths. Given this, it is perfectly reasonable for someone to challenge us to provide support for this claim. (Papineau 1993: 155)

That support will involve providing evidence that inductive generalizations are reliable. The problem here, though, is obvious. The only evidence we can have of reliability is evidence about how things have gone in the past. On the basis that things have worked out in the past we must infer that they will continue to be reliable in the future. So any reliabilist defence of induction assumes induction, something that Hume has shown cannot be an adequate answer to the problem he posed.

Papineau and others have claimed that this is not a disaster. Hume was right to point out the circularity in this kind of reasoning but wrong to think that this automatically made it a bad thing; circularity can be benign as well as vicious. Philosophers who think this will distinguish between two kinds of circularity: "rule circular" and "premise circular". Premise circularity is indeed bad. A premise-circular argument is an argument of the form:

I love Inverness Caledonian Thistle.
Chocolate is good.
Therefore I love Inverness Caledonian Thistle

The conclusion in a premise-circular argument is one of the premises. However, as Van Cleve (1984), Papineau (1993) and others have pointed out, the reliabilist justification of induction is not circular in that way. The argument proceeds something like this:

Most of the inductive inferences I've drawn in the past from true premises have had true conclusions.
Therefore inductive inferences are reliable and will generate generally true conclusions from true premises.

Nowhere in that argument do I explicitly make use of the claim that induction is reliable. Rather, my premises just appeal to the fact that when I have made inductive inferences in the past I have tended to arrive at true conclusions. The circularity arises because *the rule of inference* that takes me from the premises to the conclusion is precisely the rule of inference that I want to justify, namely the inductive rule.

We can justify this sort of rule circularity by drawing an analogy between induction here and the case of deductive arguments. Imagine that someone questions the validity of a deductive rule inference, say the rule *modus ponens*: if p, then q; p, therefore q. What could we say in response? The standard way to justify logical rules and systems is to offer soundness and completeness proofs for the system in question. This can be done for the propositional calculus; students are expected to learn such proofs. But these proofs make use of deductive rules. So our justifications of deductive rules seem to present a case of the same rule circularity as the reliabilist defence of induction. Not many philosophers are sceptical about deductive inferences as a result of this; rather they generally take the soundness proofs offered of deductive logics as evidence of the reliability of deduction.

Reliabilists will typically claim that what is good for deductive logic should also be good for inductive logic, so an inductive proof of the reliability of induction is all the proof that we could want.

Unfortunately this won't work, at least not in the very simple form presented here. Inductive justifications of induction face a problem which no deductive justification of deduction does. It is a now-famous problem first expressed by Nelson Goodman in his classic work *Fact, Fiction and Forecast*.

Take an emerald. You can see that the emerald is green and, having seen lots of emeralds, you may be inclined on that basis to say that all emeralds are green – a good induction, it would seem. But consider this. We can introduce a new property, the property of being grue. An object is coloured grue if it is green before the year 2020 and blue thereafter. Every emerald that we have seen up until now, in the year 2008, as well as being green, is also grue. Using our basic inductive inference, we seem entitled to infer that "all emeralds are grue". On the face of it two uses of the same inductive rule lead to contradictory claims. The first claim, "all emeralds are green", tells us that the first emerald we view in 2020 should be green, our second inductive inference tells us that "all emeralds are grue", and so the first emerald we view in 2020 should be blue. Use of our simple inductive rule, then, cannot be reliable at all since it leads to contradictions.

We can adapt the grue case to demonstrate a similar problem for the inductive justification of induction. This is elegantly set out by Colin Howson:

> Call an inductive inference made by the rule "right" if it concludes to a true assertion and "wrong" if it concludes to a false one. Call an inductive inference "ring" if it has been checked and found to be right or not been checked and is wrong. Suppose the majority of checked inductive inferences have been found to be right. It follows that they are also ring. Using as a justified premiss "the majority of checked inductive inferences are ring" . . . we conclude [using the inductive rule] that the majority of inductive inferences are ring. But only a finite number have been checked, leaving a potential infinity unchecked. It follows that the majority of all inductive inferences are wrong, and hence that the rule is unreliable!
>
> (Howson 2000: 30–31)

So we can provide an inductive argument to demonstrate the *unreliability* of induction.

Typing mechanisms

Talk of grue properties and ring inferences no doubt sounds highly artificial, but it highlights in a very clear way a fundamental difficulty for reliabilists. Reliabilists claim that when a true belief is generated by a reliable mechanism it counts as knowledge. When we talk of a belief-forming mechanism being reliable or not, we mean a *type* of mechanism; and when we come to assess whether any particular true belief counts as knowledge, we have to assess whether the belief in question was formed by a mechanism that we deem reliable. The problem is that the particular process by which the belief was arrived at can be classified in many different ways, just as a particular emerald can be classified as green or grue. The worry is of course that if we classify the mechanism one way, then it will be an instance of a reliable process, and so knowledge; classify it another way, then it will not.

We do not need fancy arguments of the kind offered by Goodman and Howson in order to see this. Suppose I am looking out my window late at night and I think I see a fox, and indeed in fact there is a fox in my garden. So I have formed a belief, a true belief, that there is a fox in my garden. What mechanism is responsible for the formation of that belief? One obvious answer is that it is my visual system. So the question of whether my true belief counts as knowledge depends on whether my visual system is reliable or not. In general, I imagine, my visual system is reliable. So it looks as if the reliabilist should say in this case that I *know* there is a fox in my garden. But the process by which I identified the fox could be classified in other ways. It could be classified as seeing through my window or the process of seeing through my window late at night in poor light. Suppose, further, that I am generally wrong about what I think I see through my window late at night. Well, in that case my belief does not count as knowledge as it is formed by an unreliable mechanism. So, as in the grue case, depending on how we classify the mechanism, we can end up with contradictory answers about whether or not my belief counts as knowledge.

Here is one last example due to Robert Brandom to illustrate the same point. Imagine I am pursuing my lifelong interest in viewing barns around the country. I am looking at a barn right now and I believe that there is a barn in front of me. And indeed there is a barn in front of me. Does my belief constitute knowledge? The answer to that question for the reliabilist should be straightforward. All we need to find out is how reliable my visual system is. Does it generate more true beliefs than false ones? But things can become complicated when we take into account facts external to the perceiver. Let us imagine that I have wandered, in my search for barns, into a particularly strange county known as Barn Façade County. In this peculiar part of the world the people have an odd hobby of building barn façades, objects that look to all normal viewers like barns on first viewing but in fact are nothing like that. Now imagine that I am in that county and I am looking at the one and only true barn in that county surrounded by hundreds and hundreds of fake barns; does it seem right in those circumstances to say that I know I am looking at a barn? Intuitively the answer seems to be no; after all, it is just a happy accident on my part that I am looking at the only barn in Barn Façade County. If I were in fact looking at a barn façade I would not be able to tell that apart from a real barn, so my visual system would have generated a false belief. Considering all the fake barns in Barn Façade County and my inability to distinguish fake barns from the real McCoy, it seems as if my visual mechanism for discriminating barns is in fact unreliable and so I do not really have knowledge. But that is not the end of the story. Barn Façade County is part of a larger state, the Great Barn State, in which the making of barn façades is frowned upon. Nowhere else in the state would I come across a barn façade. Am I a reliable discriminator of barns where I am? Well, if I now classify the mechanism by which I form the belief by making reference to the Great Barn State, then the answer is yes. In the state as a whole I shall be more often right than wrong when I believe I see a barn in front of me. So my visual system is a reliable discriminator of barns and I do know there is a barn in front of me.

Here again we have the same result: classify my belief-forming mechanism one way by reference to Barn Façade County, and it is unreliable; classify it another way, by reference to the Great Barn State, then it is reliable. Reliabilism gives contradictory answers about whether I know or not depending on how I categorize the process by which I form my belief.

This is a serious problem for reliabilism and undermines one of its initial attractions for a naturalist. Reliabilism seemed to offer us a way of getting rid of difficult notions like justification. The normative element in our account of knowledge is replaced by purely factual considerations concerning the reliability or otherwise of our belief-forming mechanisms. But the examples we have worked through show that this is not as straightforward as we initially thought. Whether a mechanism is reliable or not depends on how you describe, type or classify it. Reliability then seems not a purely factual matter but one dependent on our interests and classifications.

How should a reliabilist respond to these problems? Clearly what the reliabilist needs is some way to pick out the *right* classification of the mechanism in these cases. Is there an objectively correct way of classifying mechanisms such that we can make purely factual judgements about whether or not they are reliable?

Natural kinds and evolution

One response, which might be appealing to a naturalist, is to claim that certain classifications are themselves natural – what philosophers call natural kinds. If "green", for example, is a natural-kind term, and "grue" is not, then we have an apparently good reason as naturalists to reject inferences involving "grue".

But what makes a natural kind natural? In the green/grue case, we might be tempted to define natural by reference to what we find natural. This would be similar to the way that Hume explained induction. Our inductive habits are a gift from nature, just what we find it natural to do. The trouble here is that often what appears to us to be a natural classification turns out to be less than natural from the perspective of science. For example, we distinguish naturally at the culinary level garlic and onions. But for the botanist, this marks no interesting distinction. Both are alliums (as are some lilies) (Dupré 1993). More obviously, the classification of things into charm quarks and mitochondrial DNA is very unnatural to most of us. It takes a good deal of scientific training to learn what these things are and their significance. Even things that sound related to everyday concepts such as "energy" or "work" have quite different senses or meanings in the specialized disciplines of the physical sciences. The new-age therapist who offers to rechannel my energies means something quite different from my old physics lecturers when they talked of the conservation of energy.

The classifications of developed science are weird and wonderful compared to our everyday talk. The "natural" in natural kinds might then be better explained by appeal to science. Natural kinds are those that feature in our empirically well-confirmed scientific theories. So grouping things together as electrons, water molecules or water voles is considered natural because these are classifications employed in successful sciences. Part of what science is in the business of doing is discovering for us the way the world is; and that involves, in part, classifying it correctly.

The trouble with this response is that it seems circular. To see this let us pretend for the sake of argument that "all emeralds are green" is a well-established scientific claim. The reason we think inductive inferences involving green are sound and those involving grue are not is that green is a natural kind and grue is not. So we are right to conclude "all emeralds are green" and wrong to conclude "all emeralds are grue". The reason we think green is a natural kind and grue is not is that "green" features in our best science of emeralds and grue does not. For example, we know from our science that all emeralds are green. So our justification of our inductive inference (or claim that a mechanism is reliable) is that it uses natural kinds or classifications; and our reason for thinking the kinds are natural is that they appear in our best-confirmed science.

The charge of circularity was also levelled at Quine; and it seems the reliabilist could respond in a similar way. Naturalists are not interested in providing a foundation for science. Rather, their account of science and knowledge is to be informed by our best science. If scientific laws and natural kinds cannot be defined independently, that does not show that there is anything wrong with either concept. It just shows that we have to give up certain first philosophical presuppositions regarding what counts as an adequate explanation.

Let us assume anyway, for the sake of argument, that we can make good sense of the idea of natural kinds; how will it help the reliabilist? What reliabilism types or classifies are mechanisms. What we need is a scientific way to pick out the natural mechanisms of belief formation. An obvious way to proceed is to appeal to natural selection. Certain items have evolved through natural selection for the purpose of performing certain functions. A bat's echolocation system has evolved for the purpose of navigating and locating insect prey. We might say something similar about the belief-forming mechanisms of human beings and other animals.

This general approach to reliabilism is developed and defended by Hilary Kornblith (2002) in his ecological account of knowledge. Kornblith wants to argue that knowledge itself is a natural kind that we can see employed by animal ethnologists in their study of animal behaviour. He defends reliabilism (in part) against Brandom's criticism that there is no right way to classify belief-forming mechanisms as follows:

> Knowledge is an ecological kind: it has to do with the fit between an organism and its environment ... the current practice of biology requires that we understand the evolutionary history of an animal species as determined, in part, by adaptations to their environment, where the notion of environment is not given in any way by human interest or practices.   (Kornblith 2002: 65)

Let us think about this suggestion in relation to my example of glancing at a fox through my window late at night. Here is a sketch of the story a reliabilist might tell. My visual system has evolved in a certain environment. It has evolved to help me see objects in good light. It has not, unlike that of some nocturnal animals, been selected for good night vision. Given that I saw the fox late at night, my visual system is working in conditions that go beyond what it was selected for and so we should not think it is reliable in these circumstances. So the reliabilist appealing to natural belief-forming mechanisms might reasonably say that I do not know there is a fox in my garden in this case. Much would need to be fleshed out in a story like this, but the general strategy is clear. We can appeal to the conditions under which a mechanism evolved to pick out how it is to be classified and then make a purely factual judgement about whether the mechanism in question is reliable or not.

This won't work, though, with Brandom's example. The different classifications that lead us to say that in some circumstances our barn perceiver knows and in some circumstances he does not are not natural at all. They involve reference to classifications that depend on human interests. Natural selection does not discriminate between state and county lines.

Kornblith's response to Brandom's particular example takes the form of a challenge:

> [Cases such as Brandom's barn-façade example] are relatively rare, and this should not make us view the very idea of knowledge as a natural kind as any less natural for all that. What Brandom would need to show in order to undermine the idea of knowledge as a natural kind is more than that we construct cases that defy any sort of natural classification. It would need to be shown that at least as many . . . cases of knowledge that are of real philosophical interest do not lend themselves to a naturalistic specification of the environment relative to which a process of belief acquisition should be counted reliable or unreliable. The barn façade case does not do that work.
>
> (Kornblith 2002: 69)

Kornblith's view is, if I have him right, that although philosophers can manufacture cases where decisions about how to classify a belief-forming mechanism are in some way arbitrary, these cases are marginal. We're not, if we're honest, that concerned about whether an individual who sees a barn in a strange part of the land counts as someone who knows or not. A good naturalist account of knowledge tells us what knowledge is in the cases where it is theoretically interesting for us. There will no doubt be times where we are uncertain whether to classify certain cases as knowledge or not. Brandom has given us an example. But this is true of many complex kinds dealt with in science. Take the idea of sex, for example. There is a clear difference between the sexes and we all know how to differentiate people of different sexes. We are taught in high-school biology that sex differences can be traced to chromosomal differences. Females have an XX chromosome and males have an XY chromosome. But there are some people who do not neatly fit these classifications. For example, some individuals born with androgen insensitivity disorder have an XY chromosome but will develop in such a way as to appear female. Should we classify people with androgen insensitivity disorder as male or female? There is no clear answer here, at least as far as the scientific facts go. The best answer (in all ways) is to ask those who have the disorder. Some might think of themselves as male, some female, some neither male nor female. But the fact that some individuals fit into neither category, male or female, neatly does not show that there is no meaningful distinction between the sexes. Similarly with knowledge. Just because we can invent some examples where we are no longer certain whether to say someone has knowledge or not or where our decision seems arbitrary does not show that there is something wrong with reliabilism.

So an opponent of this kind of reliabilism has to show that there are interesting cases of knowledge which cannot be dealt with in this way. Kornblith states in the quotation above that there must be *at least as many* interesting cases where reliabilism, invoking natural selection to specify (relative to the environment) the correct classification of the belief-forming mechanism, fails as it succeeds. This is surely an exaggeration. The opponent of reliabilism does not need to show that more than half the philosophically interesting cases of knowledge aren't captured by Kornblith's reliabilist account. All they are required to show is that there is a significant class of interesting cases of knowledge not adequately described in Kornblith's way. Another scientific example can help us to see this point. Take the biological notion of species. Species are prime example of a natural kind; and species is itself a more general natural kind. A great deal of work in biology has gone into trying to give a scientific account of species. One popular account championed by Ernest Mayr became known as the biological species notion. A species is a group of "actually or potentially inter-breeding natural populations which are reproductively isolated from other such groups" (Mayr 1963: 19). What is appealing about this idea is that it does not make reference to common or shared properties. Biology, post-Darwin, has had to come to terms with the fact that vari-ation is the norm. Without variation there would be nothing for natural selection to work on. So in biology there will not be a set of essential properties that mark out an individual as belonging to one species rather than another. Mayr's idea gives us a way of defining species that allows for this variation. What marks out whether one indi-vidual belongs to a species is its potential to interbreed with others of the group. As an account of what species are, Mayr's proposal has an obvious drawback. Some animals and plants don't interbreed. There are asexual species. Mayr's account cannot tell us how to group these together. It does not matter whether there are in fact more asexual species than interbreeding species. His theory is clearly deficient as a general account of the natural kind species because there is a large class of organisms to which it doesn't apply.

The same standard should apply to Kornblith's proposal. Are there interesting cases to which his reliabilist account does not apply? The answer seems to me straightforward – yes, lots of them. Science provides the best examples. Consideration of scientific enquiry raises two related problems for a reliabilist account such as Kornblith's. First, science thrusts us into environments quite different from those in which our cognitive capacities evolved. When scientists in the twentieth century looked at photographs from bubble-chamber experiments or at images created by an electron microscope, they were placing themselves into environments wholly alien to those of their ancestors. The world of atoms, quarks and electrons is not for us a natural environment. Secondly, we can only make sense of the process of scientific enquiry by adverting to our cognitive interests. Why spend all that money and time building supercolliders and intricate particle detectors unless you have very specific investigations in mind? Those interests are not given to us by nature either. Not everyone feels the pull of questions in fundamental physics. The idea of what constitutes an appropriate environment to test something is obviously relative to what we consider interesting to investigate. In fact, in general those environments don't exist until we create them, guided as we are by our interests. The same experimental set-up, the same environment, might be appropriate for certain investigations and inappropriate for others. How we understand and classify the reliability of those methods depends on what we are interested in investigating. Thus we can have no adequate account of scientific knowledge which doesn't make some reference to scientists' interests. Kornblith's account wants knowledge to be a natural kind. For him that means there is a natural fact about the reliability of our belief-forming mechanisms. Crucially the account of reliability is supposed to be independent of our interests, but I don't think we can even make sense of such an interest-free account when we turn to scientific enquiry.

Reliabilism looks like an attractive account of knowledge for a naturalist because it promises to reduce a difficult normative notion, justification, to a purely factual one. If we can say what it is to have a belief and what it is for a belief to be true, then we have a completely naturalist theory of knowledge. The reliabilist definition has further advantages too. It can make sense of our inclination to say that animals know certain things even though they cannot offer reasons. They know because they have belief states that are reliably produced. Reliabilism also informs us of what self-conscious enquiring human beings are trying to do. They are trying to regulate and control the methods by which they form beliefs to make them as reliable as possible. But we have also seen that reliabilism has problems – problems that threaten its appeal to a naturalist. In order to claim that any particular belief-forming mechanism is reliable, we need to type or classify the mechanism. There seem to be different ways to do this, leading to different answers about whether something is classed as knowledge or not. We considered one possible answer: appeal to the idea of natural kinds. Kornblith suggested that an appeal to natural selection can provide us with an objective way of classifying our belief-forming mechanisms. But this seems an inadequate response once we begin to reflect on the sort of knowledge claims that particularly interest a naturalist. Science has taken us into environments quite different from those in which our ancestors evolved. Natural selection alone cannot offer us an objective way to classify the belief-forming mechanisms used here. Only an understanding of the role that scientists' aims and interests play in designing and controlling such experiments can make sense of scientific enquiry.

Did nature design us for knowledge?

Introducing evolutionary arguments to a discussion of reliabilism raises interesting new questions. Do we have any good reasons to think that evolution has designed us with reliable belief-forming mechanisms? Do we have good reasons to think that the kinds of brains that we have been given by nature are well adapted to discovering the truth about the world?

Interestingly, some recent empirical work by psychologists suggests that we are not very reliable at formulating true beliefs. One very famous example is the so-called Harvard Medical School test (Kahneman & Tversky 1973). Harvard Medical School students (presumably quite a bright bunch) were asked this question: "if a test to detect a disease whose prevalence is 1/1000 has a false positive rate of 5 per cent, what is the chance that a person found to have a positive result actually has the disease, assuming you know nothing about the person's symptoms or signs?" You might like to try this for yourself before proceeding further.

The most common response (47 per cent of individuals) was that the chance of the patient having the illness was 95 per cent. But that is wrong. The correct answer is around 2 per cent. If we think in frequencies instead of percentages, we can see quite readily that this answer is correct. If you were to test 1,000 people, given how rare the disease is, you would expect one of the people you test, on average, to have the disease. Now the test has in addition a false positive rate of 5 per cent, which means that of the remaining 999 people you test, about 50 of them will register a false positive. Hence the actual chance of you having the disease, given that you've returned a positive result, is 1/51, about 2 per cent. Less than one-fifth of the students at Harvard gave that answer.

Here's another example (Wason & Shapiro 1966). Subjects were given four cards, displaying two numbers and two letters, as below:

E   H   4   7

They were told that each card had a number on one side and a letter on the other and then asked this question. How many cards do you need to turn over to discover whether or not the following sentence is true: "if a card has a vowel on one side, then it has an even number on the other side"? Again you might like to pause before reading on to see what your own answer would be.

Very few people gave the correct answer, which is that you have to turn over the card on the far left and the card on the far right. Almost everyone can see that you should turn over the card marked with an E on it, reasoning, correctly, that you need to discover whether that card has an even number on it to establish the truth of the statement they have been asked to consider. Far fewer people realize that you need to turn over the card with the number 7. You need to do this because if that card has a vowel on the other side, then the claim in question will be false.

Again these results suggest that we are not very good at logical reasoning. We might be tempted to conclude, then, that the brains that nature has given us are not well suited for discovering truths. They are not reliable.

Given these results, we could construct a naturalistic argument for scepticism. Scientific research shows that human beings do not have belief-forming mechanisms that reliably generate truths, and so we are not knowers.

This would be a very poor argument, and perhaps not even coherent. Clearly even if our first instinct is wrong about the kind of examples outlined above, then we are in a position to correct our mistakes. You might like to consider your own reaction to the Harvard Medical School case. If you were one of the many who thought the answer was 95 per cent, then I hope that, after my explanation, you were able to see that the answer should have been something slightly less than 2 per cent. If we weren't able to formulate correct beliefs like that, then it would be impossible to set up the experiment in the way that the scientists did. After all, the scientists know the answer before they set up the experiment; and they are human just like us.

What this suggests to me is something quite different, already mentioned in our discussion of Brandom and Kornblith. If we understand reliabilism to be a claim about the reliability of our immediate, unreflective belief-forming mechanisms, then it won't account for what, for the naturalist, should be our most interesting examples of knowledge – namely science.

A good naturalist account of knowledge must say something about how scientific beliefs are formed and why they are to be trusted; and that requires us to say something about how our interests shape our enquiries and how reflective judgements can guide them.

The idea that knowledge consists in true belief formed by a reliable mechanism is inadequate, then, I think, for two reasons. One is that we have no principled way to type the belief-forming mechanisms that is fully naturalistic. The second is that it fails to provide illumination of what is distinctive and special about scientific enquiry. This is not to say that the general idea of reliability is not important in thinking about knowledge and our methods of acquiring it. It is just to point out that the idea of reliability on its own does not make knowledge itself a fully natural property, if by natural property we mean one independent of any of our interests.

We need to investigate in more detail the peculiarities and details of science and scientific method, and how our interests and aims influence this enquiry. This is the subject of Chapter 4.

four

Naturalized philosophy of science

Naturalists are impressed by science; science is to be a model for philosophy. An important question for a naturalist is to ask what is distinctive about science. If we know that, we can begin to make some sense of the task of making philosophy more scientific. A traditional answer to the question of what is distinctive about science is that it employs a special method. Science makes use of special modes of inference, testing or experiment that set it apart from non-scientific disciplines such as astrology and homoeopathy. Methods, whether scientific or not, are normative. They tell you how you *should* do something. Norms, as we've seen, cause trouble for naturalists. Naturalists then have two difficult tasks when it comes to understanding science. First, they need to say what distinguishes the methods of science from those of non-science. Secondly, they need to show that scientific norms can be accommodated within a naturalistic world-view.

A tale of two methods

Traditional philosophy of science has offered us two very general answers to what is distinctive about science and its method – inductivism and hypothetico-deductivism.

Inductivists say that science begins by piecing together observations. From the data we put forward a tentative generalization. We then look for analogous phenomena in the world on the basis of which we can extend our generalizations. Once we have a generalization, we use it to make predictions. If the prediction matches the new data, the theory is confirmed. The more tests our theory passes, the more our theory is to be trusted and the more chance there is that it is true.

The problem of induction still nags at inductivists, but the general idea about what is distinctive about science is clear enough. The more confirmed a theory, the more a scientist should believe it. Non-science subjects such as creation "science" or reflexology do not begin with the careful piecing together of observational evidence and are not well confirmed experimentally. Carnap, as we touched upon in Chapter 1, was an inductivist and he offered some very sophisticated formal treatments of confirmation.

Hypothetico-deductivists, on the other hand, claim that science does not begin with raw data but by postulating a theory or hypothesis to explain some phenomena that we are interested in. From that we make predictions. If the tests agree with the predictions, we hang on to our theory. If the prediction doesn't match up with the data, then we must disgard our old hypothesis and replace it with a new one. This is, as we've seen, Quine's view of science. Its loudest and most persuasive advocate in the twentieth century, however, was Karl Popper. Popper claimed, in contrast to the inductivists, that the point of testing was always to search for refutations or falsifications of our theory. When theory and observations agree, we learn nothing. Refutations, on the other hand, tell us a great deal. They tell us that our current theory is wrong and so we are forced to reject it and come up with better guesses about the nature of reality.

As with the inductivists, sticky problems arise for the hypothetico-deductivist account: for example, what counts as a good revision of a theory after it has been falsified. Different advocates of hypothetico-deductivism offer different answers. Popper told scientists that they should avoid *ad hoc* revisions and offer bold hypotheses with new testable consequences. Quine said, as we saw, that we should employ the principle of "minimal mutilation"; we should go for the simplest and most conservative change to our total science. Despite these differences, there is a basic agreement about what the general method is that makes science distinctive. Science is distinguished from non-science because disciplines such as astrology or homoeopathy do not make testable predictions, or, if they do, they fail to revise their theories according to the principles set out by Popper or Quine.

The methods of inductivism and hypothetico-deductivism are very abstract, and as articulated by Quine or Popper or Carnap do not involve much reference to actual scientific practice now or in the past. Such was the way of philosophy of science before 1962.

Kuhn's revolution (with a little help from Feyerabend)

> History, if viewed as a repository of more than anecdote or chronology, could produce a decisive transformation in the image of science by which we are now possessed.
>
> (Kuhn 1970: 1)

These are the opening words of Kuhn's 1962 classic *The Structure of Scientific Revolutions*. Undoubtedly his work made a decisive transformation in the philosophy of science. Kuhn made history of science matter to the philosophy of science, and in a way that greatly affected philosophers' views of scientific method.

Although inductivists and hypothetico-deductivists disagree over the fundamental methods of science, the pictures have in common two elements: first, scientists produce theories of the world; and secondly, the scientific method involves (in some way) the testing of those theories. One of the worries that the history of science raises for this picture is that a great deal seems to go on in science that has nothing to do with testing theories. Take, for example, the history and development of one theory: Newtonian mechanics. Newton first published the essentials of what we now call Newtonian mechanics in 1687 in his *Principia Mathematica*. Until the early twentieth century, when it was replaced by quantum mechanics and the general theory of relativity, Newton's theory held sway in the physics community. If inductivists and hypothetico-deductivists were right about the methods of science, we would expect to find that during those 200 years physics involved the testing of Newton's theory. According to the inductive method we should expect to see scientists looking for confirmations of Newton's theory; according to Popper we should expect scientists to be looking for refutations. But as Kuhn points out, this is not what we see. Much of the work done by scientists of the eighteenth and nineteenth centuries had nothing to do with testing. For example, one of the most significant pieces of work done in the period was Henry Cavendish's experimental work aimed at discovering a more precise value of the gravitational constant G. This does not test Newton's theory but assumes it. Similarly there were important theoretical developments at this time. The great mathematicians Laplace, Lagrange and Hamilton provided new mathematical treatments of Newton's theory. Again these were not new rival theories but alternative ways of presenting the same theory. Within the standard pictures of science it is unclear how to make sense of the kind of work undertaken by experimentalists such as Cavendish or mathematicians such as Lagrange.

Kuhn provides an account of science that does better. The key idea in Kuhn's writings, which can help to us to make sense of the kind of work done by Cavendish, Lagrange and the others, is that of a paradigm. He gives the term two senses: paradigms as disciplinary matrices and paradigms as exemplars. Let us take the idea of paradigms as disciplinary matrices first. According to Kuhn, scientists within a discipline take a number of things for granted. For example, in the nineteenth century physicists would have accepted the three laws of Newtonian mechanics and Newton's law of gravity. They would have agreed that certain kinds of instruments should be used in scientific investigation; for example that telescopes be used to investigate the movement of planets. These theoretical and practical assumptions form the framework in which they will conduct their scientific investigations. The scientist's job is not so much to test the paradigm but to make as much of the world fit or mesh with the central theoretical concepts of the paradigm as possible. During their scientific training scientists have learned various techniques or methods for doing this. They have learned, for instance, certain model solutions and certain techniques of mathematical approximation. Scientists adapt these model solutions to new situations and so explain more of the world, making use of the paradigm's central assumptions. Here's a nice example from Kuhn's writings:

> Galileo found that a ball rolling down an incline acquires just enough velocity to return to the same vertical height on a second incline of any slope, and he learned to see the experimental situation as like the pendulum with a point-mass for a bob. Huyghens then solved the problem of the centre of oscillation of a physical pendulum by imagining that the extended body of the latter was composed of Galilean point-pendula ... Daniel Bernouilli discovered how to make the flow of water from an orifice resemble Huyghens' pendulum. Determine the descent of the center of gravity of the water in the tank and jet during an infinitesimal interval of time. Next imagine that each particle of water afterward moves separately upward to the maximum height attainable with the velocity acquired during that interval. The ascent of the center of gravity of the individual particles must equal the descent of

> the center of gravity of the water in the tank and the jet. From
> that view of the problem the long sought speed of efflux
> followed at once. (Kuhn 1970: 190)

A scientist learns a solution to one kind of problem: the behaviour of a point-mass bob. This is later adapted to provide an account of a real physical pendulum by Huygens, which in turn is finally adapted to explain something apparently completely different – the speed of efflux. Kuhn calls this kind of activity puzzle solving, normal science or articulating the paradigm. This puzzle-solving activity illustrates the second sense of Kuhn's notion of paradigms – paradigms as exemplars. The model solutions that the scientists have learnt provide blueprints for extending the paradigm as in the case above to explain new phenomena. The work of Cavendish, Lagrange and Hamilton is another way of articulating the paradigm. A more accurate value for the gravitational constant G allows you to make more accurate predictions about planetary motions, increasing the fit between the paradigm and the world. Similarly, the new mathematics of Lagrange and Hamilton makes soluble certain problems that were intractable in Newton's formulation of his theory, again extending the range of phenomena explained by the paradigm.

Occasionally in the history of science, paradigms come under strain. Certain phenomena cannot be explained using the paradigm's principles, or the results of some other science come into conflict with those of the prevailing paradigm. These Kuhn calls "anomalies". Examples of this in the nineteenth century would have been the anomalous orbit of Mercury and the rise of electromagnetism. Mercury's strange orbit just couldn't be explained by making use of the standard techniques for describing planetary motion in Newtonian terms. Electromagnetic theory suggested that the speed of a light was a constant. This seemed to contradict Newtonian mechanics since the speed of any wave such as light should vary depending on the speed of the medium in which it is travelling. Tough problems like these, which confound the best scientists, can induce a "crisis" in confidence in the paradigm which may eventually result in a "revolution": the rejection of one paradigm and the adoption of another. This, as we know, was eventually the fate of Newtonian physics. It was overthrown and replaced by quantum theory and relativity.

When we replace a paradigm, we are not just replacing one theory of the world with another. Paradigm shifts involve changes in methods, problem-solving techniques, exemplars and ideas about proper experimental design. For this reason Kuhn claimed that different paradigms were incommensurable. They cannot be directly compared. What counts as good evidence and good scientific practice under one paradigm will not count as such under a different paradigm.

Galileo and the telescope

A nice example that illustrates the phenomenon of incommensurability can be found in the writings of Paul Feyerabend (1975) and his discussion of Galileo's use of telescopic data. Copernican theory (the idea that the sun and not the Earth is at the centre of the universe) predicts that the size of the planet Venus should vary markedly throughout the year as Venus's distance from the Earth changes. However, when we view Venus with the naked eye, we do not see this variation. The story then usually goes something like this: Galileo showed that when Venus is viewed through the telescope, the expected variation in size is indeed observed, thus producing a startling confirmation of Copernicanism and a refutation of the alternative geocentric theory.

However, as Feyerabend points out, to accept this as a confirmation of Copernicanism one would have to believe that observations of planetary size made using a telescope were more accurate than those made with the naked eye. But this was not accepted by advocates of the old Aristotelian physics. They had both theoretical and practical reasons to reject telescopic data. On the theoretical side, Aristotelians could appeal to the idea of the natural function of the eyes. The function of the eyes, they would claim, is to see. They can fail to perform this function adequately if they are impeded in a certain way. If it's very dark, you don't see so well. If you're drunk, your vision can also be defective. But under normal circumstances, since what eyes are for is to give you information about the world, it makes no sense to think that they systematically distort your perception of the world. Irving Block (1961, quoted in Chalmers 1999: 164) nicely sums up this conviction:

> Nature made everything for a purpose, and the purpose of man is to understand Nature through science. Thus it would have been a contradiction for Nature to have fashioned man and his organs in such a way that all knowledge and science must, from its inception be false.

So for an Aristotelian there would have been good reason to think that the telescope was inaccurate when it contradicted what you saw plainly with your eyes. Sticking a long tube in front of your eyes, like being drunk, is another way to distort your vision, to inhibit your eyes' natural function and so provide you with a less true picture of reality. But there was more to Aristotelians' suspicions of the telescope than *just* a dogmatic theoretical belief. They had good practical reasons to think that the telescope was unreliable. Telescopic data were known to produce artefacts and distortions. And Galileo had no systematic way to correct or compensate for these distortions since in the case of planetary observations he had no way to compare these data with "reliable" naked-eye reports.

Moreover, Galileo had no theory of the telescope that would allow him to distinguish real objects from mere artefacts. He had no real idea of how his marvellous new instrument worked. So he had no theoretical way to distinguish what might be real data from distortions.

According to Feyerabend, then, Galileo had no *rational* means of defending telescopic data and thus no way of upholding his telescopic observations as a confirmation of Copernican theory. He used an unreliable instrument (the telescope) to back up a theory (Copernicanism) that his rivals had good reason to think false anyway. Feyerabend claims that ultimately Galileo prevails not because he respects the canons of methodology or he has a rationally compelling case, but because of "his style and his clever techniques of persuasion, because he writes in Italian rather than Latin, and because he appeals to people who are temperamentally opposed to the old ideas and the standards of learning connected with them" (Feyerabend 1975: 141).

Feyerabend offers a real historical case where there is a change in method: a shift from relying on naked-eye data to relying instead on telescopic data as the most reliable way of discovering truths about planetary size. If we believe Feyerabend's account, it provides a nice demonstration of incommensurability. From the perspective of Aristotelian physics there were good reasons to reject the telescopic data that conflicted with its astronomical theory. From the perspective of the new Copernican paradigm, since the telescopic data fitted with the predictions of the theory, the telescope was embraced as a reliable instrument. What decides whether any scientist accepts one theory over another is not some objective, ahistorical scientific method.

Lessons from Kuhn

Kuhn's (and Feyerabend's) account of the historical development of science threatens inductivist and hypothetico-deductivist methodologies in a straightforward and dramatic way. When we look at what past scientists do, their work does not seem to fit the methods described by either inductivists or hypothetico-deductivists. Scientists engaged in normal science are pursuing neither confirmations nor refutations of their theory. They are engaged in an activity that Kuhn calls articulating the paradigm, which as we have seen involves many things other than theory testing.

That is an important negative conclusion, and the method of arriving at it should appeal to the naturalist. The argument is essentially an empirical one. The history of science refutes (or at least shows the inadequacy of) the most popular methodologies of science. But Kuhn's and Feyerabend's description of scientific revolutions also presents two problems for the naturalist. First, since both claim that there is never a compelling reason to change from one paradigm to another, their accounts of science threaten to make scientific change look irrational. If that story is right, it should shake the naturalists' conviction that science is to be admired as much as they think. Secondly, even if we could retell the story of scientific progress to remove some of the arbitrariness that Kuhn and Feyerabend claim exists; even if we could explain why scientists have changed paradigms and thereby methods from one period to the next, then we shall still have to confront another issue. If the methods of science have changed through history, that means there is no such thing as *the* scientific method, and so obviously no way to make use of *the* methods of science in philosophy.

Retelling Feyerabend's story

Let us see if we can make some headway with the first issue. Is there a way to explain changes in paradigms and so methods in science which avoids the problems of incommensurability? The best way to begin to answer this question is to think again about the case of Galileo and the telescope. A. F. Chalmers (1986, 1999) has presented a detailed description of Galileo's arguments for telescopic data. It turns out that Galileo had much more going for him than that he spoke and wrote in Italian.

The key idea to which Galileo appeals (and Feyerabend does not mention in his account) is irradiation. When apparently small bright objects are viewed at a distance against a dark background, they appear larger than they actually are. We know this (as Galileo pointed out) from terrestrial cases. If a torch is viewed late at night from a distance, it appears much larger than it does close up or during the day. Hence Galileo argued that we should expect the same to be true with the stars. When seen at night they will appear much larger than they actually are. This hypothesis can be tested, as Galileo pointed out. If we can reduce the apparent brightness of the stars or planets, then we should expect to see a reduction in the apparent size of these objects. Galileo suggested a number of ways that this might be done. We can view the star through a cloud or a black veil, for example. When we do this we see that planets "show their globes perfectly round and definitely bounded" (Galileo 1957: 46–7, quoted in Chalmers 1999), and so smaller. Stars, on the other hand, are "never seen bounded by a circular periphery, but have rather the aspect of blazes whose rays vibrate about them and scintillate a great deal" (*ibid.*)

There was more evidence too for the irradiation of planets viewed at night. Venus can be observed during the day or at twilight, and when it is so observed, it appears much smaller than it does during the night. Galileo claimed further that we could test the prediction that Venus varies in size during the year by only making observations during the day, and when we do so, we see the predicted change.

Thus Galileo was able to show that naked-eye observations provided contradictory information. In particular, he was able to demonstrate that our unaided senses are very unreliable when it comes to judging the size of apparently small, bright objects against a dark background. None of the evidence that demonstrates this fact requires us to appeal to telescopic data. However, having noted all these facts, Galileo was in a strong position to argue for the reliability of the telescope, at least with regard to judgements about planetary size. Telescopes remove irradiation. We can again see this with terrestrial examples. Moreover, the variations in the apparent size of Venus observed through the telescope are compatible with the naked-eye observations during daylight. All of the above makes a very strong case for the superiority of telescopic data for stellar observations over naked-eye data.

Galileo is able to make a rationally compelling case for the superiority of telescopic data because:

much was shared between him and his rivals . . . They shared the aim of giving a description of the motions of heavenly bodies that was borne out by the empirical evidence . . . There were low-level observations such as pointed out by Galileo that his opponents had no sensible option but to accept.

(Chalmers 1999: 168)

Incommensurability, at least in this case, seems to exaggerate or misrepresent the actual facts of the case.

Laudan's naturalized philosophy of science

The lessons of Chalmers's discussion can be developed into a general theory of naturalized methodology. Chalmers's story appeals to common interests, goals, some shared data and low-level theory to explain how a change in method can be rational. Separating out the role that theory, methods and aims play in the development of science offers a general way of thinking of methodology as an empirical discipline. This idea has been developed in some detail by Larry Laudan.

Laudan claims that methodology of the form practised by Popper, Carnap and others involves prescriptions such as the following: avoid *ad hoc* hypotheses; always favour more general theories; always favour simpler hypotheses over more complex ones, and so on. What Laudan calls classical methodology treats such statements as categorical imperatives – statements of the form:

One ought to do *x*.

Laudan suggests a naturalized philosophy of science should render them as hypothetical imperatives – statements of the form:

If one's goal is *y*, *then* one ought to do *x*.

For example, Popper tells us to avoid *ad hoc* hypotheses. Why? Because the aim of science, according to Popper, is to come up with bold, highly falsifiable theories. The more falsifiable a theory is, on this view, the better it is. Once we make this explicit we can see that Popper is really saying: if you want to develop risky, highly falsifiable theories, then avoid *ad hoc* hypotheses.

Laudan claims that once we have articulated our methodological rules as hypothetical imperatives, they can be tested empirically. Commitment to a hypothetical imperative of the above form involves commitment to the idea that:

> (P) Doing x is more likely than alternative strategies to produce y.　　　　　　　　　　　　　　　　(Laudan 1987: 205)

For example, Popper's claim becomes: avoiding *ad hoc* hypotheses is more likely to produce highly falsifiable theories than any other strategy.

The naturalized methodologists can then test assertions such as (P). We look through the history of science to find which kinds of strategy have been the most successful, for example, in producing falsifiable theories. If we endorse Popper's aim, then that's the method we should use.

Naturalized versus traditional methodology

More generally, then, according to Laudan, the naturalized methodologists' account of science can be contrasted with the traditional view of philosophers of science, as follows:

Traditional philosophy of science	Naturalized philosophy of science
Aims (FIXED)	Aims (REVISABLE)
↓	↑↓
Method (FIXED)	Methods (REVISABLE)
↓	↑↓
Theory	Theory

Traditional methodology sees science as having one overarching aim, say to discover the truth or come up with falsifiable theories. The method of science, then, is whatever allows us to reach that aim. Theories are tested by making use of this method. The naturalized methodologist, accepting the insights of Kuhn and Feyerabend, thinks there is no such thing as *the* method of science or *the* aim of science. Methods and aims change as science develops. We have already discussed one example of changing methods. Others aren't hard to find. A good example is the discovery of the placebo effect. If you give a group of people suffering some pain a sugar pill with no active ingredients, then generally they will report feeling better. Interestingly, if you give them a big red pill rather than just a sugar pill, the result is even more dramatic. Somehow the fact that you believe that the pill will make you better really does make it the case that you feel better. This is a remarkable and remarkably widespread phenomenon. There have been placebo surgical interventions (nothing is done but the patient thinks they are being operated upon) and successful ameliorative treatments for Parkinson's sufferers. (See Guess *et al.* 2002 for some fascinating detail on how placebos are being harnessed to improve people's well-being.) Methodologically the placebo effect is important because even if you get positive results for a drug from a test group, this doesn't indicate that the drug itself is doing anything to improve the health of the patients. It could be a placebo effect. To counter this, blind comparative trials were introduced. You give one group of patients the drug in question and another group a placebo. You then look to see if your new drug does better than the placebo. Double-blind trials, in which those who administer the drugs do not know who is getting the placebo and who the trial drug, were introduced when it was discovered that doctors often unwittingly behave differently with patients who are getting the real drug than those who are not. Interestingly, how positively your doctor reacts to your treatment seems to have an effect on how well you feel. Doctors are often, not surprisingly, more positive about non-placebo treatments, so non-placebo patients do better. (Double blind trials also help eliminate other kinds of bias.) These discoveries about human psychology and physiology then feed back into our methods. Our scientific theories, including those of psychology, provide another resource along with the history of science for adapting and improving our methods.

Examples of changing aims are harder to find, in part, I suspect, because it is never very clear precisely what the general aims of scientists are. Laudan offers us the following example: "Newton . . . saw as one of the central aims of natural philosophy to show the hand of the creator in his creation" (Laudan 1987: 198). But this is a not a cognitive aim that scientists (apart from advocates of intelligent design) share. Similarly, the aim of pre-Newtonian scientists was to explain all motion in terms of pushes and pulls. With the advent and success of Newton's theory of gravity, that aim was given up. The rise of quantum theory might be another example. The failure of so-called hidden variable theories meant that scientists abandoned the idea that a good physical theory ought to be deterministic and came to accept the idea of a fundamentally indeterministic science.

Laudan offers us a way of accounting for these changes that avoids worries about incommensurability. There are often good empirical reasons that scientists can recognize for adopting one method (and perhaps also aim) over another. We can appeal to discoveries in our science to explain changes in methods and employ the history of science to advise scientists about the optimal strategy for achieving their goal.

Laudan's view has other attractive features. It can allow for the fact that different sciences can have different methods. That seems right to me. I'm not sure that the methods of a theoretical physicist have anything very much in common with those of a marine biologist. On Laudan's model all this can be readily explained. Different scientists have different aims and so different methods are appropriate for realizing them.

For a naturalist, though, undoubtedly what is most attractive about Laudan's idea is that he provides an acceptable way of accounting for norms. Norms are analysed as hypothetical imperatives, and once this is done, we employ the history of science (and other theoretical information we get from science and common sense) to investigate which methods are most effective in realizing our aims. The reason for adopting certain norms becomes an empirical matter.

Worrall's trilemma

One obvious problem with Laudan's theory and indeed any attempt to say that methodological issues can be settled by an appeal to empirical data is that to test our methodologies we shall have to employ some method for choosing between competing methods. We need a principle or a set of principles to tell us which methodology we should prefer – a meta-methodology, if you like. The question then arises what could justify the adoption of this meta-methodological principle. John Worrall (1989) has argued that there are only three answers; and none of them is satisfactory for a naturalist.

The first possibility is that the meta-methodological principle too is justified by appeal by empirical evidence. But then we must have the beginnings of an infinite regress. How do we explain why scientists use that empirically discovered principle rather than any other? Again, this can only be done if we are using some standard, some methodology to judge rival theories. But then what is the status of that meta-meta-methodological principle?

Secondly, Laudan might construe the methodological principle as justified *a priori*, in which case we do not have a fully naturalized philosophy of science and we have gone back to admitting that we need to do first philosophy of some kind.

The only remaining possibility is to say that it has no particular justification, and any other principle would be just as good. But then the naturalist would be no better off than Kuhn or Feyerabend. He would have to admit that the methods employed by scientists are arbitrary.

Laudan has a strategy that he thinks avoids this trilemma. He suggests that the meta-methodological principle is the following inductive rule:

> (R1) If actions of a particular sort, m, have consistently promoted certain cognitive ends, e, in the past, and rival actions, n, have failed to do so then assume that future actions following the rule "If your aim is e, then you ought to do m" are more likely to promote those ends than actions based on the rule "If your aim is e, you ought to do n".
>
> (Laudan 1987: 206–7)

Laudan thinks (R1) is an acceptable principle for a naturalist to invoke since every methodologist will agree that it holds. It is not justified *a priori* but by the empirical observation that all those who have considered questions of scientific method would accept this principle. So a naturalist, Laudan claims, can with a clear conscience use principle (R1).

Worrall has complained that this is clearly inadequate for two reasons. First, as an empirical claim it appears to be false. Not all methodologists accept this rule. Popper, for one, rejected *any* inductive principle outright. Secondly, by appealing to the received opinion of methodologists, Laudan is slipping in a hidden norm. Why are we consulting philosophers of science rather than astrologers or religious fundamentalists? Presumably because we think methodologists know better than others how science should proceed. What we really need to know is why that is the case. We need to provide some justification for trusting the judgements of methodologists over others who might have different views on the appropriate methods for empirical investigation. Surely the only kind of justification that we would find adequate is one

that appeals to *a priori* standards of rationality which these methodologists adhere to (and astrologers don't).

Laudan can respond not unreasonably to the first worry by pointing
out that, as a matter of fact, within systems like Popper's, despite official
doctrine there are certain claims that seem to rely on inductive principles. Without something like the principle (R1), Popper would have
no reason to say that we should prefer theories that have withstood
severe tests, such as general relativity, to theories that are not falsified
because they have not yet been tested.

The second issue is more interesting. I think Laudan's response
should be to make a bolder claim. It is not just methodologists who
accept (R1), everyone does. How could we make any decisions about
what to do, given we had some aim, if we did not? Even if I could
persuade someone like Worrall that this was true, he might complain
that this is not much of an advance. The mere fact that everyone agrees
to something is no reason to accept it. Once everyone (in the Western
world who cared to think about it at least) thought that the Earth was
the centre of the universe. But we know that to be false. Why should
mere widespread agreement of any claim give us a *reason* to think that
it is true?

A naturalist has a perfectly good response to this, one that again
highlights the fundamental difference in attitude towards epistemological questions between naturalists and non-naturalists. If we think
of principle (R1) as providing something like the foundation for all our
scientific knowledge, then an objection such as the one I attribute to
Worrall seems reasonable. Why should we trust a principle just because
many people hold it to be true? Appealing to a fact like that can never
serve as a *justification*. Laudan's and other naturalists' attitude should,
I think, be like Quine's. We start thinking about science within scientific practice, not trying to provide a justification of science from
outwith science. General and weak inductive principles such as (R1)
are part of that science, one of the planks of Neurath's boat. As such
they require no further justification. They are innocent until proven
guilty. Laudan is happy to admit that we might refine or revise the
principle in future. This is, of course, something Quine would accept
in principle too. But the motivations for any such revision could come
only from within science for there is no higher court of appeal. Note,
too, that it is this difference in attitude that separates this Quinean
approach from reliabilism. Reliabilists start with a general philosophical account of knowledge. Science and its success at acquiring knowledge are then explained in terms of this theory. The Quinean naturalist

rejects that picture and so the philosophical problems that come with it. We have a successful scientific (and indeed common-sense) practice in which inductive procedures play an indispensable role. We admit, given Hume's problem, that we might be wrong about how things will go in the future. But this does not undermine our confidence in science. It just makes us fallibilists.

Methods: thick and thin

We seem to have come full circle in our account of naturalized philosophy of science. I began this chapter with a criticism of the traditional views of science as espoused by Carnap, Popper and Quine. Kuhn's work showed us that the inductivist and hypothetico-deductive models of science didn't capture what scientists in the past and now were actually doing. That in turn gave rise to a new problem. If science is as Kuhn describes it – consisting of periods of puzzle-solving normal science punctuated by scientific revolutions – then there seem to be discontinuous or irrational changes in scientific method. Chalmers and Laudan have provided us with a way of understanding how methods change so that fears about incommensurability can be put to one side. But to get Laudan's programme off the ground we have to make use of a very general methodological rule – essentially, the principle of induction. And we have rejected the idea that this involves a return to first philosophy by invoking a Quinean picture of our science. Principle (R1) is at the centre of our belief system. It can be given up – but we need a reason to do so and the only reasons of interest are those emanating from the sciences.

Given this final step, we might wonder whether there is any substantial difference between Quine and Laudan. After all, as we remarked in Chapter 2, Quine himself suggests that normative epistemology is concerned with reasoning from means to ends. Normative epistemology is supposed to be like engineering. Have we overstated the case against Quinean philosophy of science at the beginning of this chapter? In some ways yes; in other ways no.

We can distinguish between what I shall call thin and thick methodological rules. Thin rules are rules like (R1), very general and very abstract. Thick methodological rules are like those involved in designing double-blind clinical trials. They provide a richer, more detailed account of the methods used by scientists. Thick methodological rules are essential for providing a descriptively adequate account of science.

Since Quine says little about these thicker methods, it is fair to say that this characterization of science is descriptively inadequate. That said, there is no particular reason why Laudan's characterization of science cannot be accommodated within Quine's holistic picture. Although Quine does not describe such thick methods in any detail, there is nothing to stop him endorsing the claim that particular methods might be developed for particular enquiries and that these methods can be justified in the way Laudan sets out.

Some more substantial worries about Quine's account of science are raised, though, by Kuhn (and perhaps not adequately dealt with by Laudan either). Quine thinks of science as a bunch of sentences or beliefs. Kuhn's work suggests a more practical or practice-orientated account of science. As we said earlier, science is not just about testing theories. It involves learning practical techniques of experimental design, mathematical puzzle-solving and catching on to the significance of exemplars, among other things. Quine tells us nothing directly about that. Norms are involved here too. Experiments are well designed or not; exemplars are extended to new cases appropriately or not. Kuhn's work reminds us that to understand science we need to understand more than the sentences scientists accept or reject and why they do so. Even though Quine's account is sufficiently abstract to accommodate aspects of Laudan's naturalized methodology, there remain good reasons to think, given the emphasis he places on testing, that he has failed to recognize important aspects of science and its practice.

Again, though, this is a criticism of the detail of Quine's account; it does not undermine the general structure of the defence of a naturalized account of norms. We can easily explain why scientists adhere to these methods and norms. (Their scientific training has inculcated in them these standards and procedures.) And we can also fairly easily explain the scientists' right to be confident about them. (They are part of a successful scientific enterprise.)

Our picture, then, of a naturalized account of scientific aims and norms has two parts. Explicitly articulated norms and methods can and often are defended by empirical means. In doing so, we demonstrate that these methods are better at achieving our goals than some rival method. This is what Galileo did with the telescope. Other norms are defended in a more general way. The thin rules like (R1) (and perhaps also some of the practical skills Kuhn emphasizes are learnt by scientists in their training) are generally non-explicit. They can be defended, if made explicit, again by experience. They play an essential role in successful science. We would be willing to give them up if better alternatives came along, but without such alternatives we have no reason to reject them.

This account explains the reasonableness of scientific claims without having to invoke very general notions such as justification. If a belief is reached by standards and methods that are backed up by empirical data in the way Laudan describes, then that is reason enough to endorse the belief. That is an agreeable consequence given the struggles that we noted reliabilists had in trying to provide a general naturalistic account of (or replacement for) justification.

Norms and the aim of science

Does this solve all the worries a naturalist might have about norms in science? Arguably not. Another worry arises once we begin to think about the aims of science. Aren't the ends of enquiry subject to evaluation as well? What method or rules do we use to decide what we should be aiming for? This seems particularly pressing if you admit, as Laudan does, that the aims of science change. When aims change, how do scientists make reasonable judgements about what aim it would be better to adopt?

The naturalist's response concerning how to evaluate aims should be the same as his response to the worry about changing methods. When we look at concrete cases, it is not difficult to see the sort of evaluations that go into making a case for changing the ends of enquiry. If realization of our aim seems forever elusive and rival theories and methods seem more successful in promoting further aims we share, then we drop that unrealistic goal and try something different or more modest. Arguably this is what happened both during the quantum revolution and the abandonment of Cartesian physics. The aim of obtaining a deterministic physics or a mechanical explanation of all phenomena in terms of pushes and pulls by direct contact turned out to be unable to accommodate certain empirical results. Rival theories that did not respect these goals proved more successful. Also, perhaps given time, scientists come to realize that their favoured methods or theories do not actually achieve the aim set out; or at least that we may find value in a theory even though we don't share the same aim as those past scientists who put forward these theories or methods. Arguably (although I would not insist upon it) this is what happened with Newton's aim to glorify God. It became clear that you could understand and utilize Newtonian mechanics without sharing that aim.

The methods or rules of thumb used here are platitudinous, like rule (R1), the sort of thing that everyone will recognize and acknowledge in making judgements about how to choose between competing goals. In the former case, at least, we need in addition to appeal to further ends in order to make sense of the rationale of changing the objectives of our scientific investigations – aims such as the desire for scientific theories to match the data. This raises a further question: are there some ahistorical aims shared by all science? We can profitably think about this by transferring the metaphor of thick and thin from methods to aims. I am sure that scientists would describe the aims of their research in quite specific terms. They have thick aims. They are interested in the mating habits of baboons; or in giving a unified theory of physics; or making semiconducting devices small enough to be used in the development of prosthetic eyes. But they are no doubt committed to other goals. They want their theories to match the data as well as possible. They want their theories to be consistent (and perhaps, to echo Quine, also simple, elegant, fruitful). Perhaps they also take themselves to be aiming at the truth. Surely most scientists would agree to some of these thinly described aims. How can we justify the adoption of these goals? What makes them the right ends for science to be pursuing?

I'm not sure that there is any sort of answer to that question. Perhaps the naturalist might say that the search for true beliefs or at least beliefs that allow us to control and manipulate our environment are aims that we all share to some extent. How could we get by in the world at all if we did not have some beliefs that met these goals? Perhaps we don't need to worry about it too much. Maybe having aims like these is just what it is to be engaged in any kind of pursuit of knowledge. You could do other things too: write plays, tell jokes or tease your little sister. Science is an option, not an obligation. But if you are interested in learning something about the world, then you must be committed to something like making sure your beliefs match the empirical data. On the other hand, perhaps naturalists do have a problem here. Is there any way to motivate the claim that science is a good thing to pursue? And if naturalists can't say anything here, how are they to justify their attitude of admiration towards the sciences? To put it another way, if these aims have no particular justification or principled motivation, does the naturalist have any way of criticizing other sorts of enterprises that don't share these aims? Might religion, astrology or perhaps other kinds of philosophy turn out to be enterprises that serve different aims to the sciences and serve them successfully?

We shall address this later. But now I wish to turn to the question of how our understanding of science might be applied to philosophy.

Monism and pluralism about methods

We noted, as naturalists, two reasons to be interested in science and its methods. One was the recognition that science involved methodological norms. We wanted to be able to give an account of scientific method that didn't appeal to first philosophy. We have had some success there. The second reason was that we wanted to make science a model for philosophy. Quine, recall, embraces what he calls methodological monism: the methods of philosophy are no different from those of science. But we have seen that when we consider thick methodological rules, the methods of the sciences vary through time and from science to science. When we think of methods in a descriptively rich way, we quickly reach the conclusion that is no such thing as *the* scientific method. It could be argued, then, that the underlying method common to science and philosophy is captured by thin methodological rules such as (R1). The problem with this is that these methodological rules are so thin and abstract that they would probably be endorsed by everyone. Biblical scholars and literary theorists would probably accept weak inductive rules as well as chemists and botanists, not to mention the good common sense of the average man or woman in the street. Defining the methods of science by reference to such bland rules won't distinguish science from anything else. What might it mean, then, for philosophy to be done in a scientific manner?

Realism and anti-realism: a naturalistic argument for realism

We can find an answer to that question once we look at the way self-proclaimed naturalists have argued for what appear to be traditionally philosophical claims. A good place to start is with another issue in the philosophy of science: the realism–anti-realism controversy.

Scientific realists believe that scientific theories are true or at least approximately true and that the key theoretical terms in science, such as "electron" or "DNA", refer to unobservable entities. Anti-realists deny this. Philosophers who call themselves naturalists have interesting ways of arguing for both positions.

We start with the realists. Their basic argument is very simple. It involves an appeal to one thin method. One of the methods of inference employed in the sciences (some claim at least) is known as abduction or inference to the best explanation. Imagine a doctor confronted with a patient with a list of symptoms: spots, sore throat, temperature. The doctor works out that if the patient has measles, this would explain all the symptoms. He might further conclude that no other illness would explain all these symptoms manifesting themselves in the way they do. So the best explanation of the patient's condition is that he has measles. Scientists postulate entities and theories in order to explain some observed phenomena; and in good cases where other competing explanations can be ruled out we have sound reasons to think that if the explanation accounts for all the phenomena, then it is true. Abductive reasoning like this is essentially a refined form of the hypothetico-deductive method. A good theory, a probably true theory, is one not just consistent with the data but one that explains too, and explains better than any other rival hypothesis.

Realists such as Richard Boyd (1996) think that we can use the same form of abductive inference to defend scientific realism. Science is predictively successful. Quite strikingly so. There is agreement between theory and observation to one part in 10^{12} in certain tests of quantum electrodynamics. That is our first basic observation, like the doctor's observation of spots. What can explain that success? Only that the entities referred to in successful scientific theories exist and the scientific theories that describe those entities are true or at least nearly true. As Putnam (1978) puts it, "Realism is . . . the only philosophy that doesn't make the success of science a miracle." Putnam's nifty summary has led many people to refer to this realist argument as "the no-miracles" argument for realism. Since we are ruling out miracles as an explanation of scientific success for obvious reasons, only realism will do.

Boyd and other realists argue for their position by appeal to a thin method and a thin goal. Our goal in science is truth and explanation. A method that achieves this aim for us is abduction. Realists then use the method to argue that the best explanation of science's success is that it is true. Realism itself becomes an explanatory scientific theory. Here is one way, then, that we can extend scientific methods to philosophy.

A naturalist argument for anti-realism

Realists say that there is a link between predictive success and truth. Laudan (1981) claims that the history of science shows us otherwise. A whole host of scientific theories have been predictively successful: Newton's theory of gravity, the caloric theory of heat and the phlogiston theory of combustion to name only a few – but that turned out to be false and postulated entities that did not exist. There is by our current lights no such thing as gravitational forces, caloric or phlogiston. So history teaches us quite the opposite of the realist's conclusion. Successful theories are often false and posit entities that don't exist.

Laudan's argument can be presented as a kind of induction. Past theories (e.g. Ptolemaic astronomy, Keplerian astronomy and Newtonian astronomy) turned out to be false, so we infer that our current theories (relativity, say) are likely to be false too. Because of the rather gloomy view of current scientific knowledge this argument offers us, it is often referred to as the pessimistic meta-induction. Here is another way we can extend scientific thinking to philosophy. One of our thinly described scientific goals is to have a theory consistent with the data. Anti-realists claim that realism, understood as a scientific theory, does not meet this desideratum.

A historical example that nicely dramatizes the conflicting attractions of the no-miracles argument and the pessimistic meta-induction can be found in the history of optics. At the beginning of the nineteenth century, the Newtonian corpuscularian conception of light faced a number of serious problems; in particular it seemed unable to account for various diffraction phenomena. A French engineer, Augustin Fresnel, showed that many of these problems could (at least in principle) be solved if light were described as a transverse wave propagating through a luminiferous ether. Henri Poisson, an advocate of the rival corpuscularian view, thought that this led to a ridiculous result. If Fresnel's theory were right, there should be a bright white spot in the centre of the shadow cast by an opaque disc. The experiment was performed and the white spot observed. Surely such a result shows that light must be as Fresnel described it. Any other possibility would be a miracle. Later physics does not support this view. Subsequent work by Maxwell and Einstein consigned the ether to history. If there is no ether, there is no vibrating in the ether and there is nothing in the world like Fresnel's description of light. Surprising predictive success pulls us towards realism; knowledge of the history of science pushes us back to anti-realism.

Is there a way for a naturalist to choose between these arguments? If we accept Laudan's account of the history of science, then perhaps realism is indeed undermined. But it seems open to the realist to refine his argument in certain ways. For example, realists might claim that we should only be committed to entities that play an indispensable role in the success of a theory (see Kitcher 1993). Since, for example, the ether did not play such a role, no realist should ever have been committed to its existence. A more detailed reflection on the actual history can make this more plausible. Fresnel never in fact had a worked-out mechanical model of the ether. The ether had to be incredibly dense to support light vibrations, and yet so light and rare that it would allow objects like you, me and the Earth to pass through it without much, if any, effect. What Fresnel got right, a realist might argue, was the idea that light was a wave. What he got wrong was his (incomplete) model of what that wave vibrated in. Indeed, we can see that much of the mathematics that Fresnel used to describe light waves is retained in later electromagnetic theory. So the realist might plausibly argue that a more detailed look at the history of science should lead to an optimistic meta-induction. As science develops it weeds out inessential elements and retains those parts that do the explanatory work, getting closer and closer to the truth. So it's not obvious that a more nuanced reading of the history of science won't be able to save the realist argument from Laudan's criticisms. Moreover, the realist might complain that an anti-realist like Laudan has no explanation of science's success. On the other hand, an anti-realist might reject the very idea of explanation, at least as understood by the realist. The idea that a good explanation of something is a reason for thinking it is true is presumably something anti-realist philosophers in general deny. Good explanations are often false, they might say, again pointing to the historical record.

We have two accounts of how philosophy can be more scientific; or how scientific ways of thinking can be used to advance philosophical theses. On one account scientists (and philosophers) make inferences to the best explanation. Our aim is to formulate true, explanatory theories, and inferences to the best explanation allow us to achieve that goal. The other appeals to consistency with the data as a goal, and offers an inductive argument for anti-realism. Realists might object that the anti-realists' analysis of the data is superficial. Anti-realists will object that realists' use of inference to the best explanation is question begging.

Neither realism nor anti-realism: the natural ontological attitude

Just to complicate matters further for the naturalist, there is a third possible position in the realism–anti-realism dispute that also claims to be a form of naturalism. Arthur Fine advocates what he calls the natural ontological attitude (NOA), which he takes to be neither realist nor anti-realist. According to Fine, both realism and anti-realism add an unwanted philosophical gloss to science. Anti-realists, Fine claims, want to do something strange to our homely notions of truth or evidence. When developed as a positive doctrine, anti-realism comes in many forms: empiricism, idealism, verificationism, pragmatism. Empiricism asks us to draw a distinction between observable and unobservable entities. Science aims, according to the empiricist, only to be empirically adequate; in other words to make correct predictions at the level of observable phenomena. Claims about the unobservable are not to be believed (van Fraassen 1980). Verificationists and pragmatists want to change our ordinary concept of truth. Truth is what is verifiable or what we are fated to agree upon in the long run (see Putnam 1981). Fine says that we should reject these extra-scientific layers.

Realists too wish to add something odd and extra-scientific, says Fine. "What the realist adds on is a desk-thumping shout of 'really' . . . The full-blown version of this involves the concept of truth as correspondence with the world, and the surrogate use of approximate truth" (Fine 1996: 129).

Fine recommends that we ditch this too. Instead we should adopt the more modest NOA. He offers the following description of what such an attitude amounts to:

> I certainly trust the evidence of my senses, on the whole with regard to the existence and features of everyday objects. And I have a similar confidence in the "check, double-check, check, triple-check" of scientific investigation . . . So if scientists tell me that there really are molecules and atoms, and . . . who knows maybe even quarks, then so be it. I trust them and, thus, must accept that there really are such things with their attendant properties and relations.   (Fine 1996: 127)

This might sound just like realism (see Musgrave 1996). But there are, I think, at least three reasons why Fine insists that it is not. First, Fine does not accept the correspondence theory of truth. In fact, he does not accept any theory of truth. This is one way in which he sees his position as mediating between realism and anti-realism. Pragmatists and realists can both agree that many scientific claims are true. They differ in their interpretation of what true means. Pragmatists say that it is what we agree upon in the long run; realists say that it is correspondence to reality. Fine agrees with both realists and pragmatists when they say that certain scientific claims are true. However, he disagrees with both when they try to develop a philosophical theory of what truth is.

Secondly, Fine rejects the general nature of the realist argument. We don't think that scientific claims are true because that best explains their success. We think that scientific theories are true (if we do) because of the detailed evidence that scientists lay out for their particular claims. Correspondingly, our commitment to the truth of the claims of various sciences will vary with how good the evidence is (and obviously how much we know about that evidence). So NOA recommends that we take each science as it comes rather than try to come up with overarching arguments for realism or anti-realism.

Finally, Fine is not committed to the idea of progress. "Nothing in NOA dictates that [scientific] change be assimilated as being progressive; that is, as a change where we learn more about *the same things*. NOA is perfectly consistent with the Kuhnian [or Laudanian] alternative, which counts such changes as wholesale changes of reference" (Fine 1996: 130). Again, we can see Fine rejecting both an all-out realist approach – science is progressive – and an all-out anti-realist approach – science is not progressive. What we need to do is look to the particulars of each case to decide the question.

Thus Fine's NOA is different from realism because it avoids making any commitment to extra-scientific claims such as the correspondence theory of truth, the explanatory power of realism or the progress of science. How are we to decide between these three different views? Do naturalists have some further ideas about how scientific evidence, say, might resolve this dispute?

Below, I intend to do the following. I want first to look at how the same general strategy used to defend realism is employed by contemporary metaphysicians to argue for the existence of a variety of weird and wonderful entities. We shall then compare that method with a real historical case study of how scientists decide questions concerning the existence or otherwise of certain entities. With that case study in place, we shall be better positioned to make a judgement between realism, anti-realism and NOA.

On what there is, at least according to some naturalists

Quine, we noted in Chapter 2, believes in the existence of mathematical objects such as numbers and sets. His reason for so believing is that numbers and sets play an indispensable role in our best scientific theories and we as good naturalists should be committed to whatever entities our best science finds indispensable. We can see how this could be a consequence of the defence of scientific realism that we've looked at. The best explanation for the success of science is that the entities postulated in our scientific theories exist. Scientific claims cannot be made without the use of mathematics. As Putnam (1975) says,

> one wants to say that the Law of Universal Gravitation makes an objective statement about bodies ... What is that statement? It is just that bodies behave in such a way that the quotient of two numbers associated with the bodies is equal to a third number associated with the bodies. But how can such a statement have any objective content at all if numbers and "associations" i.e. functions are mere fictions?
>
> (*Ibid.*: 74)

So science postulates or at least implies the existence of mathematical objects like functions and numbers. If we believe that our science is true, we must also believe that mathematical objects exist.

Others have adopted the same or a similar strategy to defend a variety of claims about what there is. David Lewis (Loux 1979) claims that our ordinary and indeed our scientific talk commits us to the existence of what he calls possible worlds. We'd all agree that a sentence such as "there are way things might have been which are different from the way they are" is true. That claim involves a commitment to a certain kind of entity "ways things might have been", and so if we're going to understand that sentence as true, we have to accept that those entities exist. Lewis calls those entities possible worlds. Possible worlds are, says Lewis, worlds just like our world, full of concrete objects, people, trees, houses, gardens, electrons, except that those objects are arranged in different ways to the way they are in our world. There's a possible world, for example, where there's an object very like me but is only five foot five inches tall. There's another possible world in which there is a football team very much like Inverness Caledonian Thistle, but which wins all its matches. These worlds, as Lewis puts it, are causally disjoint from our world. They don't exist in the same spatial and temporal realm, and we have no empirical access to them. Nevertheless, we have to believe that such worlds exist if we want to make sense of counter-factuals such as "it's possible that I might have been five foot five", or "it could have been the case that Inverness Caledonian Thistle were a great football team".

In a similar vein, David Armstrong (1983) has claimed that we should be committed to the existence of universals. According to Armstrong, we need universals to make sense of certain aspects of our science. An important feature of science is that it contains laws, claims such as: the speed of light is a constant and independent of the speed of the source; all electrons are negatively charged; and all male sea-horses give birth to their young. An interesting philosophical question arises about what makes something a law. The most straightforward answer is that a law is a true universal generalization. This account is widely thought to be inadequate because there are many things that we would recognize as true universal generalizations that we don't think of as laws. Here's a classic example. Take the claim that there is no gold sphere in the universe with a diameter greater than fifty kilometres. That's true, I take it, and it's also a universal generalization; it says that, for all x, it's not the case that if x is a gold sphere then x has a diameter of fifty kilometres or more. But it's not a law; it's just an accident of the universe that there's no such sphere. There could have been a sphere of that diameter. Contrast the claim we have just made about gold spheres with a similar one we might make about a uranium sphere. It's not the case that anywhere in the universe there exists a uranium sphere with a diameter of fifty kilometres or more. This too is a true universal generalization; and it seems to be a law as well. It's impossible to gather that much uranium in one place. If you have more than a certain critical mass of uranium, you set off a chain reaction causing a massive explosion. The difference between the non-existence of the gold sphere and the non-existence of the uranium sphere appears to be that it could *never* be the case that there was a uranium sphere of that size but there *could be* a gold one. The idea that a law is just a true universal gener-alization cannot capture that contrast.

This is where Armstrong's account comes in. In order to account for the difference between merely accidentally true universal general-izations and genuine laws we need to postulate the existence of uni-versals. Real laws state relations between universals. Here's a simple case. Let us just say that the claim, "all emeralds are green" is a law. According to Armstrong, that means there's a relationship of necessity between the universal "green" and the universal emeraldness.

Emeraldness necessitates greenness. So a law of nature is a kind of second-order universal, as he puts it – a universal that relates other universals. Armstrong's claim is put forward in the same naturalistic spirit as the argument for scientific realism. He offers an abductive argument in favour of universals. Postulating universals best explains what a law of nature is.

In a way Quine and Lewis's view is more modest than Armstrong's. Quine and Lewis take themselves to be uncovering the implicit onto-logical assumptions in science and common sense. Armstrong is putting forward a new explanatory theory. But the basic idea is the same. The existence of certain entities is required to explain science and its success. Metaphysics is to be pursued as part of or in the same way as science, and when we do that we find the world contains many strange entities such as possible worlds, numbers and universals.

That seems a very surprising result. Naturalism, as described in the Introduction, seemed like an austere sort of philosophical position. Naturalists wanted to rid the world of various kinds of spooky entities. But it turns out that, if Lewis, Armstrong and Quine are right, a naturalistic approach to philosophy endorses the existence of a whole bunch of entities that common sense suggests are rather strange.

Many philosophers have, of course, disputed these particular claims. Some have tried to say that we can do without numbers in our science (Field 1980). Others say that you can explain what is meant by "ways things could have been" without believing in possible worlds; sets of propositions will do instead (Stalnaker 1976). Some say we don't need universals to explain laws of nature; tropes (abstract particulars) will do the work better for us (Campbell 1990). But these kinds of responses all accept the general strategy put forward by Quine *et al.*: we should be committed to entities that are required to explain certain features of our science and its success. What they dispute is whether the particu-lar entities Quine and others believe in are indispensable or that entities postulated form part of the best explanation of statements of possibility, laws of nature or whatever is under discussion.

I shall call this approach to ontological questions "constructive methodological naturalism". It is the way most ontological questions are pursued in contemporary philosophy. The naturalized ontologist must put forward arguments for the indispensability and the explana-tory worth of the entities he takes to exist. His opponents must dispute the indispensability or explanatory worth of those entities. That's how we are supposed to decide what there is.

On what there is, at least according to some scientists

Here's an important question for a reflective naturalist to ask. Do scientists' judgements about what exists match the way that Quine and others do ontology?

A good case study for us is the early history of atomic theory. Throughout the nineteenth century, the hypothesis that gases and other chemicals were made from atoms and molecules was used to explain and systematize a great deal of phenomena. Chemists knew that when two gases combine to form a compound, the volumes of the gases would be some simple integral proportion. For example, two volumes of hydrogen combine with one volume of oxygen to form water. From this, Avogadro hypothesized that equal volumes of gases contained equal numbers of molecules and was able thus to explain not only the law of combining volumes but also the Charles–Boyle Gas laws (a volume of gas varies directly with temperature and inversely with pressure). Further experimental work by Cannizzaro and Meyer led eventually to a determination of atomic weights that paved the way for the development of the periodic table. In physics, Maxwell and Boltzmann used the atomic hypothesis to develop the kinetic theory of heat and statistical mechanics, which provided the beginnings of an explanation of the phenomenological laws of thermodynamics. Given all this work, to which the idea of the atom was indispensable, one might expect that the scientific community in the nineteenth century was in agreement that atoms existed. How could one go about determining atomic weights if there were no atoms? In point of fact, though, there was widespread scepticism about the existence of atoms. One of the sceptics was Maxwell himself. The attitude of many scientists is well expressed in an early-twentieth-century chemistry textbook: "the atomic hypothesis has proved to be an exceedingly useful aid to instruction and investigation . . . One must not, however, be led astray by this agreement between picture and reality and combine the two" (Ostwald 1904, quoted in Maddy 1997: 138).

A few years later, this scepticism had dissolved. Why? The new confidence about the existence of atoms had both a theoretical and an experimental aspect. On the theoretical side, in 1905 Einstein published a paper on Brownian motion. It had been known for a long time that pollen particles suspended in a liquid solution produced a strange random motion. Einstein showed that, assuming the kinetic theory of heat, one could make precise predictions about the movement of these (microscopically) visible pollen particles as they bounced off molecules.

The hard experimental work of making these measurement was undertaken by Jean Baptiste Perrin. In a series of experiments he was able to verify Einstein's predictions with remarkable precision, thus producing a demonstration of the existence of atoms that could be "seen".

The effect of this work was almost complete conversion of the scientific community to the existence of atoms. A later edition of Ostwald's textbook demonstrates this dramatically. The original cautious agnosticism about atoms is replaced by this statement:

> I have satisfied myself that we arrived a short time ago at the possession of the experimental proof of the discrete or particulate nature of matter ... the agreement of Brownian movement with the demands of the kinetic theory ... [which has] been proved through a series of researches and at last most completely by J. Perrin, entitle[s] even the cautious scientists to speak of an experimental proof for atomistic constitution of space-filled matter.
>
> (Quoted in Maddy 1997: 141)

We can find a similar sort of story in our current science. The Standard Model in particle physics is a strikingly successful theory by any standards. It accounts for an exciting range of phenomena at the subatomic level and has been significant in discovering a new zoo of exotic particles. An important aspect of the Standard Model is the so-called Higgs mechanism. In the theory, particles with mass, quarks for example, obtain this mass through interactions with a field, the Higgs field. Massless particles, like photons, don't interact with this field. The Higgs mechanism requires the existence of a further particle, the Higgs boson. Do scientists believe in the Higgs boson just because it's an indispensable part of a highly successful scientific theory? Well, it appears that many scientists are at least agnostic about this. "The problem is that no one has ever observed the Higgs boson in an experiment" (European Organisation for Nuclear Research webpage). One of the motivations for building the enormous and enormously expensive Large Hadron Collider (LHC), which is due to come into action in 2008, has been to try to uncover some direct experimental proof that this particle exists. Particle physicists want to "see" the Higgs boson before committing to its existence. If ontological commitment were as easy as Quine claims, such a search would be unnecessary. It should be enough that it forms an indispensable part of our best science.

When we reflect upon cases such as the history of atomic theory and the status of the Higgs boson, we see a strong disanalogy between the methods of ontological commitment employed by scientists and those suggested by Quine, Armstrong and Lewis. It is important to a scientist to have some kind of direct experimental support for the existence of the entity in question. If no such support is forthcoming, then agnosticism appears a scientifically respectable attitude.

Maddy on mathematics and science

I doubt whether anyone other than a philosopher has ever entertained the thought that universals or possible worlds exist, but certainly sophisticated scientists are well aware of the phenomena that Quine points to, namely that mathematics seems to be an indispensable part of scientific knowledge. A reasonable further question to ask then is: how do scientists view the mathematical part of their theories? This question has been discussed in some detail by Penelope Maddy (1997). Her main examples concern the use of continuum mathematics. Science, replete as it is with differential equations, is full of applications of mathematics that assume the existence of continua. Maddy makes three important points in relation to scientists' use of continuum mathematics. First, when we look at physics textbooks we find that mathematical treatments of physical phenomena are often presented with further assumptions that we know are false. "We use continuous functions to represent quantities like energy, charge and angular momentum, which we know to be quantized; we take liquids to be continuous substances in fluid dynamics, despite atomic theory" (Maddy 1997: 143). It would be silly to argue from these kinds of examples to the truth of mathematics and the existence of real mathematical continua. The mathematics has application only because we idealize the situation in a certain way. We treat things that are not continuous as though they are. This is not to say that we must think that the science here is simply false. There may be appropriate ways of describing fluid mechanics so that we may say it approximates to how things are. However, in doing so we would also be denying the literal truth of the part of the theory that involves the application of continuum mathematics.

Maddy's second point is that even where mathematics is applied without idealizing assumptions, scientists' attitude is not automatically one of full belief in the structures associated with the mathematics. For example, general relativity makes use of continuum mathematics, and it is therefore assumed within the theory that space and time are (or space-time is) continuous. However, scientists themselves think that the issue of the continuity of space and time is an open one. Maddy, for example, quotes the Nobel-prize winning physicist Richard Feynman: "I rather suspect that the simple ideas of geometry, extended down to the infinitely small space, are wrong", and another physicist, Isham: "[F]rom the view point of quantum theory, the idea of a space-time point seems singularly inappropriate: by virtue of the Heinsberg uncertainity principle, an *infinite* amount of energy would be required to localise a particle at a true point" (quoted in Maddy 1997: 149, 151). So even when scientific theories involve no idealizations, scientists often have good grounds to doubt the literal truth of certain structural claims implied by the use of continuum mathematics.

Maddy's final point is that even where scientists are not explicitly questioning the structural assumptions implied by the mathematics, their attitude to the bearing of empirical evidence upon their theories is quite different when it comes to mathematical existence claims compared to other theoretical assumptions, such as the existence of atoms or Higgs bosons. As she puts it, "scientists feel free to use whatever mathematical apparatus they find convenient and effective without regard for the abstract ontology required, and more to the point without regard to the physical structural assumptions pre-supposed" (Maddy 2001: 110). Success of the theory is not taken to confirm the mathematics. Mathematics is treated expediently.

So scientists don't commit themselves to the existence of some unobservable entity until they have some direct empirical support for such a position. Nor do they believe that the indispensability of mathematics to physics commits them to the existence of mathematical entities – either because they think that the structural assumptions implied by the mathematics are or might be false, or because the mathematical part of the theory is not taken to be confirmed or disconfirmed by empirical evidence.

One response that Quine might make to this is that scientists are wrong. They have failed to realize the implicit ontological commitments in the claims that they make. Although this is certainly one possible position, it seems to violate the spirit of naturalism. It would be very strange for someone who proclaimed himself a naturalist to say that science and scientists were getting fundamental questions wrong. I think this point is decisive against the metaphysical moves we find in Lewis, Armstrong and Quine. Their methods of inference to the best explanation or appeals to what your best overall scientific theory of the world commits you to are not the methods of science. When we reflect upon what scientists actually do, their methods for deciding such ontological questions are more complicated and more sophisticated. A properly naturalized metaphysics or ontology should take this on board. If we are to proclaim ourselves as naturalists, then our decisions about what does and does not exist should generally reflect the ways that scientists themselves go about deciding such questions. An important and interesting constructive task for a naturalist would be to provide a more detailed and nuanced discussion of the methods of ontological commitment actually used in the sciences. Only then would we have a chance to try to adapt those methods to philosophical questions.

I shall not attempt to do anything like that here. It would be a massive undertaking. We would need to look at the many ontological disputes that have occurred in science and how they have been resolved. However, even the examples we have briefly sketched here suggest something that looks disastrous for the project of constructive methodological naturalism. Ultimately questions of ontological commitment are decided in science by certain kinds of experimental results. We need to "see" in some sense that atoms or Higgs bosons exist. Without that kind of direct experimental corroboration, these entities remain merely hypothetical for many scientists.

Constructive versus deflationary naturalism

The above discussion suggests that a better way to decide what there is, is just to follow the real methods and results of science. This attitude recalls Fine's NOA. We might call this kind of naturalism "deflationary", in contrast to the views of Quine, Lewis, Armstrong and most contemporary ontologists. Whereas constructive methodological naturalism involves a commitment to a definite method for resolving ontological matters, NOA does not express any such particular claim. Rather, it invites us to look at the detail of science and try to come up with an account that correctly describes how scientists decide such questions. In light of Maddy's remarks about mathematics, we might also investigate the difference between questions that scientists regard as empirical (such as the existence of atoms) and those that they consider pragmatic (such as the existence of mathematical continua); and how such judgements change, if they do.

NOA seems to me to be the right position for the naturalist to adopt. We should reject special general realist or anti-realist arguments and look to the details of science to decide what there is and whether and to what extent we think our theories are true.

There are three possible problems with this position. First, it seems exceedingly bland. NOA tells us only about science. It does not tell us how to extend this kind of naturalism to other areas of philosophy. Secondly, there remains the unanswered question of why we should value science. Thirdly, having decided that there is no unique scientific method, we need some other way to discriminate between respectable and valued scientific disciplines and non-sciences.

An answer to the second and third problems would provide an answer to the first. If we can say what science is and why we value it, then we would be in a position to explain the NOAers' attitude to other disciplines. Minimally, we would say that when others are developing ethical or political theories or whatever it may be that the assumptions and theories produced there should be consistent with those of science. This is a fairly weak constraint but it is nevertheless a constraint of sorts.

Unfortunately, the other two problems strike me as very hard. We can say, of course, that we value science because it is a successful enterprise. But what is success? Who judges that, and who decides what counts? One obvious answer is that we decide; and early twenty-first-century people agree that the theories and technology produced by our science are things, in general, to be valued. This response seems a little weak. People value other things too, and some people don't care a jot about science. Others think it is obviously dangerous, bringing with it the threat of nuclear destruction or an erosion of social ties. What can a NOAer say to them?

The best answer that we can give is simply to repeat what I said above: the aims of science overlap with basic pre-scientific aims that we all share to some extent. We want to be able to predict, control and manipulate our environment. Science allows us to do this, only more so. To those who worry about the impact of advanced science on our lives, the advocate of NOA can encourage them (like realists and anti-realists) to be more nuanced in their approach. The dangers of some scientific technology must surely be balanced against the obvious benefits – from transport and communications to medical breakthroughs.

Fine himself recommends that criticism of the direction of science and scientific funding should have its basis in a deeper knowledge of the work and practice of science. As he puts it, "To pursue NOA's third way means to situate humanistic concerns about the sciences within the context of ongoing scientific concerns, to reach out with our questions and interests to scientists' questions and interests" (Fine 1996: 174).

As to the question of deciding what the sciences are that we are reaching out to, again I'm not sure there is any very precise answer here. We have a pretty good idea which subjects are sciences and which are not. University faculties and designers of school curricula have no difficulty in deciding which subjects to designate as the sciences. But perhaps we feel that something more than highlighting our confidence in identifying science is required. We need to say what these disciplines have in common. We might be tempted in light of our discussion of the differences between metaphysicians and scientists to appeal to experimental methods. But even this fairly bland suggestion is probably too limited. Astronomy and mathematics, for example, don't employ experimental techniques.

The best answer the NOAer can give is to invite us again to look to the details of science. Science is a self-critical enterprise. It provides resources for criticizing itself and other disciplines. We have good and obvious reasons to exclude topics such as astrology or creation science. These disciplines are not successful by their own lights. Astrologers do not accurately predict people's future on the basis of planetary motions. Advocates of intelligent design, whatever the merits of the problems they raise for various parts of the theory of evolution, have no alternative scientific story to put in its place; they have no suggestions as to how to undertake research into the nature of the "intelligent designer". Science is different. The sciences have made progress – at least by their own lights. Physicists know more about the subatomic realm than before. No doubt the Large Hadron Collider will enhance that process. Evolutionary biologists know more about the evolutionary process than Darwin. Good science is, furthermore, rich in unsolved problems that this deeper knowledge throws up. We don't need any general definitions or criteria of what science is to make these points. The best naturalist criticism of astrology and other pseudoscientific subjects is in effect no different from the criticism that Quine levels at first philosophy. Either these subjects fail by their own lights or they are undermined by the results and methods of successful sciences.

Conclusion

Our struggles with science and its methods have offered us two versions of a naturalism that denies a first philosophy. The first, constructive methodological naturalism, suggests that we employ the method of inference to the best explanation. Naturalists of this stripe offer us arguments for the existence of numbers, worlds and other esoterica. The problem they have to confront is that their methods of ontological commitment do not seem to be shared by science – a serious problem for a naturalist. The second position is an attitude or a stance. It tells us to take science at face value, and not force it into a preferred mould. The worry here is that the advice seems too bland to provide the basis of an interesting philosophical programme, and we seem to lack any way of distinguishing what the (respectable) science subjects are from the unrespectable or unwanted. I have suggested how the deflationary position can answer some of these concerns.

If you dislike both, do not despair. There are other ways of being a naturalist. Instead of beginning with method, we may start with metaphysical matters and define our naturalism by what we take to exist. This, as we shall see, provides another kind of philosophical programme for the naturalistic philosopher.

five

Naturalizing metaphysics

At the end of Chapter 4 we started to move away from issues in naturalized epistemology and began to ask questions about ontology. We entertained questions concerning the existence of unobservable entities, numbers and possible worlds, among other things. In this chapter and Chapter 6 we ask: is there such a thing as naturalized metaphysics? Is there a description of how the world is in very general terms that should be endorsed by a naturalist?

Physicalism as naturalism

For many naturalists the answer to this question is straightforward. Naturalism is synonymous with another "–ism" – physicalism. Physicalism is the naturalistic successor to the materialism of Democritus and Hobbes. Physicalists have learned from science that there is more to the world than the atoms and the void. There are fields and forces and superpositions of state too. Good naturalists as they are, physicalists let scientists fill in the details concerning exactly what there is. Once the scientists have figured out what the fundamental physical constituents of the world are, then the content of physicalism can be stated very simply. According to physicalists, everything is or is in some appropriate way dependent upon the physical. (We'll worry later about what "in some appropriate way dependent upon the physical" might mean.)

We need to ask two questions. The first concerns the justification of physicalism. What is it about the claims of physicalism that demand assent? The answer for a naturalist must be that our best science supports this metaphysical view. This does indeed seem to be what physicalists say:

> Broadly empirical in character, [physicalist materialism] is supported inductively by scientific practice.
>
> (Hellman & Thompson 1977: 311)

> According to contemporary physicalists, the principles of physicalism are to be treated as high level generalisations.
>
> (Post 1987: 95)

We need to ask exactly what kinds of empirical or scientific evidence justify the claim that everything is physical.

The second question we need to address concerns matters of clarification and definition. Many things don't seem to be physical: the mind, morality, numbers. If everything is physical, then physicalists owe us an account of how we are to understand these apparently non-physical things and their relation to the physical.

I shall begin with the question of justification. Why should we believe that everything is physical? Two arguments are offered by physicalists that make direct appeal to science in order to justify this claim. I shall refer to these as the argument from reductive success and the causal argument for physicalism.

The argument from reductive success

Versions of this argument can be found in Oppenheim & Putnam (1958), Papineau (2001) and Melnyk (2003). The argument begins with an observation from the history of science. As science develops, we often find that the entities and laws of the non-physical sciences can be explained or accounted for by some more fundamental science. For example, in the nineteenth century the laws of thermodynamics were given a more fundamental explanation in terms of statistical mechanics. Concepts such as temperature in thermodynamics were identified with molecular motion, and the principles of thermodynamics were derived from the more fundamental atomic picture of statistical mechanics. In the twentieth century something similar happened with chemistry. The chemical concept of valence, which provides rules for how atoms can combine to form molecules, was explained by appeal to fundamental principles of quantum mechanics. Electrons orbit in shells around an atom. The valence roughly corresponds to how many electrons are needed to fill or empty the outermost shell. Why the electrons orbit in these shells is explained by the Pauli exclusion principle: electrons cannot share identical properties. Other examples abound: the mechanical explanation of respiration; the biochemical explanation of genes and inheritance, to name just two obvious examples.

The physicalist then argues that we should expect to see this same picture in the future. Apparently non-physical entities and the laws that govern them will be explained in terms of, or, as people sometimes say, reduced to, physical laws and entities. For example, we should expect that neuroscience will eventually do the same thing for psychology that quantum theory did for chemistry.

We can flesh out the idea in the following way: this kind of physicalist argument assumes a hierarchical structure to the world, starting at the bottom with physics and progressing through chemistry and biology eventually to psychology and maybe sociology.

Cognitive science, decision theory	Psychology	minds, brains
↓ explained by (reduces to)		↓ (composed of)
Mendel's Laws, biochemistry	Biology	cells, organisms
↓		↓
Laws of chemical composition, valence	Chemistry	molecules, atoms
↓		↓
Quantum electrodynamics	Physics	quarks, superstrings

Higher levels represent a new and greater degree of complexity. Entities at one level are exhaustively composed of entities at the lower level. For example, cells are composed of macromolecules, macromolecules are composed of atoms, atoms are composed of quarks, etc. The laws that govern each of these entities can be explained in terms of the laws of some more fundamental level. We are justified in believing in such a picture because science provides good evidence that some of the levels are related in the appropriately reductive way. We then argue inductively that eventually all the various levels will be reductively related to one another and ultimately to fundamental physics, and hence that everything is physical.

Frankly, this is a terrible argument. Granting for the moment that there do in fact exist such reductions of non-physical sciences to more fundamental physical sciences, the inductive argument is no good for three reasons. First, it is not at all clear why success in one area should lead one to expect success in another. At the very least, some argument is needed to justify the idea that all other, as yet unreduced, domains can reasonably be expected to conform to the pattern of the supposedly successful reductions. It may after all be part of the standard dualist picture to think that there should be reductions in all domains to physics except the mental realm. Is there any reason to hold that claims about the relationship of physics to chemistry support physicalism better than this sort of dualism?

Secondly, the examples referred to are hardly a fair sample. If we are to consider the argument offered in a truly naturalist spirit, the sort of inductive argument presented here should pass muster by scientific standards. To make the argument good we would have to assume that our selection of cases of successful reduction resembles drawing balls randomly from an urn. In other words, they are a representative sample from all the sciences. Clearly, though, scientists have not achieved their reductionist successes by randomly choosing one area of investigation, rolling up their sleeves and attempting to provide a reduction. They have deliberately chosen areas in which they believed such reductionist ploys were likely to succeed, given the techniques and tools available to them. But since not all areas seem so ripe for reduction, we cannot sensibly generalize from such a base.

The third problem is with evidence. If the argument is any good, all the evidence must point in the same direction. Physicalists must expect that these reductionist successes point towards the same underlying physical ontology. But that does not appear to be case. Consider the two plausible candidates for examples of successful reductions mentioned earlier: thermodynamics and the chemical concept of valence. These two "successes" might be considered data points in their inductive argument. However, as far as the ontology of the reducing sciences is concerned (and that is what is at issue), they provide no reliable pattern at all. The ontology of statistical mechanics is radically different from that of quantum mechanics. One employs a notion of particles with definite position and trajectories; the other does not. One assumes an underlying deterministic ontology; the other does not. The differences are many and varied. There is simply no general ontological picture that can be inferred from these two cases, even if we grant that they are both successful reductions.

Multiple-realization arguments

Most philosophers who call themselves physicalists do not try to justify physicalism by making use of the argument from reductive success.

They reject the argument not for the reasons I have given but because, as a matter of fact, many philosophers think that disciplines such as economics or psychology won't reduce to physics in the way that thermodynamics reduces to statistical mechanics. Their point is a simple one. Many non-physical properties can be realized in many different physical forms. Take economics and the idea of money. Money can take many different forms: paper, metal, or something stored in the memory of a computer. All these forms can be used to conduct economic transactions. As we noted above, to effect the reduction of thermodynamics to statistical mechanics, we need to say temperature is *identical* to mean molecular kinetic energy. If reductions require such identity relations, then multiple realization makes reduction impossible. The economic property of being money is not identical to any particular physical property.

Given the multiple realization of many non-physical properties, such as that of being money, most physicalists qualify their physicalism by the term "non-reductive". If the argument from reductionist successes is no good, and if multiple-realization arguments suggest that we shouldn't expect reductions of certain sciences to physics, then we need another argument for physicalism.

The argument from the completeness of physics

Once the idea of reduction is given up, the most common form of argument in favour of physicalism is the so called overdetermination or causal argument (see Papineau 1993; 1998; Spurrett & Papineau 1999; Montero & Papineau 2005 for versions of this argument).

The argument begins with an observation about physics. Physics, we are told, is causally complete: we need never leave the realm of physics in order to account for all physical phenomena. This claim can then be used as a premise in an argument of the following form:

1. Physics is causally complete.
2. Non-physical domain X has physical effects (e.g. mental events have physical causes).
3. There is no systematic overdetermination.

So non-physical domain X must be (or in some suitable way dependent upon) the physical.

Let us consider each premise in turn. Premise 1 is justified by what we know about physics as compared to other non-physical sciences. When we consider sciences such as geology, meteorology or psychology, the explanations offered there often have to move beyond the entities and laws strictly studied in these disciplines. For example, to account for weather phenomena, we sometimes need to appeal to non-meteorological phenomena. A volcanic eruption can affect the weather; some people say that if a butterfly flaps its wings in Japan, this can effect whether or not it rains in Dublin. Similarly, psychological explanations often refer to non-psychological phenomena. One of the reasons why you are in such pain is perhaps because I cut your arm off. Volcanic eruptions and butterfly movements are not meteorological phenomena. Similarly, dismemberment is not a psychological event or cause. So neither meteorology nor psychology is causally complete. Physics is different. To account for changes in physical events and processes, we need only appeal to physical events and causes. We know this because physical laws such as those found in quantum mechanics or general relativity are universal and without exception. Only physics matters for explaining why electrons or planets move and behave as they do.

Let us now consider premise 2. If by X we mean mental states and properties, then premise 2 amounts to something that sounds like a truism: mental events cause physical events. For example, my desire to type these words cause my hands to dance across the keyboard in a certain way.

An event is overdetermined if it has two independent causes each of which would have been sufficient to bring about the effect. If, for example, I wanted to assassinate my head of department, I might hire Jones the hitman. After I hire him, I hear from people in the know that he is very unreliable. Since I'm determined to get my man, I hire another hitman, Smith, to carry out the same deed. Smith and Jones both set up their weapons and telescopic sights. Just as my head of department emerges from the gate, they both fire and the bullets enter his body at the same time, killing him. In that case the death of my head of department is overdetermined. Either one of the bullets from Smith's or Jones's guns would have been sufficient to kill him. Premise 3 says that although this can happen, it doesn't happen very often.

Given these three premises, if a mental state of mine causes some physical event, say my desire to type certain words causes the movement of my hands over the keyboard, then since those movements are also physical events they must have, by premise 1, a complete physical cause. So we have two candidate causes for my hand movements. Premise 3 rules out that they can be independent causes of the event. So mental states must be identical to (or in some way suitably dependent upon – that phrase again) physical states. I say "or in some way suitably dependent upon" because multiple-realization arguments seem to have ruled out that mental and physical events are identical. This looks like a more promising way of arguing for physicalism. All we need to do now is to work out what "suitably dependent" might mean.

Supervenience

If the relationship between physical properties and objects is not one of identity, then what is it? The answer most physicalists would give is that non-physical properties and states *supervene* on physical properties and states. What does that mean? The intuitive idea, or the slogan behind supervenience, is that there can be no change in the supervening state without a change in the subvening one.

Imagine two paintings that are absolutely physically identical; it seems plausible to say that if the two paintings are identical, whatever aesthetic worth we think the first painting has, the second painting must have equally. The only way to change the aesthetic worth of one of the paintings would be to change its physical state. So we can say that aesthetic properties supervene on physical properties. There can be no change in the aesthetic value of a painting without a corresponding change in its physical state. But it looks as though we should also want to say that although the aesthetic properties of the painting depend on or are determined by the physical properties, those aesthetic properties are not the same as or cannot be reduced to the physical properties.

That's the basic idea, but the topic of supervenience has spawned a large technical literature so some further definitions and clarifications are in order. In explaining some of these more complicated ideas below, I shall assume that the non-physical properties we're interested in are mental properties – not because mental properties are the only ones thought to supervene on physical properties, but just because that's the way most people talk about supervenience. What is said below about mental properties applies equally to all other non-physical properties, states and events.

Defining supervenience

The origin of the term "supervenience" in the context of the modern mind–body problem can be traced to Donald Davidson's seminal paper "Mental Events". However, Davidson provides no more than the intuitive idea above: "there can be no change in the mental, without a change in the physical". The technical explication of this basic idea is mostly, if not solely, due to the efforts of Jaegwon Kim. From his work, several permutations of supervenience have arisen that are standardly classed into three types of relation. If M and P are non-empty families of properties, then one set of possible definitions runs as follows:

(SS) Strong Supervenience   M strongly supervenes on P just in case necessarily for any object x and any property F in M, if x has F, then there exists a property G in P such that x has G, and necessarily if any y has G, it has F.

(WS) Weak Supervenience   M weakly supervenes on P just in case necessarily for any object x and any property F in M, if x has F, then there exits a property G in P such that x has G, and if any y has G, it has F.

(GS) Global Supervenience   M globally supervenes on P just in case for any two worlds, w1 and w2, if they are P-property indistinguishable, then they are M-property indistinguishable.

To put the general idea into English: if the mental strongly supervenes on the physical, then wherever there are certain physical properties, there will be certain mental properties, and that relation holds counter-factually. That is, in any possible situation in which P is present, the supervening state M will be present. Here is an example of a strongly supervening property relation. Take the property of being a sister. For all possible situations in which someone is a sister, that person will also be female. So we can say that the property of being female strongly supervenes on the property of being a sister.

(WS) is identical to (SS), except that the relation does not hold counterfactually. Here's a possible example of weak supervenience. Think again of our paintings. We said that any two paintings that are physically identical must be identical in aesthetic worth. However, you might think that in a certain way beauty is in the eye of the beholder. For example, it is plausible to think that if there were no people, then there would be no art and so no aesthetic worth. If you do think that, then we can imagine a world in which there is an object physically identical to our painting but no one around to appreciate it. We might say, then, that in that world the painting has no aesthetic value. The relation of supervenience between the physical aspects of the painting and its aesthetic worth does not, unlike the relation between being a sister and being female, hold counterfactually.

(GS) simply implies that given the complete physical state of the universe, the complete mental state of the universe is fixed. Intuitively (although there is room to disagree depending on how one construes the modal terms), (SS) implies both (WS) and (GS). Note too that although the above definitions of (SS) and (WS) are framed in terms of relations between properties present in an individual, they need not be that restrictive. One could easily rephrase both (SS) and (WS) in terms of a relation between properties in a certain region. For instance, take some region of space. Then fix all the P-properties intrinsic to that area and (according to this form of supervenience) all the M-properties are fixed too. Terence Horgan calls this regional supervenience. I prefer to think of it as a more general definition of (WS) or (SS). In the limiting case where the subvening properties include all physical properties, (SS) becomes a version of (GS).

Let us turn then to the question of the appropriateness or otherwise of these forms of supervenience as explanations of the mind–body relation. A powerful and well-known objection to (GS) goes along the following lines. Assume that mental properties globally supervene on physical properties. Now, imagine two worlds that are physically identical and, hence, by (GS), mentally identical. Suppose there is some minor change in physical properties in one of the worlds, for example that a few hydrogen atoms are shifted in a galaxy far, far away. The two worlds now differ physically. It is perfectly consistent with (GS) that the two worlds may differ radically in the distribution of their mental properties (or that there may be no mental properties at all in one of the worlds). It seems therefore utterly mysterious what the relation between physical and mental properties is, given (GS), or why one should believe that the mental is actually *dependent* upon the physical in any interesting sense at all.

John Post (1995) has argued that although global supervenience is *consistent* with the sort of story told above, it does not *imply* its truth. It may well be that moving a few hydrogen atoms has no effect at all on the mental properties of the universe. Post suggests that (GS) be understood as programmatic. It defines the minimum structure that physicalism has to satisfy, the detail of which will be filled in later. However, when one considers what that extra detail might be, it is difficult to resist the thought that it will involve citing particular physical base properties upon which particular mental states supervene. In other words, it will involve setting out the sorts of relations that characterize (SS), at least as liberally construed by me. I do not see any way of defending (GS) as providing an explanation for the link between the mental and the physical that does not make it into a version of (SS).

Weak and strong supervenience look more promising alternatives. They are clearly explanatorily more robust forms of the supervenience relation because they tie the supervenient property more closely to the physical manifestation of the thing we take to have that property. If the mental strongly or weakly supervenes on the physical, it supervenes on the sort of physical thing that has mental properties, i.e. human bodies (or human bodies plus the local environment). That seems to be more the sort of thing we are looking for and rules out, of course, the possibility that physical properties far removed from the individual in question can have a dramatic effect on the individual's mental states, as (GS) seems to allow.

Both (WS) and (SS) imply the existence of psychophysical correlations, as suggested by my informal summary. From the above formulations, (WS) implies laws of the form $Gx \rightarrow Fx$. Whenever an individual instantiates a certain subvening property, there will always be the supervening property. (SS) implies laws of the form $Gx \Box \rightarrow Fx$. Whenever an individual instantiates a certain subvening property, there will always be the supervening property and that relation holds counterfactually too. (WS) is consistent with reading the correlation between the subvenient and the supervenient as merely accidental; and most philosophers think that accidental covariance of properties is not a strong enough relation to ground a metaphysically robust form of dependence. Certainly this is Kim's view. Hence the only relation that appears as though it might describe a physicalist version of the mind–body relation is (SS), which implies the existence of some kind of necessary connections between Fx and Gx. Let us consider this type of supervenience in more detail.

What are events?

We have talked so far of properties and states, but to understand how supervenience can play a role in the causal argument for physicalism we need to think in terms of events and causes. This is easy to do given a certain picture of what an event is. Take the event of me wondering what to write next. This event exhibits a certain property, my wondering, which occurs at certain time, while I was writing this, in a certain individual, namely me. So it is reasonable to say that an event is a property instantiated in an individual at a time. If a mental event supervenes on a physical event, then there will be some physical property instantiated in an individual, on which some mental property instantiated at the same time and in the same individual supervenes. This is Kim's view of an event. Others call these facts rather than events. It doesn't matter which name you prefer. What matters is how properties relate to things that stand in causal relations. Events (or facts) are the instantiation of a property in an individual at a certain time.

Problems of epiphenomenalism

One can best appreciate the sort of picture (SS) provides of the relation between mental and physical events by considering Figure 5.1. The Ms represent mental events and the Ps physical events.

The figure represents the general structure of mental causation on Kim's theory. We take the horizontal arrow to indicate causation and the vertical arrows the dependence relation that is described by (SS). Only P-type events directly cause other P-type events, given the completeness of physics; and M-type events supervene on P-type events.

What seems curious about this is that the figure seems to be perfectly consistent with thinking that the Ms are *caused* by the Ps. In other words, we may imagine that the figure represents a form of dualism, rather than a form of physicalism. Of course it doesn't represent a

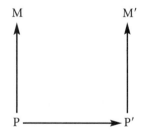

Figure 5.1 Supervenient causation

classic form of Cartesian substance dualism. We don't have two different substances here, whatever substances are. Both properties and events are supposed to be instantiated in the same subject. Nevertheless, we do have a property dualism. Given multiple-realization arguments, supervening properties are meant to be different from their subvening bases. If we follow Kim in identifying an event as an exemplification of a property at a particular time, then we are also committed to event dualism. The mental event and the physical event cannot be identical. Now if we take the (SS) relation to represent a causal relation, we have a classic form of dualism – epiphenomenalism – in which mental events are caused by physical events and cause nothing themselves.

Kim, however, places an extra condition on a property being real which would seem to rule out construing the supervenience relation as representing a form of dualistic epiphenomenalism. He claims that in order for any natural property to be construed realistically, it should do some causal work. Since, by construction, one would think that epiphenomenal mental properties or events do no causal work, they must be ruled out as real by this strengthening condition. But Kim's own analysis of what makes higher-level states causally efficacious is revealing. In his original 1989 paper (Moser & Trout 1995), he maintains that one can reasonably claim that a mental event caused a physical event if the mental event in question *strongly supervenes* on the physical base that would feature in a complete *physical* explanation of the cause of the physical event. In terms of Figure 5.1, we could say then that M *caused* P' for example on the Kim model – not because it does so directly: a direct diagonal causal arrow from M to P' is ruled out because if M causes P' directly that would violate the completeness of physics; or if it does not, then it would at least mean that P' was causally overdetermined, which Kim thinks is unacceptable. Rather, because it stands in the correct (SS) relation to the physical cause, it may itself be considered a cause. Kim sometimes refers to this as supervenient causation. So Figure 5.1 is an acceptable form of supervenient causation by Kim's lights. However, we have yet to see any reason not to interpret the figure as describing a form of dualistic epiphenomenalism. All that Kim's analysis has added is the counterintuitive idea that if one is a dualistic epiphenomenalist, then one can claim, as Kim does, that mental properties are causally efficacious because they strongly supervene on the physical.

The disturbing thought is that the relation (SS), the strongest form of supervenience, is not by itself strong enough to rule out forms of dualism. Even that is only half the problem. The kind of dualism that supervenience plus the completeness of physics permits is a version of epiphenomenalism. It seems, then, by analogy to lead to the conclusion that the mental is causally inert *no matter how* the supervenience relation is interpreted. This must undermine the causal argument for physicalism. It looks as if, if the mental supervenes on the physical, then premise 2 is false. No mental event ever causes a physical event. Kim has called this latter problem the causal exclusion problem. If mental events really do supervene on physical events and physics is causally complete, then there seems to be no causal work for any mental event to do.

Kim and many other writers on this subject are aware of these problems. For example, Kim has written:

> Mind–body supervenience, therefore, does not state a solution to the mind–body problem; rather it states the problem itself.
> (Kim 1993: 168)

> But the Thesis itself [supervenience] says nothing about the *nature* of the dependence involved: it tells us neither what kind of dependence it is, nor how the dependence grounds or explains the property covariation ... When we reflect on mind–body supervenience and compare it with the traditional options, we are struck by its failure to address the explanatory task. (*Ibid.*: 166–7)

The explanatory task is to say exactly how and why the mental supervenes on the physical, and show that this is consistent with our intuitive conception of what is involved in physicalism.

From supervenience to superdupervenience

When the idea of supervenience was first put forward, some natural-ists thought it was a philosophical panacea. We could account for all apparently non-physical properties by saying simply that they super-vened on physical properties. Aesthetic worth, morality and even the norms of justification were all said by some philosophers to supervene on a physical base and this, it was claimed, made them unproblematic. But most philosophers would now acknowledge that the formal presentation of supervenience as it stands is not adequate to ground a form of non-reductive materialism. One reason for this is that the technical notion of supervenience outlined above is non-symmetric. Strong supervenience implies that supervenient properties co-vary (admittedly necessarily co-vary) with subvenient properties. (SS) does not tell us *how or why* these properties co-vary. The intuitive idea behind non-reductive physicalism is that the physical *determines* the mental. Determination should, intuitively, be an asymmetric relation. Moreover, when one reflects upon the conventional position, it is a strange mix of views. It involves a commitment on the one hand to monism, since everything is fundamentally physical, and on the other hand property dualism (or pluralism), since the world contains irreducibly non-physical properties and events. What non-reductive physicalists need to combine these monistic and pluralistic parts of their view is an explanation of why the mental supervenes on the physical, which converts the standard non-symmetric relation of supervenience into an asymmetric relation of dependence, rules out dualism and circumvents the apparent problems of mental events being epiphenomenal. What is needed, in Terence Horgan's (1993) words, is superdupervenience.

Two grades of necessity: a first move

There are ways this can be done. Below I provide two. First, though, I wish to consider a common response to the problem that non-reductive physicalism plus supervenience cannot be distinguished from epiphenomenal dualism which I think is inadequate.

Some philosophers argue (Loewer 2001; Noordhof 2003; Bennett 2003) that all we need do to distinguish epiphenomenal dualism from non-reductive physicalism is to make a distinction between two different kinds of necessity – causal and metaphysical. Epiphenomenal dualism is the idea that there is a necessary causal connection between subvening and supervening states. Non-reductive physicalists claim that the connection between the two states is metaphysically necessary.

We can understand the distinction with the aid of a theological metaphor. Suppose God wanted to create a world exactly like ours. What would he have to do? He begins by creating a world that is physically identical to ours in all respects. Would he have anything left to do? Well, if this were a world in which non-reductive physicalists are right, then the answer is no; according to these philosophers, he would not. All the physical states of the world necessitate all the mental states and other non-physical states of our world. Just creating a world with all the same physical properties as ours is enough to bring about a world with all the same mental properties as ours. You might wonder exactly how God can create many things by just creating one, so it is useful to focus on a concrete case. If God creates a world in which there is only Adam and Eve, he can also create a world in which let us say Adam is on Eve's left. He didn't have to create Adam, Eve and the relation of Adam being on Eve's left. Creating the first two people and placing them where he did was enough. The non-reductive physicalist thinks that it is the same with mental properties. Creating all the physical properties is by itself enough to create the mental world.

The epiphenomenal dualist has a different story. After God has created all the physical states and laws, he must do something else to create a world like ours. He must create laws linking physical states to mental states. If he doesn't do this, our world won't be like his new creation.

I find this solution unsatisfactory for two reasons. First, even if we granted that this provided a way of distinguishing dualism from non-reductive physicalism, it doesn't seem to address our worries about mental causation. If physical properties metaphysically necessitate mental properties and physics is causally complete, it is still unclear how mental states can cause anything – and that's bad news if we want to endorse the causal argument for physicalism. Secondly, the proposed distinction depends upon a certain idea of causation as a contingent relation between events that not every philosopher shares. For example, Sydney Shoemaker claims: "[A]ll of the causal powers possessed by a property . . . are essential to it. This has a very strong consequence, namely that causal necessity is a species of logical necessity" (Shoemaker 1984: 222). If that's the right account of causation then it won't be possible to draw the distinction between non-reductive physicalism and epiphenomenal dualism in the way that I described, since there is no distinction between metaphysical and causal necessity on such a view. What's really required for superduper-venience is an account of precisely why and how mental states supervene on physical states, and an account of causation, particularly mental causation, which makes it clear how mental events can cause physical events.

Superdupervenience I: determinates and determinables

There are two detailed accounts of the superdupervenience relation that I think are promising candidates for solving many of the problems we have so far highlighted. The first can be found in the writings of Stephen Yablo (1992). The second has been elaborated by David Lewis (1972), David Armstrong (1981) and a later version of Jaegwon Kim (1998).

We begin with Yablo's account. Yablo claims that the relation between sub- and supervenient properties and hence the relation between mind and body should be thought of as a species of the deter-minate–determinable relation. That is, mental properties are related to physical properties as the property of being red is related to the property of being scarlet. The property of being red is a determinable. There are many ways of being red. The property of being scarlet is a determinate. Being scarlet is one way of being red, a more specific or more determinate way of being red.

This might seem quite implausible since the connection between determinates and their determinables appears to be a conceptual one. All you need to know in order to understand that scarlet is a deter-minable of red is what red and scarlet mean. The connection between the mental and the physical doesn't seem to be like that at all. Our understanding of what a belief is and our understanding of what a physical state such as a brain state is don't suggest a similar conceptual connection. To address this problem, Yablo appeals to some examples of *a posteriori* necessities made famous by Saul Kripke (1980). In days of yore, philosophers thought that if a statement was necessarily true, then it would have to be knowable *a priori*. Necessary truths were thought to be just conceptual or logical or mathematical truths. Kripke has taught us otherwise. For instance, we use to think that the Morning Star and the Evening Star were different, but we were wrong. We discovered that they were identical. The names "the Evening Star" and "the Morning Star" both pick out the planet Venus. The statement "the Morning Star is the Evening Star" is, when we reflect upon it, a necess-ary truth. It couldn't be the case that the Evening Star existed without the Morning Star since of course they are the very same thing. If there can be such empirically discovered necessarily true identity statements, then, claims Yablo, why can't there be the same *a posteriori* discovered determinate–determinable relations? Just as we may be deceived into thinking that the Evening Star and the Morning Star are distinct, so we may be deceived that the mental is not a determinable of certain physical determinates.

Yablo defines the relation between determinates and determinables as follows:

> (Δ) P determines Q iff: for a thing to be P is for it to be Q, not *simpliciter*, but in a specific way. (1993: 252)

The specific way is that described by the determinate–determinable relation: to be scarlet is to be red in a specific way. As with strong supervenience, if P is instantiated, then Q must be also. But Q may be instantiated without P; that is, such an interpretation of the mind–body relation looks open to the possibility of multiple realization. For example, something can be red in many ways. It can be scarlet, it can be vermilion, it can be burnt sienna or any of the many red colours available from your local DIY store. This leads naturally to the following analogous relation for events:

> (δ) p [event] determines q [event] iff: for p to occur (in a possible world) is for q to occur (there), not *simpliciter*, but in a certain way. (*Ibid.*: 260)

Since events are particulars, some sense needs to be given to the idea that they may occur in a certain way; in other words, what it is to be a particular event needs to be explained. Yablo does so by introducing the notion of the essence of an event. Technical complications aside, an essence is the set of properties necessary for the existence of the event, excluding trivial analytic properties and those that are consequences of the basic and (it is hoped) logically independent set of essential properties. This is a variation on the Kim model of events. Instead of an event being just the instantiation of a property at a time, an event is now understood as an instantiation of a cluster of properties – its essence. On Yablo's account physical events "subsume" mental events. The essence of the mental event is determined by the essence (or part of the essence) of the physical event. So far, this is just a more explicit version of the standard supervenience account. Mental events and physical events are non-identical; they have different essences in Yablo's terminology, but physical events determine mental events. The original part of Yablo's claim is just the thought that the determination relation is to be explained as a species of the determinate–determinable relation. In other words, the essence of any particular mental event is the determinable, which is subsumed by a physical, determinate essence. Epiphenomanalism is then side-stepped since "determinates do not contend with their determinables for causal influence" (*ibid.*: 259). For example: "[Archimedes] shouting 'Eureka!!' was causally sufficient for his cat's startled flight, nobody would think that this disqualified his (simply) shouting from being causally relevant as well" (*ibid.*: 272). That seems right. We don't want to exclude determinables from being causes merely because there is a more specific determinate we could also cite as the cause. In fact, Yablo goes further than simply saying that determinates do not compete with their determinables for causal influence. There should be, he claims, a "fit" between causes and their effects. "[T]hey should incorporate a good deal of the causally important material and not too much of the causally unimportant material . . . the cause was the thing that made the difference between the effects occurring and it not" (*ibid.*: 274). So, in some situations it is better to say that the determinable caused the event and let the determinate with all its extraneous detail drop out of the picture. Understanding the determinable event then as a cause of another determinable leads to this kind of picture:

Determinable (Socrates drinking the hemlock) → Determinable (Socrates's death)
↑
Determinate (Socrates guzzling the hemlock)

Since Socrates drinking the hemlock is sufficient to cause his death, being told that Socrates guzzled the hemlock only adds unwanted and unneeded detail. If you want to test the fit between cause and effect you need only apply this test. Could the effect have occurred without the cause in question? If yes, then there is not a fit between cause and effect. Clearly the effect in question (Socrates's death) could have occurred if Socrates had not guzzled the hemlock. If he modestly sipped the hemlock, the effect would have been the same.

The same applies to mental causation. Often the best candidate for a cause is the mental state. A full physical description adds unwanted detail. If mental states are multiply realized, then there is not an appropriate fit between cause and effect. The effect could have occurred without the subvenient physical base in question because another physical event could have been the subvening base for the same mental state.

M (Determinable: Desire for water) $\rightarrow$ P (Determinable: Reaching for glass)

$\uparrow$

P (Physical realizing state, Brain state X: Determinate)

Consider the concrete case above. My desire for water causes me to reach for a glass of that cool, refreshing-looking stuff. My desire supervenes let us say on some brain state, X. The best fit between cause and effect, though, is clearly the fit between the desire and the body movement, since some other brain state, call it Y, might have realized the same mental state. So it is possible for the glass-reaching to occur without brain state X.

This does not affect the claim that physics is complete since when any state is described in maximum physical detail the best candidate (in fact the only candidate) to be the cause in that situation is another physical state. So we can still hang on to the thought that every physical event described in maximum physical detail has a complete physical cause.

All of this works, provided you are prepared to accept that the relation between the mental and the physical is the same as the relation between red and scarlet. Yablo has succeeded in showing how you can hang on to the completeness of physics and supervenience, and save mental causation.

Superdupervenience 2: analytic functionalism

If you are not persuaded that the relation between mental properties and physical properties is like that of a determinable to a determinate, then you have other options. Another common approach, analytic functionalism, is described by Kim:

> For functional reduction we construe M as a second-order property defined by its causal role – that is, by a causal specification H describing its (typical) causes and effects. So M is now the property of having a property with such-and-such causal potentials, and it turns out that property P is exactly the property that fits the causal specification. And this grounds the identification of M with P. M is the property of having some property that meets the specification H and P is the property that meets H. So M is the property of having P. But in general

the property of having property Q = property Q. It follows
then that M is P.   (Kim 1998: 98–9)

Again this might sound very abstract, but the basic idea is fairly simple. Many non-physical properties can be identified by their causal role. Take the example of a mousetrap. What makes something a mousetrap is that it performs a certain function. It takes as input a live, free mouse and produces as an output a dead or trapped mouse. The property of being a mousetrap is having that causal role: taking a live mouse in and making it in some sense less than free. Similarly, but in a slightly more complicated way, we can define other more scientific entities by their causal role. The property of being a gene is defined by the causal role that the gene plays in inheritance. The nature of that causal role is laid down by Mendel's laws.

We can do the same thing with mental states such as beliefs and desires. For example, my belief that there is a glass of water in front of me when combined with my desire for water will cause me (normally) to reach out and pick up the glass. This partially specifies the causal role of the belief that there is a glass of water in front of me. Given such-and-such conditions (that I desire water, that I'm not tied down, etc.), I will reach out and pick up the glass. The total causal role will be specified by all the causal interactions that involve this particular belief. That's what Kim means by the specification H.

Being explicit about the causal role: Ramsey sentences

You might think that it is a big leap from specifying one particular role that a belief might play in a particular action to telling us the total causal role of any mental state. You might also be worried by the fact that in specifying the role of the belief I had to make use of another mental state, a desire. Even if we could specify the complete causal role of the belief that there is water in front of me, we would need to make use of other mental states to do so, and thus it doesn't look as if we could provide a non-circular functional specification for all mental states. And this is precisely what we need for a general account of the supervenience relation.

David Lewis (1972) offers us one neat way to see how we can generalize the idea of functional roles so that they cover all mental states. Lewis's account makes use of something called the Ramsey sentence, so we'll need to explain what that is first.

The Ramsey sentence was first employed by empiricist philosophers of science as a way of eliminating direct reference to unobservable entities and properties which, given their empiricist scruples, they found suspicious. We begin by dividing the language in which our scientific theory is expressed into two parts. One class of sentences and predicates we call observational and the other theoretical. The Ramsey sentence replaces direct reference to these theoretical terms with existentially bound variables.

Here's an example (van Fraassen 1997). Suppose we have a theory that states that water is composed of oxygen and hydrogen atoms, and suppose further that we take water to be an observational term and oxygen, hydrogen and atoms to be theoretical terms. The Ramsey sentence version of our mini-theory would say: there exist some property P, some property Q, some property R such that P and Q are mutually exclusive and water is composed of things that have property P and R and things that have property Q and R.

As I said, the Ramsey sentence was first employed by empiricist philosophers, but the formal device is not wedded to any particular philosophy. All you need to do to formulate a Ramsey sentence is divide the language of your theory into two parts. One set of predicates you will replace with bound variables (the theoretical part in the example above) and one part you won't (the observational part in the example above). We can readily adapt the Ramsey sentence method to the mind–body problem by drawing a distinction in our talk of minds and what they do between the mental vocabulary and the physical vocabulary. Lewis's idea is that we can eliminate direct reference to any mental properties or entities by replacing them with bound variables.

Consider again my first example. My desire for water and my belief that there is water in front of me will cause me to reach out and pick up a glass. Using the Ramsey sentence method, we can analyse this as: there exists some state X, some state Y such that if Jack is in state X and state Y, he will reach out and pick up a glass of water. We can get from particular cases like this to a general theory that eliminates all direct reference to mental states by thinking of our everyday talk of mind as something like a scientific theory. The theory would involve claims like the one above plus sentences such as "if someone is hit hard over the head they will experience pain"; and perhaps other claims that demonstrate some conceptual connections between our mental vocabulary, for example that toothache is a kind of pain. Once we have written out our general theory of all the causal interactions that mental states are involved in, we divide our language into the mental and physical parts and then rewrite our theory as a Ramsey sentence. This provides what Kim calls the specification H. The Ramsey sentence specifies the causal role of mental states in terms of their causal interactions.

Roles and realizers

This account tells us what the supervenience relation is: mental states are functional states defined over the physical base states. The subvening base state is the physical state which realizes that role. Strictly, of course, this kind of functionalism is compatible with dualism. It could be the case that the thing playing the role of my belief states is some Cartesian mind-stuff. But physicalists hypothesize that this is not the case. The actual thing playing that causal role will be some physical state, probably some state of my brain.

There are two different ways of thinking of the relation between the mental state and the physical state that it is supposed to realize it if you're a functionalist. You can identify the mental state specifically with the causal role. In that case, because of the multiple-realization arguments discussed above, you will say that the mental property is different from the (physical) realizing property. The brain states that give rise to my belief that there is water could be different from those that give rise to that belief in you. If you go this way, then the problem of mental causation resurfaces. Given the completeness of physics, the physical realizing state seems to be enough all by itself to produce the effect and the functionally defined mental state will have no work to do. Perhaps this is something that you can live with if you're a functionalist. We have arrived at a functional description just by defining mental states as the things that play a certain causal role. It would be odd to think that a property introduced in such a way could do any causal work.

The other way to go (as Kim suggests in the quotation above; it is also Lewis's view) is to identify the mental state in question with the realizer. The mental state, in other words, just is the physical state that plays a certain causal role. This will allow us to say that mental states are indeed causes since they are the very same thing as the physical state that causes, say, my reaching for a glass. If the mental state and the physical state are the very same thing, then they can't be causal competitors. The downside is that it appears to be incompatible with multiple realization. If mental states really are identical to some physical state, then whenever that mental state is around, the corresponding physical state must be there too.

There is some wriggle room here. You can qualify the mental state in question. Take the idea of pain. It appears that many different creatures with very different physical make-ups can experience pain. I can experience pain, for example, and so too can octopuses. It seems unlikely, then, that there is one physical state that plays the pain-role in both me and an octopus. But I can save the identity statement by being suitably discriminatory. We can identify pain-in-human-beings with the physical state that plays the role for me and you; and we can identify pain-in-octopuses with the physical state that plays that role for octopuses. So we retain identities between physical and mental states by being more precise about the particular mental state in question. We can also make some sense of calling these different things pains. We can classify them all as pains because their functional roles are appropriately similar. Pain in octopuses is presumably associated with avoidance behaviour, for example, as it is in human beings. But equally, we know, strictly speaking, that they are different properties since pain-in-human-beings and pain-in-octopuses are identical to different kinds of physical property.

Here we have a second way of reconciling the completeness of physics, multiple realization and mental causation. Mental states are identical to the physical states that realize them. Identical properties are not in causal competition and multiple realization, of a sort, can be accommodated by noting functional similarities between broadly similar mental states in different creatures.

Metaphysics, mental causation and naturalism

We began this chapter by looking for a justification for physicalism. We found that in the causal argument, but it gave rise to another problem. If non-physical states, like mental states, aren't identical to physical states as multiple-realization arguments suggest, then how can they do any causal work? This has taken us on a long detour through the ideas of supervenience, determinate and determinable relations, and func-tionalism. What is interesting about this from a naturalist perspective is how abstract and metaphysical the entire discussion is. Speculation about the relation between the mental realm and the physical realm is not informed by natural science but driven by a set of assumptions which, with the exception of the completeness of physics, are argued to be intuitively obvious. This leads or at least can lead to a kind of natu-ralism quite different from those discussed in Chapter 4. Metaphysical naturalists who call themselves physicalists do not have to endorse the idea that the methods of science and those of philosophy are continuous. Philosophy finds a special role in dealing with what Frank Jackson (1998) calls placement problems. Science tells us that everything is physical; the philosopher's job, then, is to show us how the things that don't seem physical – minds, meanings, morals – fit into the physical world. The work of placing non-physical things into the physical world is not (or least need not be considered to be) science or like science in its methods, but *a priori* metaphysical work. Jackson's own account of how to solve placement problems leads to the surprising conclusion that a naturalist should be committed to work that he calls conceptual analysis. We have seen one example of what he might mean in our discussion of functionalism. The first step in showing that mental states are identical to physical base states is to *define* the mental states like beliefs and desires via the Ramsey sentence in terms of their causal role. Given our definition of what a mental state is, it follows *a priori* that my belief that there is water in front of me, combined with my desire for water, will cause me to reach out and pick up a glass of water. That, after all, is part of what is *meant* by the belief that there is water in front of me, given that we accept the Ramsey sentence analysis.

We can then distinguish between two sorts of physicalism. *A priori* physicalism is Jackson's form of physicalism. For the *a priori* physicalist, the problem is how to relate two *vocabularies* – the mental and the physical. The method of doing this is conceptual analysis, an example of which is the Ramsey-sentence method of formulating functionalism presented above. This is to be contrasted with *a posteriori* physicalism. Yablo is an *a posteriori* physicalist. He offers us a speculation about the relationship or at least the form of the relationship between mental properties and events, and physical properties and events. This is to be seen as more like scientific work. We put forward a theory that explains various facts for us, for example how mental events can cause physical events and how the mental can be multiply realized. That there are such relations between physical and mental states is not something we can know by reflection on our concepts, but something that is (or will be) empirically discovered, just as water being identical to H_2O was empirically discovered.

Of course, to think that either approach is worthwhile, we have to assume that physicalism is right. Not everyone does. It is to those philosophers we turn next.

six

Naturalism without physicalism?

Some philosophers reject physicalism. Some of these philosophers call themselves naturalists and some do not. They divide neatly into two camps. We can think of each group of philosophers as denying one of the premises of the causal argument for physicalism.

The problem of consciousness: rejecting premise 2 of the causal argument

The larger of these two groups rejects premise 2. They believe that there is a special class of mental phenomena that have no impact on the physical. Consciousness, they claim, is not a physical phenomenon and has no effect on the physical. In fact, they make an even more specific claim. The qualitative aspects of consciousness, the redness of red, the way it feels to taste coffee, for example, are not physical. Philosophers have named the qualitative, what-is-it-like dimensions of conscious experience *qualia*. So it is to the status of *qualia* we turn first in our discussion of the adequacy of physicalism.

Three thought-experiments

Thomas Nagel (1974), Frank Jackson (1982) and David Chalmers (1996) have each offered a thought-experiment aimed to show that there is more to consciousness than can be captured by the physical.

Nagel asks us to imagine what it would be like to be a bat. No matter how much we know about the physics of a bat's sensory echolocation system, there will always be something missing in our description: what it feels like to find your way around the world using echolocation. The bat's *qualia* remain forever unknown to us.

More generally, we can put Nagel's argument like this:

1. Physics tells us about the objective structure and function of objects and events.
2. What it is like to have an experience is not an objective, structural or functional matter but a qualitative, subjective one.
3. So conscious experience is not a physical process.

Jackson asks us to imagine a brilliant but strangely abused neuroscientist, Mary. Mary has lived all her life in a black-and-white room. She has never experienced colour. Oddly for someone so confined, she has devoted her life to the physiology of vision. She knows all there is to know about the physical process of seeing. Nevertheless there is something important she doesn't know. She doesn't know what it's like to experience colour. If, one day, bored with her monochrome life, she steps outside her room and spies a red coke can, she will learn something new, namely, what it is like to experience red. But since she knows all the physical facts about vision, what it is like to experience red can't be a physical fact. We can put the argument like this:

1. Mary knows all the physical facts.
2. Mary does not know what it is like to experience red.
3. Therefore there are facts Mary does not know and they must be non-physical facts.

Chalmers tells us that it is conceivable that there could be a creature physically exactly like you or me but who lacked consciousness. Chalmers calls such a creature a zombie. Zombies might, like some of us, well up with tears at the opera, or speak passionately about the beauty of art, but there would be nothing going on inside. He would have no *qualia*. If zombies are conceivable, then they are possible and if zombies are possible, consciousness is not captured by the physical facts. We can summarize the argument like this:

1. Zombies are conceivable.
2. If zombies are conceivable, then they are possible.

3. If it is possible to have a creature physically identical to us but without consciousness, then consciousness can't be a physical thing (since consciousness does not then supervene on the physical).
4. Therefore consciousness is not physical.

All three thought-experiments have a similar form. They argue from what is knowable or conceivable or explainable by us to a claim about how the world is. They move from the claim that there is an epistemic gap between the physical and consciousness to the conclusion that there is an ontological gap. Arguments of this form are as old as Descartes's dualism. In Meditation Six, Descartes argues for what he calls the real distinction between mind and body because he can (clearly and distinctly) conceive of his mind existing without his body. In Descartes's hands at least, arguments such as these are thought to constitute a fallacy – the intensional or masked-man fallacy. Consider the following argument:

1. I know my father.
2. I don't know the masked man.
3. Therefore the masked man is not my father

This is similar in form to Jackson's argument, and can be made to look like Chalmers's argument too. Given premises 1 and 2, you can plausibly claim that you can conceive of your father existing without the masked man; hence they are different. But this kind of argument is just a mistake. The masked man might be your father. You just don't recognize him when he's wearing a mask. One cannot argue from gaps in one's knowledge to gaps in the world – or so we all thought.

Sophisticated modal arguments

The position has become more complicated now that philosophers, thanks to Saul Kripke (1980), have become more sophisticated at handling modal notions. In the following I shall concentrate on Chalmers's zombie argument, but since all three arguments have a similar form, most of what I say applies equally to the arguments of Jackson and Nagel.

The first thing to point out sounds like bad news for Chalmers *et al.* We can be mistaken about what is conceivable. Consider the example I gave earlier of a necessary *a posteriori* truth – the Morning Star is identical to the Evening Star. Ancient astronomers believed that the

Morning Star and the Evening Star were different. So they could conceive of the Morning Star existing and the Evening Star not. But since the Morning Star is the Evening Star and Kripke has taught us that true identity statements are necessarily true, it is impossible for the Morning Star to exist without the Evening Star. So there seems to be no good reason to claim that just because zombies are conceivable, they are possible.

What sounds like bad news for *qualia* fans turns out not to be so bad when we reflect a little on this example. When we try to conceive of something that is indeed impossible, such as the Morning Star not being the Evening Star, then whatever we are doing we are still conceiving of something. Plausibly what we are doing is entertaining a different possibility in which there are two planets that have some of the properties of Venus. Let's call them planet H and planet P. In our imagined scenario planet, H is a very bright object seen in the sky at the same time and the same place as the Morning Star. Planet P is a very bright object seen in the sky at the same time as the Evening Star. As Chalmers puts it: "[N]othing about Kripke's *a posteriori* necessity renders any [conceptually] possible worlds impossible. It simply tells us that some of them are misdescribed" (1996: 134). "Misdescribed" because we mistake the impossible claim that the Morning Star might not have been the Evening Star for the possible claim that something Evening-Star-seeming might have been different from something Morning-Star-seeming.

In the Morning Star/Evening Star case we can draw a distinction between something that merely looks like the Evening Star and something that really is the Evening Star; or as some philosophers put it, something playing the Evening Star-role. Anything that really is the Evening Star is necessarily identical to the Morning Star; something that merely seems like the Evening Star isn't. What we or ancient astronomers were imagining when entertaining the possibility of the Evening Star and the Morning Star being different was really something else. They were imagining a planet that is Evening-Star-like being different from a planet that is Morning-Star-like. So there is a systematic way in which things go wrong when we try to imagine something impossible. I mistake a possibility concerning some object for another possibility concerning a different but in important respects similar object. However, I'm still entertaining some kind of genuine possibility.

How does this affect the arguments concerning consciousness? Let's take Chalmers's claim that zombies are conceivable. Suppose I imagine a zombie version of me, exactly like me in all respects but this version of Jack doesn't have conscious experiences. I am definitely conceiving something when I entertain this thought. Given what we have said above, there are two options: either I am genuinely conceiving of something that is like me and does not have consciousness, or I am conceiving of something that, like the Morning Star and Evening Star case, has the appearance of being like me and the appearance of not having *qualia* – but isn't really like that. If it is the first case, then we've admitted that zombies are possible and Chalmers's argument goes through. If we want to oppose Chalmers's conclusion, we had better take the second option. In order to do that we must be able to distinguish between something really being X, and something seeming to be X, or something playing the X role. However, in the case of consciousness, argues Chalmers, this can't be done. To be like consciousness, our imagined faux-consciousness would have to play the same role as consciousness does. It would have to feel like consciousness to the individual in question. But "[i]f something feels conscious, it is conscious" (Chalmers 2002b: 256); and equally, if it doesn't feel conscious, then it isn't conscious. So there is no genuine alternative possibility we could be imagining when we think of zombies. Again, it turns out, zombies are possible and the argument proceeds as before.

The full argument for zombies goes something like this:

1. Zombies are conceivable.
2. If we find something conceivable, one of two things must be true: either (a) what we are imagining really is possible; or (b) we are mistaking a possibility concerning X for a possibility concerning something that merely looks and feels like X.
3. If (a) in the case of zombies, then zombies are possible.
4. If (b) there is something physically identical to me that looks and feels as if it isn't conscious.
5. If something feels conscious, it is conscious. (And if something does not feel conscious, it isn't.)
6. So, from 4 and 5, if (b), then zombies are possible.
7. If zombies are possible, then consciousness is not a physical thing.
8. So consciousness is not a physical thing.

If qualia *aren't physical, what are they?*

We'll worry a bit about whether this argument really is any good below, but first let's suppose it is. If consciousness is not physical, then what is it?

Jackson and Chalmers offer two possible answers. According to Jackson, *qualia* are epiphenomenal. They ride on top of physical processes but don't cause anything. According to Chalmers, the subjective qualitative dimension that we recognize in our experience is present everywhere in the universe. Physics tells us about the structure, function and objective qualities that everything has but misses out on the subjective, intrinsic character that all objects also possess. Reality then consists of fundamental entities that are neither wholly physical nor wholly mental, but have physical and mental aspects. So on Chalmers's view, as well as there being something it is like to be a human being or a bat, there is something it is like to be an electron, a lamppost and a philosophy volume. Chalmers calls the position panprotopsychism. Everything is a little bit conscious.

On both of these views *qualia* violate premise 2 of the causal argument. Although *qualia* are real, they do not impinge upon the physical domain. An obvious objection now arises. If *qualia* don't cause anything, then how come I know so much about them? Isn't it plausible to claim that my report that the coffee tastes bitter or my belief that the red colour of my shirt is unappealing and it was a mistake to buy it are caused in part by the what-is-it-likeness of the coffee and to my experience of the red colour. Certainly, that seems the most intuitive thing to say. More generally, it seems that, when we reflect on the role of conscious experiences, they are involved in many causal processes. If I sip my coffee, have an experience of an unpleasant bitter taste and then spit it out, I'm inclined to say that the bitter taste caused me to spit it out. How can we explain these simple facts about experience and its relation to action if *qualia* don't cause anything?

Jackson and Chalmers both have models to offer us about how we can have beliefs about *qualia* and how they might seem to have a role in action even though those very *qualia* don't cause anything. For an epiphenomenalist, correlated with qualitative states is some other, physical state that causes my beliefs and actions. Take my simple example of spitting out the bitter coffee. According to Jackson, this causal sequence will be like this:

$$Q \text{ (qualitative sensation of bitterness)}$$
$$\uparrow$$
$$P1 \text{ (sip coffee)} \rightarrow P2 \text{ (some brain state)} \rightarrow P3 \text{ (spit out coffee)}$$

It seems as though my experience of bitterness is in part the cause of my spitting out the coffee because there is a correlation between the bitter experience and the behaviour. But it isn't really a cause; it is just associated (maybe by some physical–phenomenal law) with some physical state P2 that does the real causal work. This would be consistent with our experience since we don't after all have direct experience of the bitter *qualia* causing anything; to us it just seems the most natural thing to say given the correlation between the experience and behaviour.

Chalmers's model is slightly different. It looks like this:

N (sip coffee/subjective feel) → N2 (brain state/experience of bitter taste) → N3 (spit out coffee/subjective feel)

For Chalmers there is a straightforward causal connection between all three states. However, as well as a physical aspect each state has a subjective mental aspect. In the case of state N2, this subjective aspect is the experience of the bitter taste. Again this theory is consistent with our experience. We can say that the mental state pain does in a sense cause me to spit out my coffee since it is one aspect of the state, the other part being the brain state, that causes me to spit. More strictly, though, if we focus on the physical aspects of all the states alone, then we need only ever allude to physical properties to explain why I spit. Laws relating all the physical properties will be sufficient to account for the spitting. The subjective feeling of bitterness plays no essential causal role.

Both views can save the phenomena. They can explain why we think that there is a causal connection between certain phenomenal states and non-phenomenal states when there is none. They face other problems, though, which make them seem even more counterintuitive.

Epiphenomenalists face a hard problem in explaining how such qualitative states could ever have evolved. If phenomenal states play no causal role, then there is no way that they could ever have arisen through natural selection. A creature can only gain a selective advantage from an attribute if having the attribute contributes in some way to its increased fitness relative to its rivals. But since *qualia*, according to the epiphenomenalists, do nothing, there can be no advantage for a creature in having such states.

It is open to the epiphenomenalist to claim that what gets selected are the physical states correlated with the qualitative states. So *qualia* are not selected but are a by-product of a normal selection processes. This leads to a further curiosity, however. An apparent advantage of the epiphenomenalist over the panprotopsychist account is that the epiphenomenalist isn't committed to everything being conscious. The epiphenomenalist seems free to say sensibly that only complex creatures like you, me and maybe bats too are conscious. The worry then is how consciousness ever arrived in the natural order of things. What happened between bacteria and bats that brought conscious states in its wake; and why did it happen if it doesn't offer any advantage for the creatures in question? If consciousness is only a feature of certain kinds of creatures, then epiphenomenalists owe us an explanation of what is distinctive about the physical make-up of these creatures such that we can expect them to be conscious. They need to explain why there are phenomenal–physical laws that they posit for these kinds of creatures here but not elsewhere in the universe.

One response that might be offered to this thought is to "go global" about phenomenal–physical laws. Epiphenomenalists might claim that every physical state has associated with it some phenomenal state. That would allow them to sidestep the question of the sudden emergence of such laws. The laws didn't emerge at all but were present from the beginning of time. This would bring the epiphenomenaist position very close to Chalmers's view and a new problem it would share with panprotopsychism.

If everything is a little bit conscious, that doesn't make the problem of consciousness easy to solve. One of the features of our conscious experience is that it has a certain unity. My experience of the world does not consist of lots of competing conscious states each offering its own view on how things seem. The problem for a view like that of Chalmers is to explain how unifying lots of different things that are a little bit conscious can give rise to a state with the property of human consciousness. What are the rules of combination between fundamental states that give rise to our unified field of conscious experience? Again, that seems like a very hard question.

We can see that if we accept the arguments for the non-physical nature of *qualia*, there is still a great deal of work to do to explain how consciousness fits into the rest of the world. We need to understand the relationship between conscious states, beliefs and actions and we need to understand, at least in the case of Chalmers's view, how primitive conscious states can give rise to the complex yet unified form of consciousness that is typical of human beings.

There is much that is counterintuitive in the pictures presented by the epiphenomenalist and the panprotopsychist but, I suppose, they are free to point out that everyone has some problems in understanding consciousness. Perhaps at the very least they have a clear idea of where the problems lie and where future work needs to be done. Of course, whether that work is worth undertaking in the first place depends on whether you are persuaded by the three thought-experiments that consciousness is special and non-physical.

Qualia's threat to naturalism: ontological and methodological problems

So far we have looked at the arguments in favour of *qualia* as something non-physical and sketched how the world might be if you accept this conclusion. I want now to reflect on what attitude naturalists should take towards these accounts of consciousness.

Let us first take the positive part of Chalmers's (and Jackson's) theory: the idea that something extra and non-physical is needed to explain consciousness. If you're a metaphysical naturalist and you identify that position with physicalism, then, of course, you stand opposed to Chalmers. However, if you call yourself a methodological naturalist, whether constructive or deflationary, then you can be more relaxed. There is nothing wrong in principle with positing new entities in science. We might think of the dispute between physicalists and *qualia*philes as analogous to the disagreement, mentioned in the introduction, between Cartesians and Newtonians over the existence of gravity. What the methodological naturalist needs to do is to figure out which is the better theory.

What is of more interest to a methodological naturalist is how we should choose between the three competing theories: epiphenomenalism, panprotopsychism and physicalism. Deflationary methodological naturalists such as Fine want to stay as close to the details of science as possible. If we take the case of atoms or the Higgs boson as our paradigm, then what is needed is some kind of discriminating empirical evidence. Unfortunately, it looks as if that is impossible. The way panprotopsychism and epiphenomenalism have been constructed rules out the possibility of any empirical evidence to distinguish between these theories. Moreover, they are also likely to be empirically indistinguishable from physicalism. One straightforward way of being a physicalist about consciousness would be to identify the states that epiphenomenalists claim cause *qualia* with those very *qualia*. The causal chain of events representing my sipping, tasting and then spitting out the coffee would look, for such a physicalist, as follows:

P1 (sip coffee) → P2 (some brain state = experience of bitter taste) → P3 (spit out coffee)

Because *qualia* (if they exist) are taken to be epiphenomenal, there is no (obvious) way to establish their independent existence in any experiment. We are, of course, free to speculate that things may be different in the future. It could be the case, for example, that in providing an account of how human consciousness emerges from the elements of protoconscious parts, Chalmers's theory will offer us some surprising predictive consequences. Perhaps there are certain situations in which the unity of our consciousness might break down, if the panprotopsychist is right. Clearly there is no such empirical evidence at the moment. So you would expect any naturalist who held empirical data to be the ultimate arbiter in any scientific dispute to be at best agnostic about the existence of non-physical *qualia*.

Let us now consider the negative part of Chalmers's argument: the thought-experiments that purportedly show the inadequacy of physicalism. Different methodological naturalists might take different views about the value of these arguments. On the one hand, it could be pointed out that thought-experiments are part of science too. Both Galileo and Einstein use certain kinds of thought-experiments to motivate their kinematical theories. We could think of what Chalmers is doing as analogous. This might be particularly attractive to constructive methodological naturalists. Just as Quine or Lewis think they have arguments that demonstrate the indispensability of numbers or possible worlds, we could think of Chalmers as providing an argument for the indispensability of something extra-physical to explain consciousness. On the other hand, a deflationary methodological naturalist might point out that both Galileo and Einstein produced theories that eventually had testable consequences; and it was the empirical success of their theories that eventually swayed the rest of the scientific community. It is not clear that anything similar is or could be true for the dispute over consciousness: physicalism, epiphenomenalism and panprotopsychism are empirically indistinguishable, at the moment at least.

In fact, the methods used by Chalmers are most similar to those of some of the physicalists discussed in Chapter 5. One way we looked at to make sense of the relation between the mind and the body was to analyse mental states in terms of their causal–functional role. Given such analyses, certain facts follow *a priori*. Given certain physical facts and a functional definition of mental properties, it is a conceptual truth that where there are certain physical properties, there must be certain mental properties. For naturalists of this stripe there is nothing objectionable in the methods Chalmers and others use to reach their conclusions. They are broadly the same methods they use themselves to articulate their physicalism, *a priori* and conceptual. Analytic functionalists think that everything non-physical can be defined functionally and reduced to something physical. Chalmers pretty much agrees with all of that – except in the case of consciousness.

Is the zombie argument any good?

It is long overdue to consider whether the arguments for non-physical conscious states are any good and whether naturalists, whether metaphysical or methodological, have anything to fear here.

The crucial step in allowing us to make the move from the conceivability to the possibility of zombies is that conceivability errors have a systematic form. When we conceive of something impossible like the non-identity of the Evening Star and the Morning Star, then we are actually entertaining another possibility: in this case that something like the Evening Star is not identical to something like the Morning Star. What is crucial in the argument for zombies is that in the case of consciousness we cannot make that distinction. Appearing to be conscious really is being conscious.

One way to avoid Chalmers's conclusion, then, would be to reject this model of modal error. If we could show that at least in some cases, when we try to conceive of something impossible, that we are not entertaining any genuine possibility, then we could block the argument for zombies.

That seems the right sort of thing to say. Consider the claim that there is a highest prime number. For the mathematically uninitiated such a claim no doubt sounds possible. So they might claim that they could conceive such a possibility. Equally, they might think they could conceive a possibility where there is no highest prime. We, the mathematically more sophisticated, know that there is no genuine possibility corresponding to the first case. Necessarily there is no highest prime number. Nevertheless, of course, we can say that our mathematically naive individual was thinking of something. They presumably know what a prime number is. So they can entertain the thought that there is a number with the property of being prime that is higher than any other number with that property. But the fact that they are entertaining such a thought does not mean there is any such possibility. All they know and are entertaining is a *description*. It does not follow that any genuine possibility satisfies that description. Of course, there may be some kind of genuine possibility that our friend is entertaining. He might flesh out his story by claiming to imagine a great mathematician announcing that he has proved there is a highest prime. But that isn't really, on reflection, a possibility to do with prime numbers. It is a possibility concerning the pronouncements of great mathematicians.

It seems to me that something similar could be said about the zombie possibility. We know the description that a possible world must satisfy to count as one with zombies. We know that it is a world exactly like ours except that consciousness is absent. But as with the case of the highest prime, nothing guarantees the existence of a real possibility that satisfies such a description.

Chalmers might claim that what is conceived by the naive mathematician and what is entertained in the zombie case is disanalogous in important respects. There are two moves that might be made. First, one could idealize. This is indeed something Chalmers suggests:

> We need a logically possible world [a genuine possibility] for every ideally conceivable scenario if we are to make sense of the various rational notions in question . . . A world can be described in many different ways, but such descriptions will always yield the same results . . . as the equivalence between the descriptions will be revealed on ideal rational reflection.
> (Chalmers 1999: 482)

Reflecting in an ideally rational manner, we can rule out the possibility of a highest prime number. If we have a full grasp of the mathematical concepts and everything entailed by them, then we should be able to see that there can be no highest prime. In contrast, Chalmers might argue, a full grasp of the relevant physical concepts and our concepts of consciousness won't rule out zombies. But what is *ideal* here, and how does Chalmers know he has managed it or what its results would be?

In the case of mathematics, it is easy to idealize. Mathematical concepts are unusually clear and well defined. The concepts used in our science are much more open-ended. Physical concepts are open to various kinds of refinement which can in turn change what we think is and is not possible. For example, for Aristotelians it was impossible that there could be more than one world. Each element has its proper place in the cosmos to which it naturally moves. Earth tends towards the centre of the earth; water to the surface of the earth; air to the lower atmosphere and fire to the upper atmosphere. If there were another world, then:

> [T]he parts of earth in another world are such as to move to the centre here and fire there towards the extremity of our world. Yet this is impossible: for if this happens, earth in its own world must move upwards, while fire must move to the centre, and similarly earth from this world must move from the centre naturally in moving to the centre in that world, because of the way in which the worlds are mutually positioned. For either we ought not to lay down that the simplest bodies in the many worlds have the same nature, or in saying that they do we must make the centre single, as well as the extremity; yet if this is so, there cannot be more than one world. (Aristotle: 276b11)

For Aristotle, therefore, it was inconceivable that there could be other worlds just like ours given what we mean by earth, water, air and fire. Now, of course, we reject Aristotle's physics and so we reject the conclusion. We think it possible that there may be other universes like ours; some cosmologists take this suggestion very seriously. Nevertheless, this is an excellent example of changing beliefs and concepts altering our conception of what is properly conceivable. There are other examples from modern physics. It was often held that no two objects could conceivably occupy the same space. Quantum theory shows us that this is (arguably) false. In an Einstein–Bose condensate all the particles occupy the same position. And of course mathematics itself provides some clear examples. It was once inconceivable that space could be anything other than Euclidean. But now we reject that.

Given such facts, it is difficult to see how we can say with authority that what we find conceivable is possible (and conversely that what we find inconceivable is impossible).

Chalmers could respond in the following way. Assume that we have a complete knowledge of the final idealized physics. From our ideal grasp of such physics we should be able to say definitively whether it rules out zombies. If our complete conceptual grasp of finalized microphysics does rule out zombies, zombies are impossible. If it doesn't, they are possible. The trouble here, of course, is that since we don't have such a grasp of the final idealized microphysics, we can't say if such a possibility is ruled in or out. Our current ignorance allows no conclusions one way or the other.

This is where the second sort of response might come to the rescue. Chalmers might claim we know *enough* about physics and consciousness now to know that zombies are conceptually possible. Physics, however it develops, concerns facts about structure and function. Consciousness, as our three thought-experiments show, cannot be captured by facts concerning structure and function, and so no physical discoveries will ever show zombies to be impossible. But I think we have reasons to be at the very least suspicious of this claim. The upshot of this way of arguing is that conscious experience is epiphenomenal. As was discussed above, that seems counterintuitive. There seem to be good reasons for thinking that conscious experience plays a causal role in belief formation and action. This fact seems to me enough to allow for the possibility that our physics (or more probably our understanding of human physiology) may develop in ways that explain consciousness without postulating new fundamental entities. At the very least, we should conclude that Chalmers's argument does not show us that we *must* postulate something new in our ontology to account for consciousness.

Let me summarize the above line of thought. The fact that we understand a sentence does not show that there is any possibility being entertained. As the case of the highest prime shows, all we need to know to understand a claim about a possibility is a set of descriptive conditions that the putative possibility would have to satisfy. That is consistent with there being no such possibility. If we try to circumvent this problem by moving to an idealized understanding, then we won't get very far. No one has such an understanding of physical concepts, so no one is in a position to say definitively what is and is not possible. The weaker claim that we know enough about what physics is like to know that zombies are possible seems to me, at best, a restatement of the non-physicalist intuition. Science forces us to revise our conceptions of what is and is not possible, of where a concept can be meaningfully deployed and where it can't. Who knows how things will look in the future?

This echoes in an important way something we learnt from Quine. Part of Quine's criticism of Carnap is that there is no principled way to distinguish between the linguistic frameworks changed for pragmatic reasons and the scientific theories within those frameworks revised in the light of empirical data. Part of Chalmers's case for zombies involves seeing our concepts of the physical and the phenomenal in a similar way to Carnap's linguistic frameworks. Our understanding of concepts, on this view, furnishes us with modal intuitions about what is and is not possible that are not to open to revision in light of new scientific knowledge. But Quine and the history of science show us that this is highly questionable. Modal intuitions, as much as anything else, are revisable in light of new knowledge. Scientific knowledge forces us to update the kinds of things we think are possible and where and how our concepts can be meaningfully employed, as well as which laws and theories we hold to be true. There is no special position for a philosopher to occupy to tell us definitively what is and is not possible, no matter how our future science develops.

Chalmers and others might object that nothing I have said helps us to understand consciousness. Showing that Chalmers's argument, which moves from an epistemic or explanatory gap to an ontological gap, is not sound does not help to bridge the original explanatory gap. True: the explanatory gap remains because we simply don't know very much about consciousness and its relation to the brain and other physiological processes. As we learn more, perhaps we shall be better placed to consider whether zombies are possible. Perhaps we'll find that as our theories and understanding of consciousness evolve, we shall be inclined to say that there is no such possibility. Maybe we'll find that we're inclined to agree with Chalmers that we need to posit something new to account for consciousness. Our attitude should be like that of the good (deflationary) methodological naturalist. Show us your different theories, let's see what they explain and let's see how they fare against the data. Just now we have no such worked-out theories and thus no reason to endorse any particular account of consciousness.

The patchwork of laws: denying premise 1

The argument we have just looked at against physicalism is of a fairly conservative sort. Chalmers agrees with the physicalist about everything except the place of consciousness in the world. A more radical and very different reason for rejecting physicalism comes from Nancy Cartwright. Cartwright doesn't call herself a naturalist but an empiricist. However, as we shall see, her arguments are very much in a naturalistic spirit.

Cartwright argues against what she calls fundamentalism, the idea that the world is governed by a small set of laws that apply everywhere and at all times. She offers in its place the dappled world or the patchwork of laws – which she characterizes as the view that "nature is governed in different domains by different systems of laws not necessarily related to each other in any systematic way" (Cartwright 1999: 31). Fundamentalism is closely related to the completeness of physics. The completeness of physics implies that the laws of physics apply everywhere and at all times. So Cartwright's arguments can be taken as arguments against premise 1 of the causal argument.

The argument offered against fundamentalism in the first chapter of Cartwright's text *The Dappled World* is very simple. Cartwright claims that when we look at the world about us we can find many kinds of phenomena that cannot be explained by our best fundamental physics. A simple example of an experiment that defeats theoretical treatment would be to drop a $1,000 bill from a window on a blustery day. We have no way to begin to explain the complex motion of our valuable note with our supposedly fundamental physical theories in this kind of example. So, Cartwright argues, we have no reason to think that the fundamental laws apply here.

Cartwright's argument against the universality of laws involves an application of a form of reasoning we saw used in Chapter 4 by scientific realists. Realists claim that we should believe in our scientific theories because they are successful. Cartwright points out that our scientific theories are successful in a very limited range of circumstances. We can often provide successful explanations for phenomena using our physics in our laboratories, where we can carefully control the circumstances and weed out possible interfering factors. This gives us good reason to think the laws are true in these circumstances, but no reason for thinking they hold in the unruly world beyond the laboratory walls. For many cases, like the $1,000 bill blowing in the wind, we cannot apply our fundamental laws and so have no reason to state that the laws hold here.

You might think that fundamentalists have an obvious response to Cartwright's claim. Everyone knows, they will say, that we have no explanation for situations such as the $1,000 bill in terms of the fundamental laws of physics. The reason why we do not, though, is equally obvious – mathematical and practical complexity. We can't apply our fundamental physical laws to this situation because either we don't have enough information about the initial conditions or we lack the mathematical know-how to say anything useful.

Cartwright's response is straightforward and robustly empiricist:

> Many will continue to believe that the wind and other exogenous factors must produce a force ... That view begs the question. When we have a good fitting molecular model for the wind ... then we will have good scientific reason to maintain that the wind operates via a force. Otherwise the assumption is just an expression of fundamentalist faith.
>
> (1999: 28)

One could, of course, write down various systems of equations that one might think captured certain aspects of the interaction, and show that they were mathematically intractable. For example, one might devise a highly complex force function for the wind. But so what? That only shows it is possible to devise mathematically intractable equations; it does nothing to show that it is the right force function. Only if you already believe in fundamentalism would you find any such arguments compelling. As Cartwright says, "I am prepared to believe in more general theories when we have direct empirical support for them" (*ibid.*: 31).

Models and laws

The full argument against fundamentalism is in fact a little subtler than I (and Cartwright in chapter 1 of the *Dappled World*) have just presented it. The quotation above talks of "a molecular *model* for the wind", which introduces something new to the argument that we have not yet discussed. Part of the temptation towards fundamentalism, thinks Cartwright, is that it rests on a misunderstanding of how laws apply to real-world situations. Laws, according to Cartwright, do not simply describe how the world is in very general terms; they have to be "fitted out", as she puts it, by models.

This will take a bit of explaining. Consider a plausible candidate for a fundamental law that holds everywhere and at all times, $F = ma$. Now, one way to understand a law like this, many philosophers claim, is that it expresses a generalization of some sort between the properties of force, mass and acceleration. The laws of physics, on this view, are no different from generalizations such as "all emeralds are green". Wherever there is a mass being acted upon by a force, the properties of force, mass and acceleration will stand in the relation described by the law. Further, we have good reason to think that the regularity holds because we have tested it many times and found that the relation between these three properties matches what the law says. Just as we have good reason to think that all emeralds are green because every emerald we have tested conforms with the law.

Cartwright's first point is that the law, $F = ma$, unlike "all emeralds are green", does not by itself tell us anything about the world. The property of being a force is not like the property of being green, something that reveals itself to an observer. To test a law such as $F = ma$ we need to find something that is a force. The law taken on its own does not tell us how to locate forces. We need to introduce what Cartwright calls *interpretative* models. In the case of classical mechanics these provide us with concrete accounts of what it is to be a force for certain kinds of systems. We find these models explained and expounded in elementary textbooks of physics. Physics students typically learn, for example, to write down equations for gravitational force, $F = Gm_1m_2/r^2$; for a spring force, $F = -kx$, where k is a constant and x measures the displacement from the rest or equilibrium position; and for a pendulum $F = -mg\sin\theta$, where θ measures the angle of displacement of the pendulum. Without models like these the student or indeed scientist has no way to apply the general law $F = ma$. Part of why science is a creative enterprise, rather than just the mindless plugging of values into equations, is that the working scientist has to be able to adapt these models of fundamental theory to new situations. He has to have the imagination to see that things that do not immediately seem like springs or pendulums can be successfully explained or accounted for using these equations. We quoted a nice example of this kind of work from Kuhn in Chapter 4. Bernouilli was able to explain the speed of efflux by making use of pendulum models. In such cases, we have good reason to say that our fundamental laws apply. But the application is not straightforward. Talented scientists are required to see how the models bequeathed to us by our theory can apply in unfamiliar circumstances.

Many applications of physics are not as neat. Sometimes the models and so the equations that we use to help us to understand the system we are interested in are not constructed from our basic interpretative models. Sometimes we have to apply principles and ideas from elsewhere. Cartwright discusses in detail the case of superconductors. Descriptions of superconducting materials, even those that try to provide a fundamental description of the interactions giving rise to superconducting behaviour, are generally a mish-mash of fundamental principles and what Cartwright calls phenomenological or *ad hoc* principles – principles introduced because they give us the right answer. Most physics is like this. We idealize and abstract and make use of whatever is at hand in order to get our theory to work. Although fundamental laws are in play here, they can't take the sole credit for our successful predictions for without the phenomenological models supplementing the fundamental laws, we will not get the answers we are after.

When we look at the relation between our best science and the world, we find three sorts of situations. In the best case, our fundamental theories and the models we use to interpret the theory fit well. The simplest examples of cases such as these in classical mechanics are pendulum motion, the orbit of the planets, the motions of springs, etc. Here we have good reason to say that our fundamental laws hold. In the second case, which Cartwright claims makes up most of what practising physicists do, we make use of both fundamental laws and principles, and ideas from outside fundamental theory to construct models that work well enough in the practical contexts we're interested in. Finally, there are some situations, for example the $1,000 bill flapping in the wind, where our laws make no purchase on reality even if supplemented by additional phenomenological principles. In the latter two cases, we have no reason to think that our laws hold here and are responsible for all physical behaviour. Thus in general we have no reason to believe in fundamentalism and so no reason to accept premise 1 of the causal argument.

Cartwright develops this negative point against fundamentalism into a positive metaphysical alternative. She suggests that we take things at face value. The world is made up of lots of laws applying in lots of different circumstances, sometimes overlapping, sometimes running out altogether. "Metaphysical nomological pluralism is the doctrine that nature is governed in different domains by different systems of laws not necessarily related to one another in any systematic or uniform way; by a patchwork of laws" (1999: 31). I think this is a good description of how science actually looks. We find scientists using different laws and theories in different domains without any necessary systematic connection between these laws. But as a metaphysical view, I find it less appealing. The argument used by Cartwright against fundamentalism looks as if it can also be used against the patchwork of laws. What is the evidence, the *direct* evidence, that the universe is made up of a patchwork of laws? There is none that I can see. Perhaps it is true that we have good evidence that the many laws making up the patchwork hold true in certain circumstances, but that is quite different from having evidence for the *general thesis* that the world is made up of a patchwork of laws. Inasmuch as we think of Cartwright's view as a metaphysical position at all, it must go beyond what we have direct evidence for, and so must be vulnerable to the same objections as fundamentalism.

I think the proper conclusion of Cartwright's work should be to reject all general metaphysical positions such as physicalism or the patchwork of laws. We have no good reason to insist that the laws of physics as applied by actual working scientists apply everywhere and at all times; equally we have no particularly good reason to deny it. Both views are pieces of metaphysics, extraneous to actual science; and good naturalists should, I think, be suspicious of such metaphysics. The physics we know and some of us love does not support any metaphysics.

What is physics?

Cartwright's work, grounded as it is in a close study of physics and its practice, is naturalist in spirit, even if she does not apply that term to herself. It begins with the detail of scientific practice and uses that to criticize a widely held metaphysical view. The completeness of physics can, though, be challenged in a more straightforward way.

I have used the word "physics" rather loosely throughout the last two chapters. Sometimes I have used it to mean the sort of thing done by physicists. Sometimes I have used it more generally, to include broadly physical events such as bodily movements. The causal argument for physicalism as I have presented it embodies this ambiguity. Premise 1, the completeness of physics, seems to refer to fundamental physics of the sort studied by science. Premise 2, the causal premise, seems to refer to the broadly physical. The sorts of physical events that we are inclined to say are caused by mental events are bodily movements. Perhaps this ambiguity is not too serious. Physicalists presumably think that the broadly physical itself supervenes on the fundamentally physical. The causal argument can then be rejigged to support this conclusion, along the following lines:

1. Fundamental physics is causally complete.
2. Broadly physical events cause fundamentally physical events.
3. Therefore, ruling out overdetermination, the broadly physical supervenes on the fundamentally physical.

We can then make use of this conclusion in our original argument and run it as before to get the physicalist's desired conclusion.

There is another important ambiguity, though, in our use of the term physics that threatens the causal argument. When we talk of fundamental physics, what exactly do we mean? If by "physics" we mean current physics, then even setting aside Cartwright's powerful criticisms, the doctrine is almost certainly false. Not even the most optimistic advocate of fundamentalism would claim that physics, as it stands now, is complete. After all, that is why it is still an interesting area of research and why we are willing to spend so much on shiny new supercolliders at CERN to investigate the existence or otherwise of the Higgs boson. We expect the laws and theories currently employed by physicists to be revised in as yet unknown ways. On the other hand, if what is meant by physics is simply the discipline that is complete or provides a complete account of everything, then the claim that physics is complete is vacuous. If it is neither of these things, then it seems to be a claim about a we-know-not kind of physics. If we cannot identify in a non-trivial way exactly what we mean by physics, then we cannot construct any argument to show that all non-physical states and properties depend upon the physical.

Some physicalists have made great efforts to avoid defining physics in such a way as to make claims about completeness false, trivial or indeterminate. We can divide their responses into three types. First, there are those like Andrew Melnyk (2003), who define physics with regard to current physics and offer some way to finesse the problem that such a view is almost certainly false. Second, there are those like David Papineau (1993; Spurrett & Papineau 1999), who offer a negative definition of physics: physics is defined as everything but the mental. And finally there are those, like Jeffrey Poland (1994), who define physics and the physicalism that goes with it as a kind of research programme.

Consider first Melnyk's idea. He defines physics in terms of those "theories that are the object of *consensus* among current physics". He seeks to avoid the worry that this claim is obviously false by suggesting that although, so defined, the probability of physicalism may be low, it is better supported by the evidence than any rival metaphysics.

Melnyk does not explain in his extensive work on the issue exactly what theory of evidence he has in play when he makes these claims, but in light of Cartwright's detailed account of how theories actually apply to the world, I think we have no good reason to think that physicalism is any more probable than the patchwork of laws. Cartwright has shown us that current physics lends no support to physicalism at all. Even setting aside the issues raised by Cartwright's work, Melnyk's account faces an obvious difficulty. The two fundamental theories that are the object of consensus among current physicists are general relativity and quantum field theory. These two theories are, however, inconsistent. They cannot both be completely and literally true. The probability of any inconsistent conjunction of theories being true is presumably zero.

A more promising strategy might be Papineau's proposal that we define physics as everything but the mental. A first obvious objection to this is that what is and is not mental is not any better defined that what is and is not physical. But let's set this aside for the moment as there seem to be other equally difficult issues to address. The first is that defining physical in this way seems to make the conclusion of the causal argument a contradiction, at least if the argument is meant to support some kind of identity claim. Papineau's causal argument would seem to run as follows:

1. The non-mental realm is causally complete.
2. Non-mental events cause mental events.
Therefore, barring overdetermination, non-mental events are mental events.

Montero & Papineau (2005) suggest that we can overcome this new problem by defining the physical as the not fundamentally mental. So the proper conclusion of the causal argument is that mental events are identical to something fundamentally non-mental.

Even if we accept this, I think this strategy for defining the physical undermines the naturalistic justification of physicalism. When we think of physics as something like fundamental physics, there is a clear motivation for saying that physics is complete. Physical laws seem to have no exceptions. Cartwright has shown us that reason is not as good as many philosophers think it is. However, when we move away from fundamental physics and define physics as everything bar the mental, there seems no good scientific or empirical reason to insist upon completeness. Many non-mental happenings seem best explained by appeal to mental states. To take one well-known example, already discussed, consider the placebo effect. It is known by scientists that patients will often feel better and actually are better when you give them a pill with no active ingredients. Somehow just thinking or believing that you will get better can actually have this effect. Whenever a new drug is being tested, measures need to be taken to make sure that any measured positive result the drug might have is not the result of the placebo effect. Blind and double-blind trials are a standard part of medical practice invented precisely to eliminate these effects. Given the existence of such phenomena and the more prosaic facts that we used to illustrate the plausibility of the second premise of the causal argument, such as the fact that I believe it is raining will cause me to take an umbrella with me when I go out, I see no good empirical reason to believe that the non-mental is complete.

Part of why Papineau and others (see especially Montero 1999, 2001) think we need a negative definition like this is that without it we shall not be able to make sense of traditional disputes in the philosophy of mind. In particular, we shall not be able to make sense of the thought-experiments of Nagel, Jackson and Chalmers with which we began this chapter. Each of these begins with the assumption that one can imagine situations in which everything is physically identical and yet there can be variation in non-physical states, or that we can know everything about the physical and still our knowledge would be incomplete in some way. If what we mean by physics is not well defined, these arguments and counterarguments have little point. We don't know what we are talking about when we say, for example, "Mary knows all the physical facts". Given my analysis of Chalmers's zombie argument, I think that's no bad thing. As I argued above, our knowledge of what is possible or conceivable or knowable is highly defeasible given the limited nature of our scientific knowledge. We should be suspicious of these arguments for that very reason. Noting the ambiguities in the term physical is another way to make that point.

In another and more important way, however, troubles with the term physics don't really affect the dispute between those who call themselves physicalists, such as Papineau, and those who don't, such as Chalmers. The difference can be stated quite clearly. Chalmers thinks that something new needs to be posited to account for conscious experience; Papineau doesn't. This would be a better way to put the dispute since it is a very local dispute about one small feature of the universe. The grand old labels materialism and dualism and the newer shinier one physicalism appear to designate very general metaphysical views. They purport to tell us how everything is. Those who are engaged in disputes in the philosophy of mind have a much narrower focus. They are interested only in the nature of consciousness. It would be better for everyone if this were made clear. Then we would see their views for what they are: theories or theory sketches of consciousness.

There is no need for something like the causal argument in order to make sense of this dispute; and that is just as well given that the argument seems to have little empirical justification once we replace physical with non-mental.

Frank Jackson offers a definition of the physical that combines elements of both Melnyk's and Papineau's suggestions. He says that "physical properties and relations . . . are those we need to handle the non-sentient, they are broadly akin to those that appear in current physical science [and] they are those we need to handle the very small" (Jackson 1998: 8). Familiar problems arise here again. If we take the first and third parts of the definition, it looks as if we can raise our original problem for Jackson's definition. If physics is simply whatever handles the very small and the non-sentient, then it has no definite content. If it is what we currently employ to explain the small and non-sentient, then it is likely to be false. Jackson's second condition seems to be of some help in navigating between the horns of this dilemma since it defines physics as like current physics, but not exactly like it. The trouble is that the phrase "broadly akin" is very vague. Interpreting this, we confront the same problem. If we interpret the phrase very liberally, then again physics is without clear content. Interpret it very restrictively, and it is likely to be false to say that such a discipline is complete. Our initial problem is not solved. We still have no clear content for the physics in physicalism.

Finally, let us consider Poland's (1994) view that we define physics and so physicalism as a kind of research programme aimed at answering certain highly general questions. Specifically, Poland thinks that anything worth calling physics will have to address the following questions:

- What are the fundamental constituents of all occupants of space-time?
- What are the fundamental processes that underlie all causation and all interaction between such occupants?
- What parameters are relevant to the unfolding of all space-time and hence to all change?
- What is the nature of space-time itself, its origin (if it has one), and its destiny?   (*Ibid.*: 125)

This still won't solve our problem. On the one hand, it still does not give us determinate content for the physics in physicalism because we have no clear idea of what a physics that answers these questions satisfactorily will look like. But equally, in so far as Poland does make clear commitments, it might rule out things we currently accept as genuinely physical. In particular, the third point is problematic. Arguably quantum mechanics teaches us that not all change takes place in space-time. Evolution of quantum states takes place in a Hilbert space. One way to think of the conceptual problems of quantum mechanics such as measurement is that it is difficult to see how to relate the Hilbert space of quantum evolution to the real space or space-time of macroscopic objects.

Poland's view, even if it does not satisfactorily tell us what the physical is, hints at a different way to think of physicalism and related metaphysical ideas. Rather than understanding them as general descriptions of how things are, perhaps we would do better to think of them as playing a methodological role. They are something like pictures or metaphors that guide (or might guide) scientific research. Metaphors are often literally false – Juliet is *not* the sun, for example. Similarly the claim that (current) physics is complete is literally false. Perhaps metaphysical views like physicalism or indeed the patchwork of laws are akin to the religious ideas that inspired Newton and Einstein or the numerological and astrological notions that inspired Kepler – useful in setting some scientific work going but not justified in any way by the results of mature science. Thinking of metaphysical theories as inspirational pictures or metaphors strikes me as an interesting project and perhaps the best way to understand how science and metaphysics relate to one another from a deflationary naturalist perspective. But it is not a suggestion I have any space to develop here.

Conclusion

I am one of a minority of naturalists who do not call themselves phys-icalists. My reasons have nothing to do with consciousness. Physics, and science in general, is a messy business. There is no general meta-physical picture that our best science supports. Add to that the fact that it is not clear what physicalists mean by physics in the first place, then the best attitude a naturalist can take may be one of metaphysical agnosticism. The best description of how things are that one can achieve is to list the many different things that our many empirically well-supported sciences say about the world. That is not a unified metaphysics but it may be the best that any naturalism can do. If that sounds like NOA, it should be no surprise by this stage in the text.

seven

Meaning and truth

Naturalists' problems with meaning and truth have plagued us throughout. In Chapter 2 we found reason to question Quine's naturalized epistemology because of problems with his account of language. In Chapter 3, we noted that even if we accepted reliabilism as an account of justification, without a naturalistic account of belief and truth it falls short of making knowledge a natural property or state. In Chapter 4, we found realists such as Boyd claiming that the *truth* of scientific theories *explained* their empirical success. Such an argument requires an account of truth that shows how it can play this explanatory role. And once we turned to metaphysical matters in Chapters 5 and 6, we have to confront the awkward fact that meaning and truth don't seem to be physical or natural properties. So what in the world is a "meaning", or the property of being true?

Essentially two approaches seem to be on offer for the naturalist. One begins with a substantive account of what it is to have a mental representation (e.g. a belief about the world). This theory of representation provides the basis on which a theory of truth can then be developed as some kind of relation between the naturalistically explained representation and the world. The other approach begins with what is often called a deflationary or minimalist account of truth and then attempts to provide a theory of meaning in which the idea of truth plays no substantial role.

In the following we look first at naturalist accounts of representation and then turn to the deflationary view of truth.

Natural representations

I can think of a chicken. I'm doing it right now. Thinking, let us say, is something that goes on in our heads. Right now, then, there is some state in my head, in my brain most probably, that has the property of representing a chicken. What makes that brain state (or whatever it is) a representation of a chicken? What makes it *about* chickens?

A good place to start for a naturalist is not with the complicated representations of people but with simpler kinds of "natural" representation. It is plausible to maintain that certain things naturally indicate or represent others. For example, smoke indicates fire; the rings on a tree indicate its age; certain kinds of spots indicate measles. No human agent is involved in these representations. What all these examples have in common is that there is a regular causal connection between the thing indicated and the indicator. Fire *causes* smoke; measles *causes* spots, etc. So a plausible basic theory of natural meaning is:

> Some state, X, means Y if and only if there is a reliable causal connection between X and Y.

Often writers in this area refer to the reliable causal connection for obvious reasons as reliable indication; and the general approach is usually referred to for equally obvious reasons as indicator-based semantics (IBS).

Clearly the definition we have given above will not be adequate to account for the complexity of all human representations. We can think of things that don't exist, such as fairies and goblins, and abstract objects, such as numbers and sets. Clearly there can be no causal connection between goblins and my representation of goblins, so some other story will need to be told here. But let's set that worry aside for now. We have the beginning of something promising. If we can construct a plausible theory for some basic human mental representations, we can worry about these more difficult cases later.

Problems of misrepresentation

One very obvious problem with our theory is that it appears to make it impossible for it to be the case that I could represent something as being X without in fact it being the case that X. This doesn't seem right.

I'm often wrong about how things are and I can have a representation when the thing I'm representing isn't present. Currently, I'm thinking of a chicken. But there is no chicken round here. If my mental state, X, representing chickens stands in the same relation to chickens as smoke does to fire, then I can't have a chicken representation without there being a chicken causing it. But I can. So our theory is clearly inadequate.

Our basic theory of natural indication also suffers from what is known as the disjunction problem. Suppose I'm a reliable indicator of chickens. When there are chickens around and I'm looking at them, that reliably causes a representation in my head. Let's again call that state X. So according to IBS theory the state X represents chickens.

Now let's further suppose that under certain conditions I'm unable to distinguish chickens from ducks. Let's suppose this is true when it's dark and there is only very poor ambient light. So there is also a reliable causal connection between my mental representation, X, and ducks-in-the-dark. Now, in such circumstances, we would clearly want to say that I *misrepresent* ducks as chickens. But the IBS theory doesn't allow us to say this. Since there is a reliable causal connection between ducks-in-the-dark and X, we are forced to say that X represents ducks-in-the-dark. In fact, given our story and the IBS theory, X represents chickens or ducks-in-the-dark. This gets the content wrong. X really should represent just chickens. The problem is that situations such as the one imagined show us that the content fixed by the IBS theory is less determinate than our intuitions say it should be. A good theory of content should remove the disjunction.

The problem is familiar to naturalists. Representation involves norms of some kind. We can represent correctly or incorrectly. Simple causal stories don't seem to be able to accommodate norms. If something causes something else, that's just a fact plain and simple, with no normative force.

Teleosemantics

There are a variety of answers available to the naturalist to deal with this problem but I want to concentrate on what seems to me the most promising – the teleosemantic approach. There are many different versions of this approach – the main players are Fred Dretske (1981), Ruth Millikan (1984, 1993) and David Papineau (1987, 1993), and they all offer slightly different twists on the basic idea. However, at the heart of all three approaches is the idea of a teleofunction, or what Millikan calls a proper function. She defines it as follows:

> [F]or an item A to have a function F as a "proper function" it is necessary (and close to sufficient) that one of these two conditions should hold. (1) A originated as a reproduction (to give one example as a copy or a copy of a copy) of some prior item or items that, *due* in part to possession of the properties reproduced, have actually performed F in the past, and A exists because (causally historically because) of this or these performances. (2) A originated as the product of some prior device that, given its circumstances, had performed F as a proper function and, that under those circumstances, normally causes F to be performed by means of producing an item like A. (Millikan 1993: 16)

That might sound terrifyingly abstract but the basic idea is simple enough. Consider the heart. Its proper function is to pump blood round the body. Why? Well, because creatures with hearts that pumped blood round the body survived and reproduced other creatures with such hearts. Creatures that did not have hearts or that had hearts that did not pump blood round the body failed to reproduce as successfully. Our ancestors were able to survive and reproduce (in part) because their hearts pumped blood around their bodies.

When we are considering the proper function of some item we are in effect asking: what was that item selected for in evolutionary history? Whatever feature of the object in question explains its continued existence through evolutionary pressures is its proper function.

Hearts do many other things than pump blood round the body. They make a kthump-thump noise, for example. That noise performs certain useful functions for us. It allows doctors to assess our health using stethoscopes, for example. But since this noise and any of the functions it performs were not selected for by evolution, it is not part of the proper function of the heart.

Note too that the proper function of an item can be something it rarely performs. The proper function of the sperm tail is to propel the sperm to an ovum, but most sperm do not get to do this. Still, the reason there are any sperm and sperm tails at all is that in our evolutionary past they were selected for that function.

Very importantly for naturalists, something can still have a proper function even if it is not actually performing that function. If some unfortunate person has a heart that does not pump, then, since it was selected for such pumping, that is still its proper function. This is what allows us to say that the heart is malfunctioning: malfunctioning here just means failing to do what it was selected for. So we have introduced a normative element into our story without appealing to anything more than evolutionary history. All we need to add to the story to get from hearts and sperm to minds and meaning is that certain brain states were selected for the function of representing the world or tracking the environment. This will solve our problems about misrepresentation. If I have some brain mechanism that, let us say, has been selected for the purpose of producing chicken representations in the presence of chickens and that mechanism is activated by ducks-in-the-dark, then that state is malfunctioning or misrepresenting. So we have a fully naturalistic account of misrepresentation.

It is important to see here that strictly speaking the evolutionary part of the story is merely an explanation of misrepresenting. Any teleosemantic account is parasitic upon an account of correct representation. Exactly how to characterize correct representation is where the various versions of teleosemantics diverge. Dretske's account of correct representation is just the basic indicator-based semantics account I have described above. Representation is first explained as the systematic presence of some representation caused by an environmental stimulus: chickens causing a representation of chickens. We then say that the mechanism producing the chicken representation has evolved for the purpose of indicating chickens. If it produces a chicken representation when there are no chickens, it is malfunctioning and so misrepresenting.

Millikan's account is a bit different. Instead of focusing on how states of the environment produce representations, the input to the system, she focuses on how the representation is used, the output and its benefit. So, to take one of her favourite examples, bees perform complex figure-of-eight dances to alert others in their hive to the location of nectar. When the bee dance is interpreted by other bees in such a way as to guide them to nectar, it has successfully performed its function. It has represented correctly. It is the correspondence between the bee movements and areas of the world where there is nectar (what Millikan calls a mapping), as interpreted or used by other bees, that constitutes correct functioning and so correct representation. Misrepresentation occurs when the system malfunctions in some way. For example, if bee 1 dances in such a way as to indicate nectar 100 metres south-west of the hive and bee 2 arrives there to find no nectar (perhaps because in the intervening time someone has picked all the flowers), then the dance misrepresents.

Learning, novel content and relational proper functions

It is of course very unlikely that human beings have brain states specifically selected by evolutionary pressures for the purpose of representing chickens; and absolutely impossible to imagine that they have brain states selected for the purpose of representing things like MP3 players or car batteries. So we need to expand on the basic story a little. One teleosemantic answer to the question of how we can represent things like MP3 players is to appeal to learning. This might seem like a cheat. It seems that we're introducing something entirely new, with nothing to do with natural selection. But if you consider Millikan's definition of proper function above, it is very abstract. Nowhere does it make explicit mention of biological evolution. So being selected does not have to mean being selected by natural selection. Learning can also be construed as a form of selection process. For example, we might think of learning as something like this: we try out various ways of responding to a stimulus in our environment. Some of these prove more successful than others. We have some kind of general ability to recognize those more successful attempts and so select (and reproduce) those behaviours in the future. For example, a crude story about how we learn the meaning of some particular concepts might go as follows: we start in response to parental pointing and cajoling to pick up objects and emit various sounds. We might pick up a carrot and say "carrot". When we do this we gain some sort of reward or approval from our teachers. Then we might try the same trick again with another object. We pick up an apple and again say "carrot". (I am imagining a learning environment very rich in fruits and vegetables.) This does meet with the same approval. So we learn to limit our utterances of "carrot" to long orange things. When we do this we meet with more success, and are rewarded by our parents. Our simple story has all the elements needed for proper functioning. First, we have variation. We as creatures are able to vary our responses to our environment. Secondly, we have selection. In learning we recognize that some responses are better than others. And finally, we have reproduction. We are capable of reproducing our successful behaviours. I'm not suggesting that my story is an accurate account of how children learn words. But the sketch does show us how the notion of proper function can be extended to learning and so suggests how teleosemanticists might explain within their basic framework how it is that human beings represent things such as chickens, ducks and MP3 players. The mental states that represent these things have been selected through learning to have that function.

Another thing human beings can do is have entirely novel thoughts. To take a very dramatic example, no one thought of space and time in quite the way that Einstein did before he developed his theory of relativity. And you don't have to be Einstein to have novel thoughts. All of us can entertain thoughts that no one and certainly none of our ancestors has had before. Consider the sentence: "Einstein often ate cream crackers, out of a plastic tub during the summer before sundown." I'm pretty sure that no one has ever written or thought such a sentence before now. But you understand it and I understand it. Indeed, many of the sentences in this book will never have been written before in English. That's not because I'm a creative genius. I'm not. Not even close. It's because it is part and parcel of every human being's ability to speak and think in a language that they can produce novel sentences.

This looks like a problem for teleosemantics. If no one in the past has used these representations, then they can have no selection history – even if we include learning as a kind of selection.

One teleosemantic answer to this problem lies in the second half of Millikan's definition of proper function, what she calls elsewhere *derived proper functions*. Another biological example will help us to understand the idea. Consider a chameleon. What we all know about chameleons is, of course, that they can change their skin colour to match their environment. The skin-colour-changing mechanism of the chameleon has as its proper function to match the skin colour of the creature to its environment. Millikan calls proper functions of this sort relational proper functions, since the function of the device is to relate one thing to another. Now imagine that a chameleon finds itself stranded on a rock. The rock is a peculiar hue of brown. No chameleon has ever sat on a rock this colour before and so no chameleon has ever changed its skin pigmentation to match such a rock. If the chameleon is able to change its colour to match the background, it will have done something that none of its ancestors has done. We can still say, though, that this new colour has a proper function. Its proper function is *derived* from the more general relational proper function of the colour-changing mechanism. The relational proper function of the colour-changing mechanism is to match the environment. The proper function of the actual colour the chameleon turns is derived from this function. Its function is to match this particular shade of rock. So even though it is a colour that no chameleon has ever turned before, since the colour is part of the normal functioning of the relational proper function, we can still say that it has a proper function. Thus teleo-semantics can accommodate novelty, if what is new is part of some relational proper function. Its functionality is *derived* from the more abstract relational function. We can adapt this story to explain our grasp of language and novel sentences. Consider our novel sentence about Einstein. What allows us to formulate novel sentences and thus have novel thoughts is that language is compositional. There are rules about how to put sentences together to form meaningful expressions; and given a finite number of concepts we can employ those rules of combination to construct an unlimited number of sentences. We can think, then, of the combinatorial rules of language as a relational proper function. They have evolved for the purpose in part, let us suppose, to allow us to represent and reason about our environment. When combined with concepts that we might have acquired through learning, these rules allow us to formulate novel thoughts such as the one I offered above about Einstein. Thus novel beliefs and represen-tations can still have proper functions. They, like the chameleon's novel shade of brown, are derived proper functions – derived from some more general function like that of a compositional language to rep-resent and reason about our environment.

It is not clear to me that all aspects of novel thought can be dealt with in this way. Einstein's original thoughts about the nature of space and time are not explained simply by appealing to the compositional nature of language. When we are told that talk of space and time should give way to talk of space-time, we are being asked to entertain a new concept – one that we certainly can't explain by appeal to learning since no one thought of space and time like this before to teach Einstein the concept. And it doesn't seem likely that we can explain the content of Einstein's thought by appeal to Millikan's notion of a derived proper function. It is not obvious (to me at least) what more general relational proper function we would be appealing to explain the content of this representation. We might say that the more general mechanism is one whose function is to fix true beliefs. But that by itself wouldn't fix for us the peculiar content of Einstein's claim. I think there is still a problem here for teleosemantics in explaining how it is that human beings can formulate new, untutored concepts.

Teleosemantics, then, has a reasonable sounding story to tell us about both how error is possible and how at least some kinds of novel content can be accommodated with an evolutionary and historical theory of meaning. There are, though, some problems.

Swampman: a comic interlude

One objection raised against the teleosemantic theory is that, if the theory is correct, then only a creature with an evolutionary history can have mental representations. Many people think that cannot be right. Imagine I have gone for stroll, as is my wont, down by the local swamp. I get struck by a bolt of lightning and die instantly. At the same time, out of the swamp gas, a creature who is molecule by molecule identical to me just before my death spontaneously coalesces. Let's call him Swampman. He goes back to my house and begins talking at great length about Inverness Caledonian Thistle's back four and the problems of accommodating normative notions in a naturalistic framework. To all eyes he seems indistinguishable from me.

But he is distinguishable from me in an important respect. He has no pedigree, no evolutionary history. Should this make a difference? Teleosemantics says it should. Many people's intuitions say it should not. So there must be something wrong with teleosemantics.

From a naturalist perspective, the teleosemanticist has a perfectly good response to this thought-experiment. Teleosemantics is put forward as an empirical theory of mental content and it is not to be dismissed *a priori* by some imaginary example. Science often subverts what we think is intuitively obvious. Once people thought it was obvious that the world did not move or that glass is a solid. Now, through science, we know better. Teleosemanticists can claim then it might be the same with Swampman. Although he seems like a thinker, informed scientific reflection will show us that our intuitions are wrong.

Others go further, dismissing the idea of Swampman out of hand as impossible. Here's Daniel Dennett positively bristling with impatience:

> Does Swampman have thoughts and use language, or not? Is a cow-shark a shark? It swims like a shark and mates successfully with other sharks. Oh but didn't I tell you? It is atom for atom indistinguishable from a shark except that it has cow-DNA in all its cells. Impossible? Not *logically* impossible (say the philosophers). Just so obviously impossible as to render further discussion unnecessary.   (Dennett 1996: 76)

Dennett's complaint, if I understand him correctly, is that Swampman is *physically* or as we might say, given some of the worries raised in Chapter 6, *naturally* impossible. In other words, Swampman is not possible given the kind of world described by our best science.

I don't think that's right. There is at least one way to tell the Swampman story in which it would be compatible with what we know about physics. The tale involves time travel, so let me defend this idea first.

If we take general relativity seriously (as you should if you are a naturalist), then there is no reason to suppose that time travel is impossible. Indeed, there are certain space-time structures, Gödel space-time structures (Gödel 1949), in which time travel would be no more problematic than space travel: venturing out along certain routes could take an individual back to where they were (temporally speaking) earlier. We call such parts of space-time "closed time curves". Let us imagine that we are in such a world. Within this world there exists a twin boy and girl. They have been separated at birth. One day each independently decides to go back in time – until approximately a year before they were born. There they meet up, fall in love and soon have twins of their own. But their children are actually just their young selves; they are each their father and mother. This is possible, since each of them contains the right sort of genetic information to be the parent of the other and, of course, we trivially have the right sort of genetic material to be our own parents. The story is a beguiling mix of science fiction and Greek tragedy, no doubt, but also philosophically important. The result is two human beings with no ancestry (or at least no evolutionary history) whatsoever. So on the teleosemantic view neither of these individuals can be described as a creature with representational states: they are both Swampbabies. But that seems intuitively wrong.

Thus a naturalist can accept the possibility of Swampmen. The chances of actually meeting one depend on how likely it is that we live in a universe in which time travel is possible. Perhaps it is not very likely, but not very likely is quite different from (naturally) impossible.

That leaves us, then, with the teleosemanticist response that our intuitions shouldn't be allowed to override good science. The quality of that response depends on how good the science of teleosemantics is. Below we shall consider some further problems for teleosemanticists which call into question the quality of their explanation of mental representation.

The indeterminacy of content

Teleosemantics encounters a problem that is very similar in structure to the disjunction problem discussed above. Consider the humble frog. Frogs have a mechanism that responds to the presence of flies in their environment. When there is a fly in the vicinity, the frog's tongue strikes out to catch it. It seems natural to understand what's going on here in the following way. The frog represents a fly in its environment and that representation in turn causes the frog's tongue to flash out. It seems equally natural to say, then, on the teleosemanticist account, that the frog has an internal brain state that represents flies. It has evolved for the function of capturing flies and so flies are what it represents.

We don't have to say that, though. We could say instead that the frog's brain represents not flies but small black dots. We can equally well tell an evolutionary story that explains the existence of the black-dot representation in frogs. It is because the frog's brain can represent black dots in its environment that it has been able to catch flies, survive and reproduce. There seems nothing we can appeal to in evolutionary theory to help us decide which one of these interpretations is the correct one. Both stories seem to account for the emergence of the mechanism in the frog's brain equally well. But obviously the content of "fly" and "black dot" is different. Not everything that is a black dot is a fly. Imagine a frog in captivity, fed black food pellets attached to a wire moved in front of the frog. As the food pellets move across his visual field he responds as he would to a fly. His tongue flashes out to grab the pellet. On the first story we told about what the frog represents, we should say that it misrepresents the pellet as a fly. On the second story, the fog correctly represents the pellet as a black dot. So what we say the frog represents and indeed misrepresents depends upon which evolutionary story we favour. But as we've just said, there seems to be nothing in the theory of evolution itself to allow us to pick out one story as the correct one, and so nothing to allow us to determinately fix the content of the frog's representation.

Two solutions: Dretske and Millikan

Dretske and Millikan, as we noted earlier, offer slightly different accounts of what constitutes a correct representation. Correspondingly they have different solutions to what we should say the frog represents. Dretske (1990) focuses on the stimulus that causes the representation.

If we have some state that can be plausibly said to indicate more than one thing, such as the brain state of the frog, then we apply the following rule: if the state indicates both X and Y, but indicates Y in virtue of indicating X, then we should say that its proper function is to indicate X. So consider our frog again. The frog indicates flies only in virtue of the fact that all flies are black dots. Our captured frog fed black food pellets demonstrates that. So we should say that what the frog represents is black dots. However, it is not clear that this removes all the indeterminacy or will provide the intuitively correct content of the frog's representation. For example, the frog's representation also reliably indicates a certain pattern of stimulation on the frog's retina. Whenever the frog sees a fly, it's retina is stimulated in a typically flyish manner. So it looks as if what the frog represents might be that his retina is stimulated in a certain way. In fact, given Dretske's preferred account for resolving indeterminacy, it appears as though we should say exactly that. The frog's representation only indicates black dots in virtue of indicating a certain pattern of stimulation on the frog's retina. That seems very counterintuitive. Worse it looks as if we could pick any point in the causal chain between the fly and the frog's representation and say that it is what the frog represents since there is a reliable causal connection between every element in the chain and the frog's representation. The threat of indeterminate content will be difficult to get rid of on any stimulus-based account such as Dretske's.

Millikan's account concentrates in contrast on the output or the benefit for the system. She distinguishes between what she calls consumers and producers of representations. A mechanism in the frog's brain first produces the representation; this is the initial stimulus but it is made use of or consumed by another part of the frog's brain, which causes the frog's tongue to lash out. It is this consuming or interpreting mechanism that fixes the content. The proper function of the consuming mechanism in the frog is to enable the frog to capture food. That is its benefit, and so what it has evolved to do. Thus what the frog represents is food. The point of having the representation is precisely that it guides the frog to capture food.

Like Dretske's account, Millikan's way of fixing the content has some counterintuitive consequences. For example imagine a primitive creature called a kimu (Pietroski 1992). Kimu are food for another organism, the snorf. It just so happens that snorfs hunt kimu only around dawn. One kimu is born with a genetic mutation that causes it to be attracted to red things. So every dawn, as the sun rises, this kimu moves east. Doing this takes it up a mountain and away from its snorf predators. Pretty quickly this mutation spreads through the kimu population. According to Millikan's account, since the benefit of having the representation that moves it east is that it avoids snorfs, that must be what it represents. The content of the kimu's representation, according to Millikan's theory, then, is snorf-free. But that seems highly implausible given that we may suppose the kimu has no way of recognizing the presence or absence of snorfs. If a snorf painted itself red, the kimu would come running (if they do run). So, the thought goes, by focusing solely on the benefit, Millikan's theory gets the content wrong. It would be much more plausible to say what the kimu represents is red or something similar in this situation.

Also, like Dretske's account, Millikan's benefit-based account does not remove all forms of indeterminacy. There are different, more or less determinate ways to classify the benefit. Does the frog benefit because the fly is food, or because the fly is a very specific form of food; for example it provides the frog with certain kinds of proteins? There seems nothing in the evolutionary history of the frog that can tell us, so no good reason on Millikan's account to claim that the frog represents food rather than, say, some specific protein.

Perhaps some indeterminacy of content is not such a worrying thing with frogs. For simple organisms we should not expect the content of their representations to be totally determinate. Maybe the best way to characterize what a frog represents is black dot or fly or food. Nevertheless, if accounts such as Dretske's and Millikan's are to move from what frogs represent to what people like you and me represent, then they must have something additional to say about human representations. Clearly for us there is a difference between representing flies and representing black dots. The content of human representations is determinate in a way that frog representations may not be. The determinacy of content remains a difficulty for all versions of teleosemantics.

Knowledge of content

There are other features of human thinking that an adequate account of representation should explain. It may be that frogs can represent flies or something similar, but no one thinks that the frog is aware of the fact that it is representing flies. Clearly human beings are aware of at least some of what they are representing. In general we know what we are thinking and saying. Communication, it seems, depends on this fact. What I'm trying to do (sometimes at least) when I talk to others is to inform them of my beliefs about the world. If I say to one of my students, "the notes are on the internet", what I'm conveying to my student is a belief about where my philosophy notes are to be found. If I weren't aware of my beliefs about where the notes are, I wouldn't be able to tell the student where (I believe) they should be able to find them. Of course, it is not *always* true that we know what we are thinking or saying. You don't have to be a follower of Freud to think that there is something to the idea of subconscious beliefs and desires. There are other kinds of example too. Once I was asked to lecture on a course on medieval philosophy and found myself mumbling things like, "according to Scouts there is a formal but not a real distinction between the universal and particular" but I didn't, if I'm honest, know what I was talking about. Such things, though, are unusual (perhaps not unusual enough in philosophy lectures). Generally we know the content of what we say (or at least intend to say) and believe.

This sort of thought is related to Brandom's criticism of reliabilism, which we discussed in Chapter 3. Recall that Brandom argued that an essential part of being a believer of any sort is that one can offer reasons for holding one's beliefs. According to Brandom, our ability to offer reasons for beliefs is what distinguishes thinkers such as you and me from merely reliably indicating entities such as thermometers or even rusting iron. We don't have to agree with Brandom that being in a position to offer reasons is constitutive of thinking. Teleosemanticists such as Dretske and Millikan have provided us with a nice story about representation, so that we can say that frogs and other animals that don't engage in explicit reasoning can be thinkers. That story also allows us to say what distinguishes real representers like frogs from mere indicators like rusting iron. Frogs have an evolutionary history and certain states selected for the purpose of representing; rusting iron does not. Still, we can see that when we move to the realm of human representations, offering justifications for our beliefs is part of what we do; and to be able to do that we of course need to have explicit knowledge about what we think. The reason why this seems difficult to accommodate on the teleosemantic story is that what fixes the content of representations belongs to the long-distant evolutionary history or a period of our very early learning. It is therefore, presumably, something that none (or at least very few) of us knows anything about.

Dretske and Millikan's accounts of mental content have counterintuitive consequences. When we move from the very basic representations of frogs and other animals to the sophisticated representations of human beings, teleosemanticists encounter three unresolved problems. First, human beings are capable of inventing new concepts, as Einstein's account of space-time shows. It is unclear how this can be accommodated by a historical theory of content. Secondly, human representations seem to have a richer, more determinate content than animal representations, and it is not clear how to explain this fact on a teleosemantic account. Thirdly, human beings know what they think. Given the way the content of mental states is fixed according to the teleosemanticist, it is difficult to see how they could, if that theory is right. Whether these problems show that teleosemantics faces insurmountable difficulties or, like any scientific theory, has some interesting problems still to solve, I leave to the reader to decide.

Constructive versus deflationary theories of truth

Teleosemantics takes the representative aspects of beliefs and desires, their content, to be a real property in the world. The aim for the semantic naturalist is to explain representation in terms of natural properties. If teleosemanticists can succeed in their aim, the next step will be to provide a naturalistic theory of truth. There might be several ways this could be done. Our basic IBS account of meaning explains correct representation in terms of a causal relation between what is represented and the representation. It would be natural, then, to explain truth as correspondence to the facts and explain the notion of correspondence by appeal to the causal relations that characterize correct representation. Millikan's account appeals to an abstract mapping relation between the representation and the world, which is in turn cashed out in terms of a successful behavioural response. If this can be fleshed out, then that would provide another non-causal model for a correspondence theory of truth. Another way to go might be to explain truth in a pragmatist fashion. Truth is what is useful to believe. This might dovetail nicely with certain benefit-based accounts of teleosemantics. We explain the content of the representation in terms of its benefits and thereby also explain why it is true. Papineau (1987) suggests something like this. All these strategies assume that, like the representation relation itself, truth has an underlying nature, which must be explained by appeal to natural properties such as causation.

Some naturalists think that there is something fundamentally wrong with these projects. Naturalists are not forced to look for natural properties that correspond to supposedly problematic properties like good or justified or true; there are other possible approaches we can take. It may be that the best way to understand a concept like "water", for example, is to look for some underlying natural property that all things called "water" have in common. But this is certainly not the attitude we take to all our concepts. We talk about things that we believe have no underlying nature because they don't exist. We don't need to give a naturalistic explanation of goblins because there are no goblins. Similarly and perhaps more interestingly, we don't think certain logical concepts have an underlying nature that we need to discover. Take, for example, the predicate "exists". When we describe something as blue, cold and round, we tend to think that this description ascribes certain properties to the entity: those of being blue, cold and round. It seems reasonable to investigate what those properties are. A naturalist might try to explain the underlying nature of the property of being blue, for example, just as teleosemanticists try to explain the underlying nature of representation. However, if we now say that there is a blue, cold round and existing thing, existence adds nothing new to our description. We don't think of existence as ascribing an additional property. We use the word "exists", at least in part, because it performs a certain function for us. For example, it allows me to say: "there exists a student in my class who will get the highest grade" without me necessarily knowing who that student is. Existence is not a substantial property in the world awaiting scientific discovery. A proper understanding of the concept of existence involves in part recognizing that "exists" functions in the way I have explained. Some naturalists think the same can be said for the concept "true". It, like existence, does not have an underlying nature to be discovered.

One early idea along these lines was the redundancy theory of truth, first suggested by Frank Ramsey (1927). Ramsey pointed out that the use of the truth predicate is often simply redundant in a sentence. For example, suppose I utter the sentence " 'Snow is white' is true". That sentence asserts no more or less than if I'd just said "snow is white". Ramsey's suggestion, then, was that we could simply eliminate the truth predicate given that there appears to be an equivalent sentence that does not use the word "true". However, there are some sentences where this kind of elimination doesn't work. Imagine I say, "Everything the Pope says is true". I can't eliminate the use of the predicate "is true" as I did before. If I do that, I end up with a partial sentence, "Everything the Pope says", which is nonsense; and clearly does not assert the same thing as the sentence "Everything the Pope says is true". The use of the truth-predicate seems indispensable in such sentences.

Nevertheless, Ramsey's theory gives a good indication of what it might mean for the truth not to be a substantial property. Truth on this theory is superfluous. It can be eliminated and so needs no explanation in terms of some underlying natural property. A lot of contemporary philosophers think that Ramsey was on the right lines. Their goal is to provide a theory of truth as a non-substantial property that can deal with the problematic cases that undermine Ramsey's redundancy theory.

The minimalist conception of truth

The most common contemporary account of truth that seeks, as Ramsey did, to characterize truth as a non-substantial property is minimalism or disquotationalism (Quine 1970; Leeds 1978; Horwich 1999; Field 1994, among others; I shall refer to the position as minimalism from now on). Minimalists agree with Ramsey that there are many sentences where the phrase "is true" appears redundant. One way to express this is that sentences like "snow is white" are materially equivalent to sentences like " 'snow is white' is true". Minimalists suggest that truth or our concept of truth is exhausted by the complete list of sentences that express these equivalences – sentences of the form: " 'Snow is white' is true if and only if snow is white", " 'grass is green' is true if and only if grass is green", " 'lying is wrong' is true if and only if lying is wrong", etc. Philosophers sometimes refer to these sentences as T-sentences; and their general form " 'p' is true if and only if p" as the T-schema. Everyone who can competently use the word "true" should accept instances of the T-schema as obvious. Anyone who grasps the concept "true" has a disposition to accept instances of the T-schema. Very importantly, minimalists also claim that there is nothing more to the concept of truth to explain what all these T-sentences have in common. Truth has no underlying nature.

The point of having the truth predicate according to the minimalists is "solely for the sake of a certain logical need. On occasion we wish to adopt some attitude towards a [sentence] but find ourselves thwarted by ignorance of what exactly the [sentence] is" (Horwich 1999: 2). Consider again the sentence, "Everything the Pope says is true". If we reflect on what I mean by asserting this sentence, then my intention is clearly to endorse whatever it is the Pope says, including sentences of which I have no explicit knowledge. Another way to express that claim would be as follows: "If the Pope said 'grass is green', then grass is green and if he said 'snow is white', then snow is white and if he said 'Inverness Caledonian Thistle are underrated', then Inverness Caledonian Thistle are underrated", etc. But this is very cumbersome. It would be better if we could find a finite sentence that summarized all of the above. This is what the truth predicate allows us to do. Any sentence that the Pope utters we know, from the minimalist definition of truth, is equivalent to another sentence involving the truth predicate. Let's say the Pope just says "grass is green" and "snow is white". These two sentences are equivalent to " 'snow is white' is true" and " 'grass is green' is true". The T-schema allows us to transform two quite different sentences into two sentences with a property in common, namely that of being true. We can then generalize over this property, and end up with the neat sentence "everything the Pope says is true".

Here's another example. Suppose you want to assert the law of excluded middle. One way of doing that might be to assert the conjunction of all its instances: "Everything is green or not green, and everything is old or not old, and everything is pretty or not pretty", etc. Again, this is very cumbersome. The T-schema tells us that every instance of the law is equivalent to another sentence involving the truth predicate. For example, "everything is green or not green" is equivalent to " 'everything is green or not green' is true". If we replace every instance of the law with its equivalent, we can then generalize over our new class of sentences. All these sentences have the common property of being true. So we can formulate the law neatly as: all sentences of the form p or not-p are true.

The point of having the predicate "is true", then, is that it allows you to make certain kinds of generalizations or allows you to talk about sentences that you do not, or perhaps cannot, explicitly entertain; and that's all there is to the idea of truth.

Propositions or sentences

In explaining the minimalist conception of truth, I have talked throughout about sentences; I have assumed that the bearers of the property true are sentences. However, it's difficult to maintain that the truth-bearers are sentences if you're a minimalist. The problem is that the sentence " 'snow is white' is true if and only if snow is white" is only guaranteed to be obviously true if the sentence quoted on the left-hand side of the biconditional *means* the same as the sentence on the right-hand side. For example, the sentence "snow is white" in some foreign tongue might mean grass is blue, and so if we asserted " 'snow is white' is true if and only if snow is white" of that language we would be saying something false. If we want to use sentences as truth bearers, then we have to flesh out the T-schema. We have to say: " 'snow is white' is true-in-English if and only if snow is white". Unfortunately by doing so we won't get a general definition of the truth predicate but instead a definition of a different but related predicate, true-in-English, true-in-Swahili, true-in-Russian or whatever it might be. That seems less than we hoped for, even from a minimal account of truth.

One way to overcome this problem is to think of the bearers of truth not as sentences but as propositions. A proposition is normally understood as what is expressed by a sentence. So the sentence "snow is white" in English expresses the same proposition as "la neige est blanche" in French. Propositions, unlike sentences, are language independent. If we define our T-schema by reference to propositions, then the truth predicate also becomes language independent.

Thus our revised minimalist definition is that the concept of truth is exhausted by a complete list of propositions of the form: "the proposition that snow is white is true if and only if snow is white" or more generally, "the proposition that P is true if and only if P". This is Paul Horwich's view.

An immediate problem for this position and one that would particularly concern a naturalist is to say exactly what a proposition is. Propositions seem to be strange abstract entities. So if Horwich's account of truth is going to be adequate by naturalists' standards we shall need to be reassured that he can provide an adequate account of the nature of propositions. We leave this until later. First it is worth considering how much the minimalist theory can explain.

Minimalist explanations of the importance of truth

The minimalist theory makes truth sound unimportant. Truth or the truth predicate is merely something that allows us to make certain kinds of generalization. But truth clearly is very important. Isn't truth what we aim for in our scientific enquiries? Don't we need true beliefs in order to facilitate successful actions? Isn't the concept of truth central to all deductive reasoning: truth is preserved in valid inferences? Isn't the concept of truth essential to a proper understanding of knowledge? It seems reasonable to think, then, that any genuinely adequate account of truth will need to shed light on these matters, and it seems natural to think that a theory in which truth plays such a minimal role will not be able to account for the importance of truth in these domains.

Horwich has shown in his work that the minimalist theory can go a long way to explaining many of these claims made about truth. Let us briefly consider the first two.

Scientific realists, as we saw in Chapter 4, claim that science aims to give us a *true* theory of the world. We tend to think that in searching for truth, scientists are looking for something deeply significant. But if all there is to truth is provided by the minimalist conception, they are mistaken. Truth is not an interesting property but a fairly trivial one. Nevertheless, the minimalist conception of truth does provide a way to make sense of the realist's claim.

We would expect realists to endorse the following long, complex sentence about the aims of science.

> If electrons are negatively charged, then scientists aim to form-ulate the proposition that electrons are negatively charged, and if the Higgs boson exists, then scientists aim to formulate the proposition that the Higgs boson exists, and if whales are mammals, then scientists aim to formulate the proposition that whales are mammals, ...

And so on for every possible proposition of science. We can see this sentence is very similar in form to the other cases minimalism handled above. Applying the T-schema, we can derive the following generalization:

> If the proposition that p is true, then scientists aim to formu-late the proposition that p.

This is just a somewhat cumbersome way of saying that scientists aim for the truth. Thus minimalism can provide an adequate explanation of what is meant by saying that scientists aim for the truth without invoking any more than the minimalist conception allows.

Consider now the second kind of case. It seems reasonable to say, for example, that if Dave wants a glass of wine and he believes that by coughing and pointing to his glass, he will get one, and his belief is true, then he will get a glass of wine. This is a particular instance of the claim that true belief facilitates successful actions. The minimalist can explain this reasoning as follows:

1. Dave desires that he have some wine.
2. Dave believes that if he points and coughs, then he'll get some wine.

From this we can deduce (if Dave is rational) that

3. Dave will point and cough.
4. Dave's belief is true.
5. (The proposition if Dave points and coughs then he'll get some wine is true) if and only if (if Dave points and coughs, then he'll get some wine). That's an instance of the T-schema.
6. Therefore, if Dave points and coughs, he will get some wine (from 4 and 5).
7. Therefore, Dave gets some wine (from 3 and 6).

Again the minimalist's theory can explain why we are inclined to say that true beliefs facilitate successful actions. Similar stories can be told for the other features of truth mentioned above.

The liar paradox

Minimalism encounters a difficulty (common to all theories of truth) with the so-called liar paradox. Recall that, according to the minimalist, all there is to the concept of truth is the complete list of propositions of the form: "the proposition that p is true if and only if p". But consider this proposition:

(A) This proposition is false.

If we plug that into the T-schema, we get the following:

(B) The proposition that (this proposition is false) is true if and only if this proposition is false.

Far from being a platitude, as instances of the T-schema are supposed to be, (B) is necessarily false. If the left-hand side is true, then the right-hand side is false and vice versa.

Horwich avoids this problem by simply exempting these kinds of sentence from his truth definition. Only the platitudinous T-sentences will be part of the minimalist definition. This seems a little *ad hoc* to me. It would be nice to have a principled reason to exempt sentences such as (B) from our definition. You might be inclined to think that until the minimalist has something more constructive to say here, his definition of truth cannot be wholly adequate.

What are propositions? Conceptual role semantics

Setting aside worries about the liar paradox, minimalism about truth is, as we have seen, a very attractive theory for a naturalist. It explains the role and function of truth so as to remove any need for the naturalist to find some natural property that corresponds to truth. However, as noted, if the minimalist definition is to be genuinely general, the bearers of truth must be propositions. The minimalist then owes us a theory of meaning that can explain the content of propositions. If no adequate account can be given here, then minimalism will not be a viable theory of truth for the naturalist.

Certain kinds of theories of meaning are unavailable to the minimalist. Many philosophers of language from Frege onwards have claimed that the meaning of a proposition is its truth conditions. If you accept such a theory, you cannot be a minimalist. If truth plays an essential role in explaining meaning, there must be more to truth than is given by the minimalist definition. Therefore a minimalist must provide a theory of meaning that does not make explicit use of truth or truth conditions.

Horwich's own account of what a proposition is involves what he calls a use theory of meaning and what many others call conceptual role semantics (CRS). Like teleosemantics, there as many different versions of CRS as philosophers who advocate the view (see Block 1978; Brandom 2000; Horwich 1998; Peacocke 1992), and not all such philosophers think of themselves as providing a naturalistic theory of meaning. For the sake of brevity I shall outline the simplest version of the theory and explain some of its problems.

What is the meaning of the word "and"; and what is involved in knowing the meaning of "and"? Plausibly anyone who knows what "and" means must know that from P and Q, one can infer P and one can infer Q, for any propositions P and Q. The meaning of "and" is given by the role it plays in inference (how it is used) and knowing the meaning is just knowing the role it plays in inference (again, how it is used). This very plausible story for the meaning of "and" is generalized to all concepts in CRS.

Consider the proposition that beer is refreshing. According to CRS, the meaning of the proposition that beer is refreshing is given by the role that such propositions play in our inferences and how ultimately they guide our actions. For example, if I believe the proposition that beer is refreshing and the proposition that there is beer in front of me, then I'm inclined to infer that there is something refreshing in front of me. Moreover, if I desire to be refreshed, then I will reach out and drink the beer. This partly specifies the conceptual role of the proposition and so partly specifies its meaning. All (the relevant) inferences involving the proposition will fix its meaning. The meaning of concepts such as "beer" or "refreshing" is fixed in turn by the contribution they make to the meaning of every proposition in which they appear.

The general idea might sound very similar to functionalism, discussed in Chapter 5. That's not surprising. If you adopt a functionalist account of mind, then in effect you are advocating a version of CRS for the contents of beliefs, desires and other mental states. However, the entailment doesn't go the other way. You can be an advocate of CRS without endorsing a physicalist version of functionalism. The link with functionalism, though, should make it clear why CRS is attractive to many naturalists. Talk of *conceptual* role might not seem any more naturalistically respectable than talk of meaning. After all, what in the world are concepts? The functionalist approach shows at least one way in which it might be respectable. The functionalist advocate of CRS will hope that ultimately "conceptual role" can be reduced to causal role. The Ramsey sentence version of functionalism offers one way that might be done.

The major problem faced by all accounts of CRS is in determining which kinds of inferences fix the meaning of propositions. The simplest answer would be to allow every inference you make with a proposition a role in determining its meaning. But that would have some very bizarre consequences. It would make it impossible for two people ever to contradict one another or for someone to change their mind. For example, suppose that until last week I accepted the proposition that beer is refreshing. However, on Wednesday morning, after one too many drinks in the college bar, dehydrated and sick feeling, I vow never to drink beer again. I now reject the claim that beer is refreshing. Obviously we would say that I had changed my mind about how refreshing beer is. The view I hold after Wednesday contradicts the view I held before Wednesday. Unfortunately CRS does not allow us to say this. Before Wednesday, I was inclined to infer from the belief that: that is beer to the belief that: that is refreshing. Such inferences partly constituted what I meant by "refreshing" and "beer", according to this simple version of CRS. However, now I no longer make such inferences. What I mean by "refreshing" and "beer" must have changed. Thus the content of the claim that "beer is refreshing" is different before Wednesday when I accept it and after Wednesday when I reject it. So my two beliefs don't really contradict one another and so I haven't really changed my mind.

The obvious solution is to restrict the inferences that constitute the meaning of propositions in some way. To overcome the problem outlined above we would presumably need to restrict the inferences to those that all competent users of the language agreed to. In other words, there would be a basic core use that would constitute the meaning of propositions and concepts. Around that core different speakers could have idiosyncratic inferential connections between beliefs, but these would not constitute part of the meaning of any proposition or concept.

The problem here is that it is very difficult to specify what these basic uses or inferences would be. On the one hand, there is the problem that plausible candidates for basic inferential roles do not seem to be rich enough to individuate concepts in the way we want. For instance, we might think that everyone would agree to the inference from "that's beer" to "that's a drink". However, that won't be enough to give the meaning of "beer", since everyone will also agree to the inference from "that's wine" to "that's a drink". Given that, of course, "wine" and "beer" mean different things, we would need some further distinguishing inferential roles. But it's difficult to think what they would be, if they were to be genuinely uncontroversial. On the other hand, when we reflect a little, it is questionable whether there are *any* uncontroversial inferential connections. For example, consider the proposition "there's a cat". It seems plausible to think that a meaning-constitutive inference might involve something like the move from "there's a cat" to "there's an animal". The trouble, however, is that we can imagine competent speakers who might deny this. My crazy neighbour Tony believes that all cats are really robots designed by aliens to spy on human beings. So he rejects the inference from "there's a cat" to "there's an animal". But he has no difficulty in identifying cats. In fact, he spends a large part of his life deliberately avoiding them. I'd be inclined to say that despite his odd behaviour Tony grasps the concept "cat". If you agree with me, then it becomes difficult to accept that any kind of inference is meaning constitutive.

Quine: there are no meanings

A radical response to the problems of CRS in fixing the meaning of concepts would be to deny that there are any meanings to fix in the first place. This is essentially what Quine says.

Like advocates of CRS, Quine thinks that all there is to the notion of meaning is how words and sentences are used. Like Horwich, he advocates a version of the minimalist theory of truth. But unlike Horwich and other advocates of CRS, he thinks that facts about use do not determine meaning. Thus he concludes that there are no meanings.

Quine's argument against meaning involves a famous thought-experiment: what he calls radical translation. Imagine encountering an individual who speaks a language totally unknown to you. Let's call him Sotul (the speaker of the unknown language). You try to figure out what Sotul means by his utterances. You construct a translation manual. You try to equate the meaning of words and sentences in Sotul's language with words and sentences in your language. So ideally you want to formulate true sentences such as the following:

> "blah, blah" in Sotul's language means s, where s is some sentence in the radical translator's (i.e. your) language.

The only information you have to go on in constructing your translation is the utterances Sotul makes in response to you and your shared environment. In other words, all you have to go on is how Sotul uses his words. If there are such things as meanings and meaning is cashed out in terms of use, then you should be able to formulate translations of the form given above.

Here is how Quine imagines that radical translation works. You begin by forming hypotheses about what Quine calls observation sentences. For example, you notice a rabbit in the vicinity and that Sotul says "Gavagai" when the rabbit is around. You imaginatively project yourself into Sotul's position and try to work out the kinds of things he sees and reacts to. So you guess in this circumstance that "Gavagai" means "there's a rabbit". You can test this hypothesis next time a rabbit comes along. You shout "Gavagai" at Sotul and if he seems to agree (assuming you've worked out how he does so), you have evidence that your translation is a good one. Over time you will build up many translations of observation sentences from which you can formulate further hypotheses about which words correspond to the logical connectives like "and", the grammar of the language and eventually the meaning of individual words. This account of translation is very similar to Quine's naturalized epistemology discussed in Chapter 2. That's not surprising since Quine's aim in constructing his epistemology was to explain how, in his words, we could move from stimulus to science. Part of that story obviously involves explaining how we acquire a language. The way we acquire our native language is basically the same way the radical translator constructs his translation manual.

However, there is now a new twist to be added. Quine claims that there will always be more than one translation manual adequate to all the facts about how Sotul uses words; and so no fact of the matter about what any of his utterances mean. There are two aspects to this indeterminacy. The first arises with observation sentences. Quine calls this the inscrutability of reference. Consider again Quine's "Gavagai" example. Instead of translating the sentence "Gavagai" as "there's a rabbit", I could, for example have translated it as "there's an undetached rabbit part" since whenever there is an undetached rabbit part around Sotul assents to the sentence "Gavagai". The evidence for that translation, then, is as good as the evidence for the translation "there's a rabbit". To preserve this alternative translation, I shall have to make many other adjustments in my translation manual but, in theory at least, Quine claims that this could be done. So since all there is to go on in radical translation is how words in a shared environment are used and the use of words can't discriminate between the claim that "Gavagai" means rabbit and "Gavagai" means undetached rabbit part, there's no fact of the matter about what "Gavagai" means. This is a fairly mild sort of indeterminacy. The truth conditions of the sentences "there's a rabbit" and "there's an undetached rabbit part" are the same. So we might still say that at the level of the unstructured sentence, taken holophrastically, to use a Quinean term from earlier, they mean the same. A more serious kind of indeterminacy, linked to the problems of CRS discussed above, arises when we move away from observation sentences to the translation of sentences that are not immediately dependent upon features of our shared environment.

Suppose I've translated "schmavagai" in Sotul's language as "hawk" and the more general term "vangal" as bird. So the whole sentence: "schmavagai dip vangal" I translate as the sentence "hawks are birds". To which Sotul assents. However, I find that Sotul also says "bridbak dip vangal". My translation for "bridbak" is "bat". So Sotul seems to be saying, according to me, "bats are birds". Now, I need to make a judgement about my translation. Either I can stand by my original translation, in which case Sotul has a false belief, or I might reconsider what "vangal" means. I might decide instead that "vangal" really means "flying animal" and thus that Sotul uses the sentence to express a true belief. This kind of example makes clear that translating Sotul's utterances involves imputing beliefs to him, and so we must as translators judge what beliefs it is reasonable for him to have. The point for Quine here is that the kinds of judgements we make here about how to translate "vangal" are pragmatic. The facts about use will not determine whether it is right for me to translate "vangal" as "bird" or "vangal" as "flying animal". Since the only facts that could be relevant to meaning are facts about how Sotul uses words, any translation that successfully accounts for Sotul's disposition to use words as he does will be as good as any other. This form of indeterminacy is more radical than the inscrutability of reference since the alternative translations of the sentence "bridbak dip vangal" have, unlike the "gavagai" example, different truth conditions and values. Again, these different translations will influence how other words and phrases in Sotul's language are translated. But if we can build two consistent translation manuals that make sense of Sotul's utterances, we have no reason to claim that one is superior – at least as far as the facts about use go. According to Quine, any translation that can successfully explain how Sotul uses his words will be as good as any other. We can summarize this point by saying that the evaluations of reasonableness, weirdness and so on needed to translate Sotul's language and simultaneously attribute beliefs to him are not further facts but judgements. Nothing in the world corresponds to these judgements. We have no grounds for saying that one is right or wrong, but we may have grounds for saying that they are better in other ways. Some translations might be easier to use than others, or seem more natural to us. But this goes beyond the facts of Sotul's behaviour and use of words.

We can relate Quine's claims to the problems of CRS. Consider again my weird neighbour Tony. We might think that because Tony's use of the word "cat" is so strange, he doesn't really know what cats are and that he is talking about something else – cat-appearances or some such. On the other hand, in interpreting him, we might decide that he means the same thing by cats as we do and just has some very strange beliefs. It seems as though it is almost always possible to save the idea that someone means the same by a word as we do by explaining that they have very strange beliefs. And equally it seems that we explain away apparent disagreement between the beliefs of different individuals by claiming that they mean different things by using similar words. These alternative interpretations involve reaching beyond how any individual uses words. We are in the realm of judgements, our judgements, about reasonableness. Quine's point, to reiterate, is that such judgements have no factual basis.

Another way to motivate the indeterminacy of translation is to appeal to Quine's holism. Recall that according to Quine all the sentences that make up our science face the tribunal of experience together. Logically, at least, we may change any one of those sentences in order to remove a contradiction between our predictions and observations. Let's imagine two such individuals who have changed their theories in different ways to accommodate some anomalous observation. Let's call the first new theory T1 and the second T2. Given both theories have the same observational consequences and all we have to go on ultimately in translation is what observation sentences individuals assent to and dissent from, the radical translator can equally well translate the scientist advocating T1 as though his utterances were expressions of T2 and vice versa. Given that we can imagine empirically equivalent but radically different theories of the world, we may translate the utterances of Sotul or anyone else as expressions of any one of these theories since all these translations will respect the basic facts about Sotul's use of expressions.

What we have said about Sotul's language applies equally to our language. Radical translation "begins at home", as Quine puts it. Our own words and sentences can be translated in deviant ways that respect the basic facts about use. There is equally no fact of the matter about whether I mean rabbit or undetached rabbit part by my word "rabbit". This is perhaps not a surprising conclusion for Quine to reach since, as we noted, our initial acquisition of a language is very similar to building a translation manual.

How do Quine's views about meaning and truth help with the problems raised in Chapter 2 with regard to his naturalized epistemology? We uncovered two problems for Quine's account. Davidson objected that since the ultimate basis for our language was private sensory stimulations, it was impossible to see how there could be genuine communication. Stroud objected that since all objects are, according to Quine, posits, it was difficult to see how language hooked up with the world; how any of our sentences could be true.

Given that Quine takes a minimalist line with truth, perhaps we have some kind of answer to Stroud's worries. Truth is not a relation between sentences and the world but a device to serve a certain logical need, as Horwich puts it, and nothing else. Perhaps too we have some sort of answer to Davidson. The claim that communication requires that we share meanings perhaps assumes that there are meanings to share in the first place. But if there are no facts about meaning there can similarly be no facts about correct communication. Quine (1990) says in a later work, "success in communication is judged by smoothness of conversation, by frequent predictability of verbal and nonverbal reaction, and by coherence and plausibility of native testimony ... what is utterly factual is just the fluency of conversation and the effectiveness of negotiation that one translation serves to induce" (*ibid.*: 43). Communication, then, is a purely pragmatic matter of getting along sufficiently well to predict what others are inclined to do given the noises they make. (See Kemp 2006 for a development of this view.)

On the other hand, it is difficult not to come to the conclusion that Quine's views make these problems much worse. Quine, unlike Horwich, takes the truth bearers to be sentences, not propositions. This means that even the minimal concept of truth must be relativized to a language. Worse, there is no fact about what language one is speaking, so no fact about how to make the relevant relativization; no facts about what one is saying; no facts about what others are saying to us. Our connections to others and the world, Quine may tell us, are causal and that is all we could want. But it becomes difficult to make sense even of this given that once we accept Quine's account of language, talk of causes must be one possible interpretation of how I use the word "cause". There might be other ways to interpret my language where causation or even objects play no part. Once I adopt Quine's view of language, Neurath's boat no longer seems seaworthy.

Quine tends to brush off these worries by insisting that we "continue to take seriously our own particular aggregate science, our own world-theory" (1960: 24), that "we acquiesce in our home tongue" (1969: 49). But many readers, including this one, find that difficult to take. Once I accept Quine's claim that there are many equally good ways to translate my utterances, then it seems impossible to take my home tongue or my total world theory seriously. Accepting that conclusion, like accepting the possibility of Cartesian scepticism, seems to undermine all my confidence in *my* science.

Quine's view of language, like his naturalized epistemology, is a piece of armchair reasoning. When armchair philosophy conflicts with or undermines science, naturalists are inclined to reject the philosophical arguments and retain the science – if that's possible. Rejecting Quine's account requires us to find something wrong with the indeterminacy of translation. I shall confine myself to two comments. There certainly seems to be something right about Quine's claim that translation requires judgements on the part of the translator; and therefore that there is at least some openness about what our words or sentences mean. I used something like this thought to criticize Chalmers's zombie argument. However, there is a big difference between admitting that there is some room for interpretation and claiming that we are so free to interpret the utterances of others that we can attribute almost any belief and language to them consistent with the agreement to and dissention from observation sentences. My own example of a differing interpretation is a very mild one. No radical conclusions follow from an example such as this. The threat of *radically* different translations seems merely a hypothetical one. A similar point seems appropriate with regard to Quine's second argument. Arguing from holism to the indeterminacy of translation requires us to accept that there could be radically different but empirically equivalent theories. We have some sense of how this would work if we accept Quine's general account of science. But we have seen in the course of this book that Quine's philosophy of science is simplistic and incomplete. Actual scientific enquiry involves much more than testing and revising bundles of beliefs. In the context of real scientific work it seems much harder to imagine how we might construct two *radically* different but empirically adequate theories. Without real examples of what these different theories would be, then, again we have a hypothetical rather than a real worry. Given this, a naturalist can respond to Quine in the way he did to the sceptic. The possibilities that he imagines are not real live possibilities for us.

Price: deflationism about meaning

Minimalism about truth has been combined with a positive theory of meaning, conceptual role semantics in Horwich's work and with an eliminativism about meaning in Quine's. There is a third option, advocated by Huw Price (2004, 2004b, 2008). A minimalist can try to do the same thing for meaning as he did for truth. Meaning, like truth, might have no underlying nature that needs to be explained by a scientific theory.

> [T]he interesting possibility is not that a mature theory might simply have nothing to say about the relations between language, on one side, and the world, or environment inhabited

by language users, on the other. It is rather that the theoretical notions important in describing these relations might not be the semantic notions, such as reference, truth and content itself – a mature scientific view of language might not treat *representation* as a significant theoretical relation between language and the world. (Price 2004b: 188)

Price (2004a) combines this suggestion about meaning with an analysis of two ways to be a naturalist – what he calls object naturalism and subject naturalism. Object naturalism takes as its focus extra-human reality. Object naturalists worry about how things such as numbers or morality or truth and so on fit into the natural world. Subject naturalists by contrast take as their starting point human beings themselves. "According to this view ... philosophy needs to begin with what science tells us *about ourselves*. Science tells us that we humans are natural creatures. And if the claims and ambitions of philosophy conflict with this view, then philosophy needs to give way" (Price 2004a: 73).

These two views don't appear to be in conflict. After all, for the object naturalist human beings are natural objects too and so need to be fitted into an account of the natural world. However, Price argues that the two forms of naturalism diverge or at least can diverge over their understanding of language. Object naturalists begin with the idea that our words and sentences *represent*; that's their basic function. The key task for the object naturalist is to work out what problematic sentences that talk of numbers or the good represent, if they represent anything. Subject naturalists are, by contrast, not committed to any such view. A prior question for the subject naturalist to consider is whether the object naturalist's characterization of language is correct. Is it consistent with our idea of human beings as fully natural creatures that what we do with words and thoughts is represent?

Adopting an account of language that rejects the idea that its basic function is to represent is at the very least a possible option. Horwich has offered an account of truth that denies representationalist assumptions. Truth is not a relation between words and the world for the minimalist. Rather, its import is explained in terms of how it is used: that it allows us, for example, to make certain kinds of generalization. Most would agree that truth plays the kind of role Horwich outlines. The question is whether there is anything more to the concept of truth. Price argues that attempts to characterize a more substantial account of truth and other semantic notions face a fatal difficulty.

> [Object] naturalism ... seems committed to the empirical contingency of semantic relations. For any given term or sentence, it must to some extent be an empirical matter whether, and if so, to what, that term refers ... However, it seems impossible to make sense of this empirical attitude with respect to the semantic terms themselves. (Price 2004a: 81)

The objection goes something like this. Consider two rival naturalistic accounts of representation, say Dretske and Millikan's versions of teleosemantics. Both purport to tell us that a mental state represents or refers to some object when certain conditions are fulfilled. As we saw with the frog example, Dretske and Millikan think that those conditions are different. We take them then to be disagreeing about some fact: what makes something a correct representation. We can cash out that difference in linguistic fashion. Let's call the representation relation advocated by Dretske STIMULUS and the representation relation favoured by Millikan BENEFIT. According to Dretske, our mental representation of the idea of representation must represent STIMULUS and similarly for Millikan our mental representation of representation must represent BENEFIT:

> Dretske: "Representation" represents STIMULUS.
> Millikan: "Representation" represents BENEFIT.

However, applying both theories completely and consistently, we must acknowledge that the term "represents" in the above two sentences means different things. What Dretske and Millikan are actually asserting is:

> Dretske: "Representation" stands in the relation described by STIMULUS to STIMULUS.
> Millikan: "Representation" stands in the relation described by BENEFIT to BENEFIT.

Now we see that, strictly speaking, the two theories don't contradict one another at all. Given the difference in their theories of representation, they are talking about different things.

According to Price, "the problem stems from the fact that the object naturalist is trying to ask a question that renders its own suppositions fluid. There is no fixed question, with a range of answers, but, so to speak, a different question for each answer" (2004a: 83). Thus, if you start with the presupposition that words and ideas have substantial semantic relations to the world, then you are committed to that also being true of words and ideas such as "true", "refers" or "represents". The object naturalist thus has to provide an account of what these terms represent. But in doing so he must make use of a theory of representation. Having done that, he seems no longer in a position to claim that he has correctly represented what representation is. It might be true that according to his own theory he correctly represents what he calls representation. But then there might be other theories that by their own lights correctly represent what they call representation. Object naturalists who diverge in their theories of representation have no further resources to draw upon to settle the matter. There seems no basis for saying that there is a fact about what the term "representation" represents. This has disastrous consequences for the whole naturalistic project. Recall that the object naturalist starts by wondering how concepts and words such as "good" and "number" fit into the natural world. He takes it as his task to try to find something in the natural world that corresponds to these concepts. But given that we cannot say what the relation "representing" or "corresponds" corresponds to in any non-arbitrary way, we cannot make sense of this task either. There is no correct answer because there is no fixed question that the object naturalist is asking.

Price's solution is to reject the representationalist presupposition of object naturalism. We begin as subject naturalists. We don't ask what words such as "number", "meaning" or "good" represent, but how these words are used by animals like us. Once we have explained the role that semantic terms such as "refers", "means", "true" and so on play in our language and our lives, we will have said all that any reasonable naturalist position can hope to say on the matter. But there will be no substantial relation of representation between our words and things. This is not to offer another theory of meaning as use. Rather, as Price (2008) sees it, the subject naturalist's task is an anthropological rather than a semantic one.

In summary, then, the subject naturalist position is this. We explain semantic terms in non-representationalist terms, just as Horwich did for truth. Having done that, we are unburdened of the task of trying to finds things in the world that correspond to the average naturalist's list of problematic concepts. What we need to do instead is to understand the expressive function of terms such as "good" or "number".

Price would admit that, as things stand, this is more a proposal than a fleshed-out theory. Nevertheless we have some clear models for how to develop such a theory. In the semantic case we have Horwich's minimalism. In other cases we have theories such as moral expressivism.

Moral expressivists claim that it is a mistake to think of a sentence such as "John is good" as referring to some property "good" in the world. Rather, talk of "good" expresses a certain kind of attitude. The crudest version of this idea is that it expresses a certain kind of approval. Price's project aims to do something similar but presumably more sophisticated for all our talk, including our scientific talk.

Subject naturalism can be combined with the sort of deflationary methodological naturalism discussed in Chapter 4. That might sound like a surprising claim. On the face of it these two modest views of naturalism seem to be in conflict. Price's non-representationalist account of language undercuts questions about ontological commitment. Worries about what things in the world correspond to our sentences only make sense within a representationalist framework. Deflationary methodological naturalists, despite their modesty, think that there are interesting scientific questions concerning what exists. Scientists from time to time find such questions pressing, as our discussion of atoms and the Higgs boson shows. Moreover, it seems difficult to understand science as not engaged in manufacturing certain kinds of representations. Scientists, as we showed in our discussion of Kuhn and Cartwright, build models – sometimes in their minds, sometimes in reality – that are meant to represent certain systems in the world. They imagine vibrations in a lattice to be like a spring, or model water molecules as though they were pendulums. Appropriate questions can then be asked about how well and to what extent the model *represents* the system being modelled.

These apparent tensions between Price and the deflationary methodological naturalist are easy to resolve. What deflationary naturalists are describing is the functioning of a certain kind of scientific practice and the language that goes with it. Science aims to map out certain elements of reality. It sometimes postulates entities to which we have no direct access; reasonable worries then arise about the existence of these entities. However, they way such existential questions are resolved is not by appeal to some general semantic theory. Philosophy of language has no role to play here. Rather, they are resolved by employing standards specific to the sciences. We look for direct experimental proof of the existence of these entities. The deflationary naturalists account of scientific modelling and ontological commitment in the sciences can be thought of as a detailed account of the functioning of one area of discourse, on Price's view.

Price's account can, in addition, help the deflationary methodological naturalist with one problem we noted at the end of Chapter 4. The deflationary naturalist's position seems so closely bound to those of the sciences that it is difficult to see how we could extend it to other areas, and for that reason perhaps it does not seem very interesting. We can see from the subject naturalist perspective that trying to extend an account of scientific thinking, reasoning and talk to other areas of discourse would be a mistake. Other linguistic practices function in different ways. What we need to do instead is, as the deflationary naturalist has begun to do for scientific practice and talk, describe those functions.

I find such a combination of views appealing. But I must admit to certain nagging doubts about Price's non-representationalism: his view seems very similar to Quine's. Quine must also be counted as non-representionalist. If there are no meanings, then there is nothing to do the representing in the first place. In addition, Price's argument against object naturalism is very similar to Quine's. Both insist that what is wrong with the idea of substantial semantic notions of meaning or representation is not they cannot be constructed in naturalistically respectable ways, but that too many such theories can be constructed. We can raise similar worries for Price's argument as for Quine's. It trades on a hypothetical that we have difficulty making sense of. We don't have *any* adequate naturalistic theories of representation, so it is a bit of a stretch to be told that they are too easy to construct. Our discussion of teleosemantics and CRS also suggests that things are not as hopeless as Price suggests. We do have ways of debating the merits of these theories; we find them all to be lacking in certain respects. I worry too that if we are non-representationalists, then, like Quine, we may cut ourselves off from the world forever. This is not an argument so much as an expression of a worry. To assuage my doubts the non-representationalists need to tell us more about how to understand the connection of our talk and thought to the world about us.

Minimalism about truth provides at least three options for developing an account of other semantic notions such as meaning. We can try to provide a naturalistic theory of meaning, independent of truth, as Horwich does. We can hope to eliminate meaning altogether, as Quine does. Or finally, we might try to be minimalist about all semantic notions, as Price does. None seems wholly satisfactory.

Conclusion

Naturalistically inclined philosophers of language offer us not only a variety of theories of meaning and truth, but a variety of strategies for constructing such theories. Some of those who advocate naturalistic ideas in other areas must hope that certain projects succeed while others fail. If, like Boyd, you want truth to play a role in the explanation of the success of science, then you must be committed to a robust, non-minimalist account of truth. Minimalist truth will not explain the success of science in the way that tracks in a cloud chamber are explained by the presence of electrons. Arguably the same must be true for reliabilists if they are committed, like Kornblith, to the idea that knowledge is a natural kind.

Deflationary methodological naturalists can be more relaxed. Their view is compatible with robust theories or with deflationary views such as Price's, but perhaps not much more relaxed. It would be nice to be able to shrug one's shoulders and say, as we did in the case of consciousness, it's an empirical question; let's just see which theory of language and truth fares best against the data. (Maddy 2001 in effect says this.) But it is difficult to see precisely how semantic theories can be empirically testable theories. The arguments of Quine and Price perhaps give us some reason to think that they cannot be.

The problem of understanding semantic notions from a naturalist perspective is the great unsolved problem for naturalists. It is not just that we don't know which naturalistic theory to accept; we are not even sure of the right way to approach these questions and whether any of the approaches on offer is consistent with the general naturalist orientation.

Conclusion

Naturalism: its motivations

We began our discussion of naturalism with some slogans. "Philosophy is continuous with the natural sciences"; "there is no first philosophy". Slogans, I said, don't tell us much. But as the chapters of this text indicate, only something as vague and vatic as these slogans could hope to capture the great variety of philosophical projects that go under the name of "naturalism". We find some naturalists deploring special philosophical methods, others embracing conceptual analysis. We find some who call themselves physicalists, others dualists, and yet others who reject any metaphysics; some who think that naturalism can provide a framework for a constructive ontology; others who think a kind of quietism is appropriate.

With so many contradictory views all claiming to be naturalist, we might begin to think that the term "naturalism" is empty. Almost any view, it seems, could be termed "naturalist".

That would overstate things. There is great diversity among naturalists, but some common ground too. All naturalisms begin with an admiring attitude towards science and its achievements. In many cases this admiring attitude is combined with a contempt or distrust for the way that philosophy has been or is conducted. This combination of views has a long history. Many of the advocates of first philosophy, Descartes, Kant and Carnap, shared the same admiration of science or nascent science and distrust of philosophy. Descartes, for example, uses scepticism as a device to sweep away the old Aristotelian foundations of knowledge, so that he can build an entirely new philosophy that makes room for the new mathematical sciences. Kant and the positivists are both concerned to show how pseudo-philosophical questions arise when we violate the preconditions for the possibility of thought (in Kant's case) or the framework of meaningful discourse (in Carnap's). These attempts at first philosophy are all designed to sort the good questions from the bad: in essence, to show us why science is as successful as it is and why philosophy has been so lamentable at making any progress over the millennia. Naturalism is part of this tradition. The difference is that whereas Descartes, Kant and Carnap all called for a new philosophy to ground the sciences, naturalists reverse the order of explanation. Naturalists take the view that we should start with our well-developed science and build our philosophy from there.

There is no clever philosophical argument that can force you to make this naturalist move. There is no argument to show that other approaches to philosophy will not succeed. Naturalism is a position that can claim at best only motivations. The motivation for naturalism is just the positive attitude towards science shared by Descartes, Kant and Carnap, and a recognition of the failures of their first philosophical approaches. An alternative response would be to try to construct another first philosophy. Naturalism has no means by which to argue that such an approach is impossible. Naturalism (or as we should say now, the varieties of naturalism) can ultimately only be assessed against other philosophical programmes by its results and prospects. Will adopting a naturalist orientation lead to interesting philosophy? Will it offer solutions to or dissolutions of some vexing philosophical questions? And perhaps most importantly, is naturalism a consistent philosophical position?

The varieties of naturalism and their prospects

This book has been an attempt to illustrate the kind of answers naturalists can offer to such questions. We've considered naturalist views in epistemology, metaphysics, the philosophy of science, the philosophy of mind and semantics. Along the way we have made several important distinctions among the naturalists we have looked at. First there is a distinction between methodological naturalists and metaphysical naturalists. Methodological naturalists think that the methods of science should be as far as possible adopted by philosophers. Metaphysical naturalists start not with scientific method but a view about how the world is – a view that they claim is derived from our best science.

Each of these kinds of naturalism admits of further distinctions. In the case of methodological naturalism, we distinguished two sub-types. On the one hand there are what I called constructive methodological naturalists such as Boyd, Lewis and Armstrong, who want to use what they consider scientific methods in metaphysics. In particular, they think that the method of inference to the best explanation can be used to justify belief in scientific realism, numbers, possible worlds and universals. On the other hand, there are what I call deflationary methodological naturalists, such as Fine and Maddy. They want to adopt the same methods for ontological commitment as found in the sciences and mathematics; and they criticize the arguments of constructive naturalists for failing to live up to the standards of real science.

Metaphysical naturalists too come in a number of varieties. First, there are the physicalists. They in turn divide into *a priori* physicalists, who think there is a conceptual connection between physical and non-physical vocabulary, and *a posteriori* physicalists, who think the connection is natural, not conceptual. Then there are metaphysical naturalists who are not physicalists, either because they think consciousness is not physical or because there is no good empirical reason to hold that physics is causally complete.

Most of these programmes promise something interesting for the philosopher. Constructive methodological naturalism provides a general strategy for constructing arguments for or against the existence of various entities. *A priori* physicalists have (perhaps) much interesting work to do in showing how claims about minds, morals and other problematic kinds follow as a matter of conceptual necessity from certain physical truths.

These are not projects, though, that I can engage in with enthusiasm. Both views seem to me as a deflationary naturalist to be undermined by a proper understanding of science. Providing some interesting work for philosophers to do is less straightforward for the deflationary naturalist. Since such naturalists are chary of going beyond the methods and theories endorsed by science, it might seem that they have nothing much left to do than point to science and its results. But there are number of interesting projects deflationary naturalists can pursue; we mentioned one in Chapter 4. The deflationary naturalist should try to say more precisely what the standards of ontological commitment actually used in science are. The general strategy must be to pursue any philosophical project through a detailed investigation of the sciences.

Let me briefly describe one further project that I believe is interesting for the insight it might provide into both methodological and perhaps also metaphysical matters.

Philosophers have long been concerned with the relation between different sciences. They have explored issues concerned with scientific reduction and unification. Sometimes this work has been used to support a more general metaphysical picture. The argument from reductionist success considered in Chapter 5 does precisely that. It takes reductionist successes in science to provide an argument for thinking that all sciences will ultimately reduce to physics and so an argument for physicalism. In Chapter 4 we encountered a different conception of how the sciences relate. Kuhn claimed that different sciences embody different paradigms. They employ different methods and standards of evaluation. On this basis, Kuhn argued, different paradigms were incommensurable and so could not meaningfully be compared. Both pictures involve exaggerations or misrepresentations of actual science. Things are neither as neatly ordered as reductionists claim nor as radically disjointed as Kuhn claims.

We can see this by considering ways in which different sciences and scientists interact that fit neither model. An obvious example is any kind of interdisciplinary research. When scientists from different disciplines interact it is not typically the case that the goal is to reduce one science to another. If they interact successfully, then obviously their paradigms or research traditions cannot be incommensurable. Such areas of scientific activity then seem ripe for naturalist research and new and interesting models to describe how different disciplines interact.

We might hope to gain various methodological insights by studying interdisciplinary work. First of all there are interesting questions to be raised about how scientists from different areas succeed in coordinating their research. A better understanding of this may provide useful methodological advice for future interdisciplinary projects. More interestingly, I think, would be to use interdisciplinary research to study the way different scientists represent and understand the object of their investigation. Do the different sciences represent the object in the same way? Do they share the same theoretical representations? If they don't, how much must they have in common to be able to communicate sufficiently with one another to conduct successful research? Such a study would enhance our understanding of how it is that scientists represent the world, and so perhaps improve our understanding of what our best science says about the world. That seems to me an interesting philosophical project and one I, as a deflationary methodological naturalist, intend to pursue in the future.

Troubles with naturalism

Philosophical naturalism must do more than reassure its practitioners that they have interesting work ahead. It must show minimally that it is a consistent position. One of the reasons to reject the philosophies of Kant and Carnap, and move away from first philosophy, was that their positions seemed inconsistent. Naturalists have to show that they do not confront a similar problem. Naturalists must demonstrate that their position is a principled one, which does not just arbitrarily reject other philosophical approaches or exclude important questions.

Let us take the second issue first. Many people are inclined to think that naturalism is in some way unprincipled or chauvinistic. In a narrow sense it is chauvinistic because it fails to take traditional philosophical problems seriously, and in a broader sense it is chauvinistic because it prioritizes sciences over all other disciplines.

Consider traditional philosophy first. Many of the traditional problems in epistemology begin by highlighting possibilities that the average man in the street doesn't usually consider. Scepticism asks us to consider the possibility that we might be dreaming. The problem of induction asks us to consider the possibility that the future might be very different from the past. Grue predicates and ring inferences discussed in Chapter 3 suggest the possibility that we may be misclassifying the things in our world. Naturalism doesn't offer any direct answers to these challenges. It just brushes them off. Advocates of first philosophy might and perhaps are inclined to think that is unprincipled. Indeed, they might think that, without answers to these questions, naturalism is unwarranted.

More generally, naturalists stand accused of having an unprincipled bias in favour of science, and correspondingly a failure to recognize the importance of non-scientific knowledge or enquiry. Again the point is that there are possibilities, ways of knowing or thinking about the world, that the naturalist ignores without good reason.

I think there are good naturalist answers to both challenges. Naturalists from Quine onwards do not lightly brush off first philosophical problems. Rather they do two things. First, they point to the failure of *all* philosophy to answer these questions. All direct attempts to defeat the sceptic are hopeless. It would perhaps be better, then, to try something different. Secondly, from the naturalist perspective there is a perfectly good and productive way to reconstrue these questions. They are really questions that, when we think them through clearly, are best answered by our current science. Brain-in-a-vat-type scenarios are beguiling because of our scientific knowledge. Because we think that all our knowledge of the world is ultimately "produced" by stimulations in our brain, it seems possible to entertain this sceptical hypothesis. Our proper duty then is to investigate this empirically, to try to figure out if it is a real possibility. If the traditional philosopher tells us that the brain-in-a-vat story is just a device to generate sceptical worries, then we lose all clear sense of the possibility we are being asked to entertain and, I would say, any clear sense of what the worry is supposed to be. Similarly with the problem of induction. Understood properly, it reminds us that we can never attain certainty in our empirical knowledge. But the bare possibility of being wrong does not shift our confidence in our current science. It simply motivates a principled fallibilism.

As to the second problem, we need to understand naturalists' prioritizing of science in context. Naturalism seems like an attractive view in epistemology and metaphysics precisely because science has been so much better than philosophy at the business of describing how the world is and uncovering methods for doing this. Science, as we have seen, has often undermined the epistemological and metaphysical presuppositions of past philosophers. Why not then hand over to science those traditional philosophical problems about method, knowledge and the nature of the world? Embracing naturalism in this way does not mean that we are forced to be interested in science to the exclusion of all other things. Rather, it is to acknowledge that the interests of science and traditional philosophy intersect in certain areas and that in those areas where they do so, science has been much more productive and fruitful than philosophy. Other interests on which science is silent can still be accommodated. Science tells us nothing about how we should lead our lives and what we should value more generally. Science demands nothing more of disciplines which address these questions than that they do not contradict our well-established scientific knowledge. This is in essence Price's subject naturalism; there is nothing chauvinistic about it.

What about the final concern: is naturalism internally consistent? This worry principally arises when we consider matters in the philosophy of language. Representationalist accounts of language are threatened by inconsistency because, according to Quine and Price, there are too many naturalistically respectable ways to represent the ideas of representation or meaning and no principled way to choose among them. Our choice between theories seems arbitrary and so our representation of scientific facts becomes arbitrary too. Non-representationalist accounts are threatened by inconsistency because we seem to lose all sense of our connection to the world; scepticism and loss of confidence in our scientific knowledge seem to come in their wake. Without confidence in our science, then, naturalism has no base from which to begin. Neither argument for inconsistency is entirely conclusive. We don't as a matter of fact seem able to generate the many equally acceptable theories of meaning that supposedly threaten the representationalist account. The connection with the world seems elusive on non-representationalist accounts but it is not clear that we can make no sense of it. Questions about meaning and truth are hard. Naturalism as it stands does not have good or clear answers to offer us, but it is not obvious that it is inconsistent.

Whatever the fate of naturalism in the semantic realm, there are still good reasons for the deflationary naturalist to continue their work in trying to understand better the details of science. Whether you say that science and philosophy are the same or totally different, it pays to have a better understanding of science. If you want to model philosophy on science, you'd better know what science does and says in some detail so that you can make sure your philosophy matches up. If you want to contrast philosophy with science, then you'd better know what science does and says in some detail so that you can make sure your philosophy is quite different. Naturalism of the sort I favour preaches that we should care more about the details of science and its practice rather than rest content with careless or simplistic overgeneralizations. That is a lesson we should all take heart, whatever our ultimate philosophical orientation.

Questions for discussion and revision

one First philosophy

1. Discuss the following claim. "If you accept Descartes's picture of representation, then the only way you can overcome the problem of scepticism is by postulating the existence of God."
2. Could it be that Kant is right that our intuitive understanding of space is Euclidean, even though, in light of scientific developments, we take this intuitive understanding to be false?
3. If there is more than one logic, what possible arguments could be offered to decide which is the right one? Won't any argument presuppose the logic it sets out to validate?

two Quine and the naturalized epistemology

1. If all our beliefs are revisable, is the belief that all our beliefs are revisable revisable?
2. Discuss the following claim: "Quine's pragmatic standards of theory revision provide all the norms we need in epistemology."
3. If naturalists like Quine have given up on trying to answer the problem of scepticism, have they given up philosophy?

three Reliabilism

1. Construct a Gettier-style counter-example to the claim that knowledge is true belief arrived at through a reliable belief-forming mechanism.
2. If justification doesn't consist in reliability, then what could it be?

3. Discuss this claim: "We don't need a general account of justification or knowledge; all we need is some way of making sense of science and its many methods. There is no reason to presume that those methods share anything deserving the label justification."

four Naturalized philosophy of science

1. Does the problem of grue properties and ring inferences arise for my defence of Laudan's principle (R1)?
2. Has Laudan provided a completely naturalistic account of norms, given that he has no explanation for the normative force of hypothetical imperatives themselves?
3. Does it make sense to believe that your theories are true without having a theory of truth as Fine does?
4. "Philosophy is so limited and minimal from a deflationary naturalist perspective, you might as well give up and become a scientist." Discuss.

five Naturalizing metaphysics

1. Provide two further examples of weakly and strongly supervening property relations.
2. Determinants are different with respect to their determinable properties. For example, red and blue are both determinants of colour and they are different colours. If mental states stand in the determinate–determinable relation to physical states, then any two physical states that realize some mental state must be different mental states. Hence multiple realization is impossible on this account. Discuss.
3. "Given that there are physiological differences between you and me, our mental states can't really be identical to the very same physical property; so if the analytic functionalists account is right, we can't really have the very same mental states." Discuss.

six Naturalism without physicalism?

1. Does it make sense to think there might be things that are possible but inconceivable?
2. How would Cartwright understand work in fundamental physics that claims to be aiming for a theory of everything?
3. If physicalists claimed that physics was a vague term, like "heap", could that help with the problems raised at the end of this chapter?

seven Meaning and truth

1. Does it make sense to think of evolution as producing norms in any substantial sense? After all, the process of evolution is just a natural one and
   evolutionary science properly understood surely simply describes that
   process.
2. How might you model a minimalist theory of reference on a minimalist
   theory of truth?
3. Are Quine's and Price's views of language compatible? If not, what does the
   difference consist in?

Guide to further reading

one First philosophy

For more on Descartes's philosophy, see Cottingham (1986) and Williams (1978). For more detail on Hume, Stroud (1977) is excellent and suggests that Hume is an early naturalist. Kant's difficult philosophy is clearly laid out in Gardner (1999). A more sophisticated account is Allison (1983). Carnap's views are compared in interesting ways with Kant's in Coffa (1991). A shorter and very elegant introduction to the same issues and their connections to modern naturalism can be found in Maddy (2001).

two Quine and the naturalized epistemology

Two useful and very clear introductions to Quine's philosophy are Hookway (1988) and Kemp (2006). A classic criticism of Quine's naturalized epistemology and its failure to address normative questions is Kim (1988). The claim that Quine's view leads to some kind of scepticism is powerfully argued in Stroud (1984). Davidson's objections to Quine's account of language can be found in Davidson (2001, 2005), especially chapter 4 of the latter.

three Reliabilism

Classic statements of the reliabilist position are given by Goldman (1979) and in a more elaborate way by Goldman (1999). See also Dretske (1981). The classic criticism of reliabilism is Conee & Feldman (1998). Further interesting criticism is to be found in Brandom (2000), chapter 3, and Howson (2000), chapter 3. Kornblith's view of knowledge as a natural kind is clearly presented and vigorously defended in Kornblith (2002). Some evolutionary psychologists think that interesting conclusions can be drawn from the experiments discussed in this chapter. See Barkow *et al.* (1992), chapter 2 for a discussion.

four Naturalized philosophy of science

For Popper's account of science, see Popper (1959, 1972); for Carnap's highly technical work on induction see Carnap (1950b). The two classic texts for Kuhn and Feyerabend are Kuhn (1970) and Feyerabend (1975). Chalmers (1999) provides a very clear discussion of the works of Popper, Kuhn and Feyerabend, as well as his own criticism of Feyerabend discussed in the chapter. Laudan (1987) provides a clear account of his basic ideas and the connections they have to both traditional methodology and the accounts of Kuhn and Feyerabend. Knowles (2003) provides some interesting criticism of Laudan and argues that norms are not needed in science. Boyd's and Putnam's no-miracles argument can be found in Boyd (1996) and Putnam (1975). NOA is developed and defended in Fine (1996). Maddy (1997) provides her account of mathematical naturalism and criticisms of Quine's account of ontological commitment. A further more recent criticism of contemporary metaphysics that takes its inspiration from Quine is Price (2007).

five Naturalizing metaphysics

The classic version of the argument from reductive success is Oppenheim & Putnam (1958). Melnyk (2003) provides a more contemporary account which goes to great efforts to show that contemporary science supports physicalism. The clearest statement of the causal argument is Papineau (1993). The most authoritative paper on supervenience is McLaughlin (1995). Yablo's (1992) account is further developed in Yablo (1997). The most systematic treatment of analytic functionalism is Jackson (1998).

six Naturalism without physicalism?

Chalmers's (1996) zombie argument has been developed in a number of papers. A useful overview is Chalmers (2002b). A more sophisticated account of Chalmers's theory of meaning and modality can be found in Chalmers & Jackson (2001). The criticism I offer of Chalmers is an unsophisticated and simplified version of Yablo (2000). Cartwright's (1999) patchwork view is criticized in interesting ways by Sklar (2003). A similar view to Cartwright's is articulated in Teller (2004). The first philosopher to present in a clear way the problem with defining the physics in physical is Hempel (1980). A further interesting criticism of physicalism and its troubles with physics can be found in Sturgeon (1998). Witmer (2000) provides a response to Sturgeon.

seven Meaning and truth

Millikan (1993) is a nice collection of essays developing her views. Papineau (1987) gives a similar account that starts with human representation. A good place to start with Dretske is Dretske (1981). He elaborates his stimulus view in Dretske (1990). Horwich (1999) is a very clear statement and defence of the minimalist account of truth. An interesting and powerful criticism of minimalism is Ketland (1998). Horwich's (1998) provides his use theory of meaning. A classic and very clear early version of conceptual role semantics is Block (1978). Quine's views on translation are set out in chaper 2 of Quine (1960). Later work suggests some softening of his view and subtle changes of mind. See Quine (1990) for an apparently less radical view. Price's (2004) subtle view of naturalism and his expressivism are developed in a number of recent papers. See in particular his (2007, co-authored with MacArthur) and (2008), where he compares his view to those of Simon Blackburn and Robert Brandom. These papers and others can be found on his website: http://www.usyd.edu.au/time/price/publications.html

Bibliography

Allison, H. E. 1983. *Kant's Transcendental Idealism: An Interpretation and Defense*. New Haven, CT: Yale University Press.

Armstrong, D. M. 1981. "A Causal Theory of Mind". In *Philosophy of Mind: Classical and Contemporary Readings*, D. J. Chalmers (ed.). Oxford: Oxford University Press.

Armstrong, D. M. 1983. *What is a Law of Nature?* Cambridge: Cambridge University Press.

Barkow, J. L., L. Cosmides & J. Toobey 1992. *The Adapted Mind*. Oxford: Oxford University Press.

Bennett, K. 2003. "Why the Exclusion Problem Seems Intractable, and How, Just Maybe, To Tract It". *Noûs* 3: 471–97.

Block, I. 1961. "Truth and Error in Aristotle's Theory of Sense Perception". *Philosophical Quarterly* 11: 1–9.

Block, N. 1978. "Advertisement for a Semantics for Psychology". In *Midwest Studies in Philosophy*, Peter A. French (ed.), 615–78. Minneapolis, MN: University of Minnesota Press.

Boghossian, P. & C. Peacocke (eds) 2000. *New Essays on the A Priori*. Oxford: Oxford University Press.

Boyd, R. 1996. "Realism, Approximate and Philosophical Method". In *Philosophy of Science*, D. Papineau (ed.), 215–55. Oxford: Oxford University Press.

Brandom, R. B. 2000. *Articulating Reasons: An Introduction to Inferentialism*. Cambridge, MA: Harvard University Press.

Campbell, K. 1990. *Abstract Particulars*. Oxford: Blackwell.

Carnap, R. 1934. *The Logical Syntax of Language*, A. Smeaton (trans.). London: Routledge & Kegan Paul, 1937.

Carnap, R. 1950a. "Empiricism, Semantics, and Ontology". Reprinted in *The Linguistic Turn: Essays in Philosophical Method*, 3rd edn, Richard Rorty (ed.). Chicago, IL: Chicago University Press, 1992.

Carnap, R. 1950b. *Logical Foundations of Probability*. Chicago, IL: University of Chicago Press.

Carnap, R. 1967. *The Logical Structure of the World: Pseudoproblems in Philosophy*. Berkeley, CA: University of California Press.

Cartwright, N. 1999. *The Dappled World: A Study of the Boundaries of Science*. Cambridge: Cambridge University Press.

Chalmers, A. 1986. "The Galileo that Feyerabend Missed". In *The Politics and Rhetoric of Scientific Method*, John A. Schuster (ed.), 1–31. Dordrecht: Kluwer.

Chalmers, A. 1999. *What is This Thing Called Science?* 3rd edn. Indianapolis, IN: Hackett.

Chalmers, D. J. 1996. *The Conscious Mind: In Search of a Fundamental Theory*. Oxford: Oxford University Press.

Chalmers, D. J. 1999. "Materialism and the Metaphysics of Modality". *Philosophy and Phenomenological Research* 59(2): 473–96.

Chalmers, D. J. (ed.) 2002a. *Philosophy of Mind: Classical and Contemporary Readings*. Oxford: Oxford University Press.

Chalmers, D. J. 2002b. "Consciousness and Its Place in Nature". In *Philosophy of Mind: Classical and Contemporary Readings*, D. J. Chalmers (ed.). Oxford: Oxford University Press.

Coffa, J. A. 1991. *The Semantic Tradition from Kant to Carnap to the Vienna Station*. New York: Cambridge University Press.

Conee, E. & R. Feldman 1998. "The Generality Problem for Reliabilism". *Philosophical Studies: An International Journal for Philosophy in the Analytic Tradition* 89(1), 1–29.

Cottingham, J. 1986. *Descartes*. Oxford: Blackwell.

Cottingham, J., R. Stoothoff & D. Murdoch (eds) 1984. *The Philosophical Writings of Descartes (CSM), Vols I & II*. Cambridge: Cambridge University Press.

Davidson, D. 2001. *Subjective, Intersubjective, Objective*. Oxford: Clarendon Press.

Davidson, D. 2005. *Truth, Language, and History*. Oxford: Clarendon Press.

De Caro, M. & D. Macarthur 2004. *Naturalism in Question*. Cambridge, MA: Harvard University Press.

Dennett, D. C. 1996. "Cow-Sharks, Magnets, and Swampman". *Mind and Language* 11(1): 76–7.

Descartes, R. 1641. *Meditations on First Philosophy*.

Dretske, F. 1981. *Knowledge and the Flow of Information*. Cambridge, MA: MIT Press.

Dretske, F. 1990. "Reply to Reviewers of 'Explaining Behavior: Reasons in a World of Causes'". *Philosophy and Phenomenological Research* 50(4): 819–39.

Dupré, J. 1993. *The Disorder of Things: Metaphysical Foundations of the Disunity of Science*. Cambridge, MA: Harvard University Press.

Feyerabend, P. 1975. *Against Method*. London: New Left Books.

Field, H. 1980. *Science Without Numbers: A Defence of Nominalism*. Princeton, NJ: Princeton University Press.

Field, H. 1994. "Disquotational Truth and Factually Defective Discourse". *Philosophical Review* 103(3): 405–52.

Fine, A. 1996. *The Shaky Game: Einstein Realism and the Quantum Theory*. Chicago, IL: University of Chicago Press.

Frege, G. 1918–19. "Der Gedanke: Eine logische Untersuchung (Thoughts)". *Beiträge zur Philosophie de deutschen Idealismus* 1: 58–77. In *Collected Papers on Mathematics, Logic, and Philosophy*, Brian McGuinness (ed.). Oxford: Blackwell, 1984.

Galileo. 1957. *The Starry Messenger*. In *The Discoveries of Galileo*, S. Drake (trans.). New York: Doubleday.

Galileo. 1967. *Dialogue Concerning the Two Chief Systems of the World*. Berkeley, CA: University of California Press.

Gardner, S. 1999. *Kant and the Critique of Pure Reason*. New York: Routledge.

Gettier, E. L. 1963. "Is Justified True Belief Knowledge?" *Analysis* **23**: 121–3.

Gillett, C. & B. Loewer (eds) 2001. *Physicalism and its Discontents*. Cambridge: Cambridge University Press.

Gödel, K. 1949. "An Example of a New Type of Cosmological Solutions of Einstein's Field Equations of Gravitation". *Reviews of Modern Physics* **21**(3): 447–50.

Goldman, A. 1979. "What is Justified Belief?" In *Justification and Knowledge*, G. Pappas (ed.). Dordrecht: Reidel.

Goldman, A. 1999. *Knowledge in a Social World*. Oxford: Oxford University Press.

Guess, H. A., A. Kleinman, J. W. Kusek & L. W. Engel (eds) 2002. *The Science of the Placebo: Towards an Interdisciplinary Research Agenda*. London: BMJ Publishing.

Hellman, G. & F. W. Thompson 1977. "Physicalism Materialism". *Noûs* **11**: 309–45.

Hempel, C. G. 1980. "Comments on Goodman's 'Ways of Worldmaking'". *Synthese* **45**: 193–200.

Hookway, C. 1988. *Quine*. Cambridge: Polity.

Horgan, T. 1993. "From Supervenience to Superdupervenience: Meeting the Demands of a Material World". *Mind* **102**(408): 555–86.

Horwich, P. 1998. *Meaning*. New York: Oxford University Press.

Horwich, P. 1999. *Truth*, 2nd edn. New York: Oxford University Press.

Howson, C. 2000. *Hume's Problem: Induction and the Justification of Belief*. Oxford: Oxford University Press.

Hume, D. 1739. *A Treatise of Human Nature*, D. G. C. Macnabb (ed.). London/Glasgow: Collins, 1962.

Hume, D. 1740. "An Abstract of a Book Lately Published, Entitled, a Treatise of Human Nature, etc. Wherein the Chief Argument of That Book is Farther Illustrated and Explained". *http://www.mnstate.edu/gracyk/courses/web%20publishing/hume'sabstract.htm*, accessed 7/7/08.

Hume, D. 1748. *An Enquiry Concerning Human Understanding*.

Jackson, F. 1982. "Epiphenomenal Qualia". *Philosophical Quarterly* **32**: 127–36.

Jackson, F. 1998. *From Metaphysics to Ethics: A Defence of Conceptual Analysis*. Oxford: Clarendon Press.

Kahneman, D. & A. Tversky 1973. "On the Psychology of Prediction". *Psychological Review* **80**: 237–51.

Kant, I. 1781/1787. *Critique of Pure Reason*. 1st/2nd edn. London: Macmillan.

Kemp, G. 2006. *Quine: A Guide for the Perplexed*. London: Continuum.

Ketland, J. 1999. "Deflationism and Tarski's Paradise". *Mind: A Quarterly Review of Philosophy* **108**(429): 69–94.

Kim, J. 1988. "What is 'Naturalized Epistemology'?". In *Philosophical Perspectives*, James E. Tomberlin (ed.), 381–405. Atascadero, CA: Ridgeview.

Kim, J. 1993. *Supervenience and Mind: Selected Philosophical Essays*. Cambridge: Cambridge University Press.

Kim, J. 1998. *Mind in a Physical World: An Essay on the Mind–Body Problem and Mental Causation*. Cambridge, MA: MIT Press.

Kitcher, P. 1993. *The Advancement of Science: Science without Legend, Objectivity without Illusions*. New York: Oxford University Press.

Knowles, J. 2003. *Norms, Naturalism and Epistemology: The Case for Science without Norms*. Basingstoke: Palgrave Macmillan.

Kornblith, H. 2002. *Knowledge and Its Place in Nature*. Oxford: Clarendon Press.

Kripke, S. A. 1980. *Naming and Necessity*. Cambridge, MA: Harvard University Press.

Kuhn, T. S. 1970. *The Structure of Scientific Revolutions*, 2nd edn. Chicago, IL: University of Chicago Press.

Laudan, L. 1981. "A Confutation of Convergent Realism". *Philosophy of Science* **48**: 19–49. Reprinted in Papineau 1996.

Laudan, L. 1987. "Progress or Rationality: The Prospects for Normative Naturalism". *American Philosophical Quarterly* **24**: 19–31.

Laudan, L. 1989. "If It Ain't Broke, Don't Fix It". *British Journal for the Philosophy of Science* **40**(3): 369–75.

Leeds, S. 1978. "Theories of Reference and Truth". *Erkenntnis: An International Journal of Analytic Philosophy* **13**: 111–29.

Lewis, D. 1972. "Psychophysical and Theoretical Identities". In *Philosophy of Mind: Classical and Contemporary Readings*, D. J. Chalmers (ed.). Oxford: Oxford University Press.

Loewer, B. 2001. "From Physics to Physicalism". In *Physicalism and its Discontents*, C. Gillett & B. Loewer (eds), 37–56. Cambridge: Cambridge University Press.

Loux, M. 1979. *The Possible and the Actual*. Ithaca, NY: Cornell University Press.

Maddy, P. 1997. *Naturalism in Mathematics*. Oxford: Clarendon Press.

Maddy, P. 2001. "Naturalism and A Priori". In *New Essays on the A Priori*, P. Boghossian & C. Peacocke (eds), 92–116. Oxford: Oxford University Press.

Mayr, E. 1963. *Animal Species and Evolution*. Cambridge, MA: Harvard University Press.

McCormick, P. J. 1996. *Starmaking: Realism, Anti-Realism, and Irrealism*. Cambridge, MA: MIT Press.

McLaughlin, B. P. 1995. "Varieties of Supervenience". In *Supervenience: New Essays*, E. E. Savellos & U. D. Yalçin (eds), 16–59. Cambridge: Cambridge University Press.

Melnyk, A. 2003. *A Physicalist Manifesto: Thoroughly Modern Materialism*. Cambridge: Cambridge University Press.

Millikan, R. G. 1984. *Language, Thought, and Other Biological Categories: New Foundations for Realism*. Cambridge, MA: MIT Press.

Millikan, R. G. 1993. *White Queen Psychology and Other Essays for Alice*. Cambridge, MA: MIT Press.

Montero, B. 1999. "The Body Problem". *Noûs* 33(2): 183–200.

Montero, B. 2001. "Post-Physicalism". *Journal of Consciousness Studies* 8(2): 61–80.

Montero, B. & D. Papineau 2005. "A Defence of the Via Negativa Argument for Physicalism". *Analysis* 65(3): 233–7.

Moser, P. K. & J. D. Trout (eds) 1995. *Contemporary Materialism: A Reader*. New York: Routledge.

Musgrave, A. 1996. "NOA's Ark: Fine for Realism". In *The Philosophy of Science*, D. Papineau (ed.), 45–60. Oxford: Oxford University Press.

Nagel, T. 1974. "What is it Like to be a Bat?" *Philosophical Review* 83: 435–50.

Noordhof, P. 2003. "Not Old . . . But Not That New Either: Explicability, Emergence and the Characterisation of Materialism". In *Physicalism and Mental Causation: The Metaphysics of Mind and Action*, S. Walter & H.-Z. Heckmann (eds), 85–108. Charlottesville, VA: Imprint Academic.

Oppenheim, F. & H. Putnam 1958. "Unity of Science as a Working Hypothesis". *Minnesota Studies in the Philosophy of Science*, vol. 2, 3–36.

Ostwald, F. W. 1904. *Gundriss der allgemeinen Chemie*, 3rd edn. Leipzig: Engelmann.

Ostwald, F. W. 1909. *Gundriss der allgemeinen Chemie*, 4th edn. Leipzig: Engelmann.

Papineau, D. 1987. *Representation and Reality*. Oxford: Blackwell.

Papineau, D. 1993. *Philosophical Naturalism*. Oxford: Blackwell.

Papineau, D. (ed.) 1996. *The Philosophy of Science*. Oxford: Oxford University Press.

Papineau, D. 1998. "Mind the Gap". *Noûs Supplement: Philosophical Perspectives* 12: 373–88.

Papineau, D. 2001. "The Rise of Physicalism". In *Physicalism and its Discontents*, C. Gillett & B. Loewer (eds), 3–36. Cambridge: Cambridge University Press.

Papineau, D. 2003. *The Roots of Reason: Philosophical Essays on Rationality, Evolution, and Probability*. Oxford: Clarendon Press.

Peacocke, C. 1992. *A Study of Concepts*. Cambridge, MA: MIT Press.

Pietroski, P. 1992. "Intentionality and Teleological Error". *Pacific Philosophical Quarterly* 73(3): 267–82.

Poland, J. 1994. *Physicalism: The Philosophical Foundations*. Oxford: Clarendon Press.

Popper, K. R. 1959. *The Logic of Scientific Discovery*. London: Hutchinson.

Popper, K. R. 1972. *Objective Knowledge: An Evolutionary Approach*. Oxford: Clarendon Press.

Post, J. F. 1987. *The Faces of Existence: An Essay in Nonreductive Metaphysics*. Ithaca, NY: Cornell University Press.

Post, J. F. 1991. *Metaphysics: A Contemporary Introduction*. New York: Paragon House.

Post, J. F. 1995. "Global Determination: Too Permissive?" In *Supervenience: New Essays*, E. E. Savellos & U. D. Yalçin (eds). Cambridge: Cambridge University Press.

Price, H. 2004a. "Naturalism without Representationalism". In *Naturalism in Question*, D. Macarthur & M. De Caro (eds). Cambridge, MA: Harvard University Press.

Price, H. 2004b. "Immodesty without Mirrors – Making Sense of Wittgenstein's Linguistic Pluralism". In *Wittgenstein's Lasting Significance*, Max Kölbel & Bernhard Weiss (eds), 179–205. London: Routledge & Kegan Paul.

Price, H. 2007. "Quining Naturalism". *Journal of Philosophy* **104**: 375–405.

Price, H. 2008. "One Cheer for Representationalism?" In *The Philosophy of Richard Rorty*, R. E. Auxier (ed.). Chicago, IL: Open Court.

Price, H. & D. Macarthur 2007. "Pragmatism, Quasi-realism and the Global Challenge". In *The New Pragmatists*, C. Misak (ed.). Oxford: Oxford University Press.

Putnam, H. 1975. *Mathematics, Matter and Method: Philosophical Papers, Volume I*. Cambridge: Cambridge University Press.

Putnam, H. 1978. *Meaning and the Moral Sciences*. London: Routledge.

Putnam, H. 1981. *Reason, Truth and History*. Cambridge: Cambridge University Press.

Quine, W. V. O. 1960. *Word and Object*. Cambridge, MA: MIT Press.

Quine, W. V. O. 1969. *Ontological Relativity and Other Essays*. New York: Columbia University Press.

Quine, W. V. O. 1970. *Philosophy of Logic*. Englewood Cliffs, NJ: Prentice Hall.

Quine, W. V. O. 1975. *Five Milestones of Empiricism*. Reprinted in Quine 1981, 67–72.

Quine, W. V. O. 1980. *From a Logical Point of View: Nine Logico–Philosophical Essays*. Cambridge, MA: Harvard University Press.

Quine, W. V. O. 1981. *Theories and Things*. Cambridge, MA: Harvard University Press.

Quine, W. V. O. 1990. *Pursuit of Truth*. Cambridge, MA: Harvard University Press.

Quine, W. V. O. 1995. *From Stimulus to Science*. Cambridge, MA: Harvard University Press.

Ramsey, F. P. 1927. "Facts and Propositions", *Proceedings of the Aristotelian Society*, suppl. Vol. 7: 153–70.

Savellos, E. E. & U. D. Yalçin (eds) 1995. *Supervenience: New Essays*. Cambridge: Cambridge University Press.

Shoemaker, S. 1984. *Identity, Cause, and Mind: Philosophical Essays*. Cambridge: Cambridge University Press.

Sklar, L. 2003. "Dappled Theories in a Uniform World". *Philosophy of Science* **70**(2): 424–41.

Spurrett, D. & D. Papineau 1999. "A Note on the Completeness of 'Physics'". *Analysis* **59**(1): 25–9.

Stalnaker, R. 1976. "Possible Worlds". *Noûs* **10**: 65–75.

Stroud, B. 1977. *Hume*. London: Routledge & Kegan Paul.

Stroud, B. 1984. *The Significance of Philosophical Scepticism*. Oxford: Clarendon Press.

Sturgeon, S. 1998. "Physicalism and Overdetermination". *Mind: A Quarterly Review of Philosophy* **107**(426): 411–32.

Teller, P. 2004. "How We Dapple the World". *Philosophy of Science* 71(4): 425–47.

Van Cleve, J. 1984. "Reliability, Justification and Induction". In *Causation and Causal Theories*, P. A. French, T. E. Uehling & H. K. Wettstein (eds), Midwest Studies in Philosophy, 4: 555–67.

Van Frasseen, B. C. 1980. *The Scientific Image*. Oxford: Clarendon Press.

Van Fraassen, B. C. 1997 "Structure and Perspective: Philosophical Perplexity and Paradox". In *Logic and Scientific Methods*, M. L. Dalla Chiara *et al.* (eds), 511–30. Dordrecht: Kluwer.

Wason, P. C. & D. Shapiro 1966. "Reasoning". In *New Horizons in Psychology*, B. M. Foss (ed.). Harmondsworth: Penguin.

Williams, B. 1978. *Descartes: The Project of Pure Enquiry*. Harmondsworth: Penguin.

Witmer, D. G. 2000. "Locating the Overdetermination Problem". *British Journal for the Philosophy of Science* 51(2): 273–86.

Worrall, J. 1988. "The Value of a Fixed Methodology". *British Journal for the Philosophy of Science* 39(2): 263–75.

Worrall, J. 1989. "Fix It and Be Damned: A Reply to Laudan". *British Journal for the Philosophy of Science* 40(3): 376–88.

Yablo, S. 1992. "Mental Causation". *Philosophical Review* 101(2): 245–80.

Yablo, S. 1997. "Wide Causation". *Noûs Supplement: Philosophical Perspectives* 11: 251–81.

Yablo, S. 2000. "Textbook Kripkeanism and the Open Texture of Concepts". *Pacific Philosophical Quarterly* 81(1): 98–122.

Index